D1564429

Joseph Conrad and the Imperial Romance

'The Boyhood of Raleigh' (1870) by Sir John Everett Millais (1829–96). Oil on canvas. Presented to the Tate Gallery in 1900 by Amy, Lady Tate, in memory of Sir Henry Tate.

Joseph Conrad and the Imperial Romance

Linda Dryden

First published in Great Britain 2000 by
MACMILLAN PRESS LTD
Houndmills, Basingstoke, Hampshire RG21 6XS and London
Companies and representatives throughout the world

A catalogue record for this book is available from the British Library.

ISBN 0–333–74715–1

First published in the United States of America 2000 by
ST. MARTIN'S PRESS, INC.,
Scholarly and Reference Division,
175 Fifth Avenue, New York, N.Y. 10010

ISBN 0–312–22553–9

Library of Congress Cataloging-in-Publication Data
Dryden, Linda, 1954–
Joseph Conrad and the imperial romance / Linda Dryden.
    p.   cm.
Includes bibliographical references and index.
ISBN 0–312–22553–9 (cloth)
1. Conrad, Joseph, 1857–1924—Political and social views.
2. Politics and literature—Great Britain—History—20th century.
3. Political fiction, English—History and criticism.
4. Imperialism in literature.   5. Colonies in literature.
I. Title.
PR6005.O4Z67   1999
823'.912—dc21   99–22232
                                                  CIP

PR
6005
.84
Z665
2000

This book is printed on paper suitable for recycling and made from fully managed and sustained
forest sources.

10   9   8   7   6   5   4   3   2   1
09   08   07   06   05   04   03   02   01   00

Printed and bound in Great Britain by
Antony Rowe Ltd, Chippenham, Wiltshire

For my father and mother, Eric and Eve Dryden,
with love

Contents

List of Plates

Acknowledgements

When John Lucas came up with the inspired idea that I look at the Millais painting 'The Boyhood of Raleigh' and consider its implications for Conrad's work neither he nor I knew that Millais's widow and her children became close friends of Conrad's family during his later life. Only when my research was completed did I find this out. I therefore include as a frontispiece to this volume the painting that triggered the ideas contained in the following pages. The painting is also included in acknowledgement of John Lucas's perception, and by way of thanks for the patient, erudite, and generous manner in which he guided me through my research. He is, I believe, the best of supervisors and always good-humoured even when pointing out my most naive blunders or unforgivable mistakes.

All the people who have contributed ideas and encouragement over the years that this book has been in preparation are too numerous to mention but I would like to single out a few colleagues and friends who deserve special mention. If it had not been for the close friendship, support, and excellent conferences and facilities offered by the *Joseph Conrad Society (UK)* I believe I would never have finished this work. I am especially indebted to Keith Carabine for inviting me onto the committee of the society and for his advice on, and interest in my work; to Allan Simmons and Robert Hampson for their invaluable scholarly advice, their patience in reading draft chapters, and not least their friendship; to Hugh Epstein, who has been the source of many an enlightening idea; to Cedric Watts for his generosity and astute comments; to Laurence Davies for his advice, encouragement, and excellent dinner conversation; to John Lester for his insight into Rider Haggard's novels; and to Sandra Dodson, Anthony Fothergill, Sue Jones, and Andrew Roberts for their friendship and advice. Hans van Marle and Gene Moore have been warm in their support and I am sincerely grateful to them. I am also indebted to Philip Conrad for kindly letting me have a copy of his grandfather's drawing 'Woman with Serpent' and for his interest in my project. I must also mention Bruce Harkness, whose snooker expertise enlivens our London conferences; Daphna Erdinast-Vulcan for her companionship during the 1997 South Africa Conference; and Mark Conroy just for being himself. There are many more people who have contributed ideas unknowingly either through their books, their journal articles, or their conference papers and I would thus like to extend my gratitude to all the scholars whose work has informed my research.

Special thanks are due to the Department of English and Drama at Loughborough University, in particular to Bill Overton, Elaine Hobby, John Schad, and Daveena Daley. I single out Sara Mills for very special thanks. Her belief in my work during the early stages of this research ensured that I persevered, and the stimulating research weekends that she organized in the Lake District will forever remain some of my fondest memories. Very warm and sincere thanks go to David Finkelstein of the Department of Print Media, Publishing and Communication at Napier University, who has given me expert advice and support, and ensured that I got this book published. I would also like to thank Alistair McCleery for the efforts he has made on my behalf and the time he has made available for the completion of this project. Ainsley Adams receives special thanks for his superb photography for the plate section of this book.

My most heartfelt gratitude, however, is reserved for my family. My partner, David Benyon, initiated me into the world of computers and word processing, and always provided a willing shoulder to lean on in times of stress. My children, Luc and Holly Benyon, have never complained about the amount of time I have spent poring over books and have always been proud of my successes. They have all been more than generous in their support of me; without their patience and encouragement the writing of this book would have been a very different experience. I am especially proud to dedicate this volume to my parents, Eve and Eric Dryden, who have never failed to support me in any way they could. I hope this book brings them great pleasure: it is but small reward for the years they have given me. I owe the completion of this research in part to my late father-in-law, Don Benyon, who, knowing he only had weeks to live threatened to come back and haunt me if I didn't finish: he may rest peacefully in the knowledge that his threat had the desired effect.

Further thanks are due to Loughborough University Library, Edinburgh University Library, Napier University Library, and the National Library of Scotland where I have spent many long hours of research. I would also like to thank the staff at all those libraries for their friendly help and advice. Numerous articles and journal papers were supplied by the British Library and for that I am grateful.

Permissions for the illustrations and drawings in the plate section were sought from various sources and every effort has been made to trace the owners of copyright for each plate. If any omissions have been made I will willingly make due acknowledgement in any subsequent edition of this volume. Although most of the illustrations reproduced here appear to be out of copyright, I would like to thank the following for their help in verifying this fact: A. P. Watt Ltd on behalf of The Lord Tweedsmuir and Jean, Lady Tweedsmuir; Addison Wesley Longman Ltd; and Thomas Nelson and Sons Ltd. I would also like to thank Tate Gallery Publishing Ltd for supplying the photograph of 'The Boyhood of Raleigh' and for granting permission to use it as a frontispiece. Thanks are also due to the trustees of the Joseph Conrad Estate for permission to reproduce the drawing 'Woman with Serpent'.

Abbreviations

Quotations from Conrad's work in the text are from the Dent Collected Edition, London 1946–55. Where a different edition has been cited this is clearly indicated in the text. Abbreviations of Conrad's works in the text are as follows:

AF	*Almayer's Folly*
HD	*Heart of Darkness*
LE	*Last Essays*
Letters 1	*The Collected Letters of Joseph Conrad, Vol. 1*
Letters 2	*The Collected Letters of Joseph Conrad, Vol. 2*
LJ	*Lord Jim*
NLL	*Notes on Life and Letters*
NN	*The Nigger of the Narcissus*
OI	*An Outcast of the Islands*
PR	*A Personal Record*
TU	*Tales of Unrest*

Introduction

After decades of critical neglect in which critics have favoured Conrad's 'major phase', as characterized by *Lord Jim* (1900), *Heart of Darkness* (1902), *Nostromo* (1904), *The Secret Agent* (1907), and *Under Western Eyes* (1911), his earlier novels, *Almayer's Folly* (1895) and *An Outcast of the Islands* (1896), now receive serious scholarly attention.[1] The significance of Conrad's early Malay stories within his oeuvre has been recognized by Heliéna Krenn, who examines how empire, race, and women are handled in the Lingard trilogy.[2] Many critics have noted the elements of romance in Conrad's fiction, but until Andrea White's *Joseph Conrad and the Adventure Tradition* (1993), very little research focused on how these elements of romance are woven into his work and how they contribute to Conrad's vision of imperialism.[3] The work of Krenn and White has broken new ground in the study of Conrad's early novels and opened the way for a searching assessment of the romance tropes in the Malay tales. This volume addresses that gap in Conrad studies by placing a quartet of Conrad's early Malay tales, *Almayer's Folly, An Outcast of the Islands*, 'Karain' (1898), and *Lord Jim*, in the context of the literature of imperial romance and adventure that was enjoying such popularity when Conrad began his literary career.

The promise of empire

A familiar feature over Victorian and Edwardian sideboards, the frontispiece to this book, 'The Boyhood of Raleigh' (1870), vividly captures the spirit of the literature of Empire in the late nineteenth century. The novels of writers like R. M. Ballantyne, Captain Marryat, G. A. Henty, W. H. G. Kingston, and Rider Haggard explored the exotic locations that are suggested by the colourful bronzed sailor of the painting.

Imperial romances represented simple escapism: its appeal lay in the ability to transport its readers away from everyday concerns and to immerse them in uncomplicated exotic romance. It was pure escapism laced with patriotic overtones and a zeal for imperial adventures. This is exactly the type of fiction that Conrad subverts in his early Malay novels, bringing him closer to the later fiction of Robert Louis Stevenson than to say Henty or Haggard. As Elleke Boehmer observes: 'Stevenson's Pacific tales...fed into a colonialist lineage which connected him to Conrad' (Boehmer, 46). Stevenson had successfully employed the genre of romance and adventure in *Treasure Island* (1883),[4] but by the time he came to write 'The Beach of Falesá' (1893) and *The Ebb-Tide* (1894) he too was more openly sceptical about the escapism that characterizes the imperial romance. Conrad, like Stevenson, presents a quite different imperial experience than is to be found in boys' imperial adventure stories or is suggested by Millais's sailor.

'The Boyhood of Raleigh' encapsulates a late nineteenth-century fascination with the far reaches of the Empire. The young Raleigh and his friend Trevelyan sit on a beach engrossed in a sailor's yarn.[5] The sailor's arm points into the distance, taking the eye out of the main frame and implying a world of romantic adventure beyond its confines. The gesture signifies a wealth of glamour and exoticism awaiting the intrepid explorer, while an expanse of blue sky and sea reinforces the promise of the motioning arm. The fixed gazes of Raleigh and his companion testify to the fascination of the sailor's tale. Their starched collars and velvet suits signify the order and sobriety of English society; and their fresh faces, intent on the tale they are being told, suggest the innocence and excitement of youth when confronted with an exotic adventure. By contrast, the sailor's bohemian appearance and dramatic posture speak of the distant lands from which he has returned to recount his adventures. Like the young Conrad, these boys are clearly fascinated by the sea life:[6] they have abandoned the toy ship nestled in the corner of the picture in favour of the real adventures of the sailor. Conceived at a time when the Empire was at its height, this painting symbolizes the adventuring spirit engendered by the imperial mission. It also represents the fascination with empire and its promised adventures that was the theme and the impetus for much of the popular literature of the second half of the nineteenth century.

Rider Haggard, perhaps the most famous exponent of imperial romance, was keenly aware of its commercial potential. In 1887 he wrote a defence of romance in general, 'About Fiction', for the *Contemporary*

Review where he expresses his perception of a burgeoning reading public demanding more and more fiction:

> At home the board schools pour out their thousands every year, many of whom have acquired a taste for reading, which, when once it has been born, will, we may be sure, grow apace. Abroad the colonies are filling up with English-speaking people, who, as they grow refined and find leisure to read, will make a considerable call upon the literature of their day. ('About Fiction', 174)

Haggard profited from this growth in the reading public: he wrote 34 adventure novels that made him a very wealthy and famous writer.

Haggard was born in 1856, a year before Conrad, and survived him by just one year, dying in 1925. Africa's wild beauty and ancient civilizations fascinated Haggard. His knowledge of things African was extensive: he had spent six years of his youth in South Africa, and as an adult served on commissions for agriculture, forestry, and emigration. He wrote various magazine and newspaper articles on his experiences in South Africa.[7] Yet, despite this intensely practical experience, his fiction presents a continent steeped in mystery, violence, and vaguely supernatural occurrences. Haggard's immensely successful imperial romances provided adults as well as children with the adventurous exploits of Englishmen in the Empire. They often took as their starting point the yearning of his protagonists for adventure in the unexplored reaches of Africa. One of his most famous characters, the eponymous hero of *Allan Quatermain* (1887),[8] registers a restlessness and a dissatisfaction with his quiet life in England at the very opening of his tale:

> The thirst for the wilderness was on me; I could tolerate this place no more; I would go and die as I had lived, among the wild game and the savages. Yes, as I walked, I began to long to see the moonlight gleaming silvery white over the wide veldt and mysterious sea of bush, and watch the lines of game travelling down the ridges to the water. (*AQ*, 3–4)

These are novels that revel in the exploits of virile heroes, while reducing women to ugly 'native' witches, or sultry beauties whose predatory sexuality threatens the hero's manliness.[9] But the hero, an example of perfect breeding and public school education, resists the temptation of miscegenation and is rewarded with humble words of praise from admiring 'natives'. In the best known of Haggard's novels, *King Solomon's Mines* (1886),[10] the hero leaves Africa, his pockets lined with diamonds. Even when Haggard's heroes remain in Africa in *Allan Quatermain* they ascend to the highest status in the land to live in the palaces of Zu-Vendis, the 'lost' white kingdom they set out to discover.

Similarly, the boys' adventure stories of Empire by such writers as Henty and Kingston focus on heroes anxious for thrilling adventure in tropical locations where they prove their manliness, assert English racial superiority, and plunder the land of its riches.[11] Their female counterparts are exemplary 'English roses', often threatened with abduction by villainous 'natives'. The imperial romance celebrated English manhood and assumed English 'girls' to be sexually 'pure', while the advances of the 'native girl' were to be resisted at all costs. The focus on male adventure reflected the belief that the English were the superior imperial power and that Englishmen presented an example of moral uprightness and physical excellence to all the peoples of the Empire. It all amounted to a desire to explore the geography and peoples of those parts of the world that the expanding British Empire was bringing to the attention of those at home. At the same time the imperial romance presented a reassuring picture of English superiority and rigid gender stereotypes.

It is little wonder that this literature was so popular: it was drawing on imperial adventure at a time when the Empire was most powerful, when it was a potent force in the British imagination. This is demonstrated by the anonymous review of *Allan Quatermain* in the *Spectator* on 28 April 1888 which claims that some 'touch of reality' is needed for complete enjoyment of the story and proceeds to cite some recent events in Africa that lend authenticity to Haggard's tale. These actual events prove, for this reviewer, that 'the English race has still a dash of heroism in real life as well as in books' and claims that when reading such accounts we must 'force ourselves to remember that we are not reading a book' (*Spectator*, 570). The suggestive power of Africa on the nineteenth-century imagination is laid bare in the predictions of what secret wonders the continent may hold in store:

> [W]ho will be surprised if some day or other we hear that one of those wonderful swords, with the back of the blade cut out in fretwork and inlaid with gold, which Mr. Mackenzie showed to the astonished Allan Quatermain is for sale in New Bond Street, and that an expedition is about to set out to discover the land of Zuvendis [*sic*]? After all there may well be greater wonders in the

heart of Africa than ever the romancer dreamt of. If we do not find She-who-must-be-obeyed, we may yet discover ruins mightier than those of Imperial Khor...Again, if the Zuvendis race is not made known to us, there may well be a white people somewhere in yet undiscovered highlands of Africa whose history may be none the less marvellous because they must be few, and must have lived a life of perpetual self-defence.[12] (*Spectator*, 571)

Certainly exotic artefacts, like Mackenzie's sword, were being brought back by explorers, but it seems that Haggard's imperial romances also tapped into some of the more fanciful nineteenth-century perceptions of the 'mystery' that was Africa.

The nineteenth century was indeed a period of massive exploration and imperial acquisition. By 1872 Disraeli was exhorting the citizens of Britain to embrace imperial greatness:

The issue is not a mean one. It is whether you will be content to be a comfortable England, modelled and moulded upon Continental principles and meeting in due course an inevitable fate, or whether you will be a great country, an Imperial country, a country where your sons, when they rise, rise to paramount positions, and obtain not merely the esteem of their countrymen, but command the respect of the world. (Quoted in Huttenback, 46)

Britain was one of the world's most powerful imperial nations. In the mid-eighteenth century Clive (1725–74) had established British rule in India. In 1770 James Cook (1728–79) instigated the British colonization of Australia by claiming New South Wales for Britain. James Brooke (1803–68), the 'white rajah of Sarawak', established colonial rule in Borneo in the mid-nineteenth century and was succeeded by his nephew, Sir Charles Johnson (1829–1917). Colonization of Africa had begun as early as the fifteenth century, but the nineteenth century saw extensive expansion of the British Empire on the continent. Africa was also opening up to explorers: from 1841 until his death in 1873, David Livingstone (1813–73) was mapping out great tracts of the continent. In 1871 Henry Stanley (1841–1904), in what Conrad was later to call 'a prosaic newspaper "stunt"' (*LE*, 17), famously tracked down Livingstone for the editor of the *New York Herald*, James Gordon Bennett. The world outside of Europe offered exciting new scientific possibilities in the middle of the nineteenth century: in South America, South East Asia, and the Galapagos Islands

Alfred Wallace and Charles Darwin formed new theories about human evolution.

Men who were later to make a living as writers of imperial fiction had also been travelling and working in the Empire during the nineteenth century. Captain Marryat (1792–1848), remembered mainly for his popular children's novel, *Children of the New Forest* (1847), had been a naval captain and based numerous adventure stories on his seafaring life and the exotic lands that he had seen. *Masterman Ready* (1841)[13] is probably the most famous of these. R. M. Ballantyne (1825–94), best known for his boys' adventure novel, *The Coral Island* (1857),[14] began his career by working in Canada for the Hudson's Bay Company. G. A. Henty (1832–1902) first became a war correspondent in the Crimea and subsequently travelled to Italy, Abyssinia, Ashanti, Spain, and France. His first boys' novel, *Out on the Pampas* (1868),[15] marked the beginning of a lucrative career as a writer of children's fiction. He wrote 35 other books, sometimes producing three or four a year.

Later in the century Conrad's contemporaries were also acquiring the experience and knowledge of the Empire that were to form the basis of their fiction. Haggard's experiences as a young man in South Africa inform his imperial romances. Hugh Clifford (1866–1941) went to the Malay Archipelago in 1883, the same year that the *Palestine*, in which Conrad was second mate, was destroyed by fire in the Banka Strait off Sumatra. Clifford is largely remembered today as a colonial governor in Malaya, but he published many fictional tales of Malay life alongside Conrad in *Blackwood's Magazine*.[16] Frank Swettenham (1850–1946), another writer of Malay stories, was also a Resident in Malaya during Clifford's time there.[17] Rudyard Kipling (1865–1936) was born in Bombay and after a childhood in England returned to India as a journalist. These writers were all to use their experiences in the Empire to write the type of imperial fiction for which the Victorian public was clamouring.

The nineteenth century was a time of trade and exploration, of imperial expansion, and of great wealth for the nations who embraced the ideology of empire. The seas were teeming with European ships importing exotic merchandise and valuable goods from imperial outposts. Sailors in those ships brought back exotic artefacts to grace the mantelpieces of Victorian homes; but they also brought with them wonderful tales of their adventures in the far reaches of the Empire. Millais's 'The Boyhood of Raleigh' thus captures the mood of the 1870s: the young Raleigh's engrossment in the sailor's tale signifies the birth of an empire that had reached its zenith in the second half of the nineteenth century. Replete with suggestions of exoticism and adventure in far off lands, Millais's sailor embodies the adventuring spirit of the age; and the wide blue sea dominating the background intimates the tall ships that plied the seas and delivered explorers like Raleigh to the shores of the those lands that were to form part of the British Empire.

Conrad and the romantic imperial inheritance

In 1874 Joseph Conrad left Poland for Marseilles to become a sailor in one of those vessels. This was to be the fulfilment of a childhood dream. His time as a merchant seaman was also to provide Conrad with the raw material for much of his fiction. George Palmer Putnam recounts a story from Conrad's childhood by Konstantin Buszczynski that indicates how, from a very early age, the sea and foreign adventures fired Conrad's imagination. Buszczynski recalls Conrad thus:

> 'And in there, in a corner of the courtyard,' he continued, pointing through the archway, 'that strange boy told us – his play-mates – the most extraordinary stories. They were always of the sea and ships and far-away countries. Somehow, the scent of salt water was in the very blood of Conrad.' (*Conrad Under Familial Eyes,* 143)

'Geography and Some Explorers' in *Last Essays* is Conrad's celebration of maps and explorers: in it he recalls his childhood boast to his friends of visiting the heart of Africa, an ambition echoed in Marlow's anecdote in *Heart of Darkness*:

> Now when I was a little chap I had a passion for maps. I would look for hours at South America, or Africa, or Australia, and lose myself in all the glories of exploration. At that time there were many blank spaces on the earth, and when I saw one that looked particularly inviting on a map (but they all look that) I would put my finger on it and say, When I grow up I shall go there. (*HD*, 52)

'There' is where Millais's sailor had been, where Conrad went, and where writers of imperial romance transported their readers. The Empire, with its exotic landscapes, strange people in flamboyant dress, and colourful wildlife offered boundless possibilities for romantic adventure stories: the Victorian imagination was captured.

Those far-off haunts of imperial romance and boys' adventure stories are exactly the location Conrad chose for his early novels and short stories. Yet many of his early readers were disappointed by *Almayer's Folly* and *An Outcast of the Islands*, as will be shown later. They may even have felt they had been duped, and indeed, to some extent, they were: Conrad's Sambir never conforms to the expectations of gorgeous exoticism presented in Henty's India or Haggard's Africa. His remote tropical islands are not the natural paradises of Ballantyne's and Marryat's idyllic atolls. Adventure, wealth, and return to English 'civilization' for the white hero describe the formula of the imperial romance; but, in their remote Eastern backwaters, Conrad's protagonists find only sordid or violent death. Even those characters who initially appear to conform to the conventional stereotypes of 'noble savages' or 'native' villains, like Dain Maroola and Babalatchi, reveal inner complexities that distance them from their romance counterparts. Conrad's fiction is that of a late nineteenth-century sceptic who rarely endorses the mid-century untroubled imperial confidence of Marryat or Ballantyne. Nor did he idealize the white hero as did Henty and Haggard. Rather, Conrad's fiction challenges notions of confident Empire and the assumptions of white superiority that characterize the imperial romance. His work displays an awareness of the Empire's glorious past, but shows its late nineteenth-century present to be fraught with unease and doubt about the existence of absolute truths. For, as Cedric Watts observes: 'In Conrad's writing we see a combination of nineteenth-century and twentieth-century preoccupations; he stands at the intersection of the late Victorian and the early modernist cultural phases; he is both romantic and anti-romantic, both conservative and subversive' (Watts, 46). In Conrad's fiction the romantic atmosphere of the imperial adventure has gone sour. He feels, like the Marlow of *Heart of Darkness*, that the 'glamour's off' (*HD*, 52).

The codes and ideals that govern behaviour in the imperial romance, the very notion of the English gentleman, are scrutinized in Conrad's tales and found wanting. The durability and unassailability of the values of the nineteenth century are called into question; at the century's end Conrad undertakes a serious reassessment of their worth. Many of these values, including the 'rightness' of the English imperial enterprise, are revealed through Conrad's fictions to be questionable ideals. Underlying the seemingly exotic surface of Conrad's early Malay fiction is a deep unease suggesting an emergent modernist writer who perceives an indifferent universe in which human endeavours to live by romantic ideals are doomed to failure. Conrad's vision is thus distinctly at odds with the positive affirmation of the values expressed by the white hero of the nineteenth-century romance.

The perplexities of his early readers, who expected imperial romance and discovered rather the disquieting histories of deeply flawed human beings, are perhaps explained by the way in which Conrad's tales resist easy classification and often undermine the very genre to which they initially appear to conform. For Fredric Jameson Conrad's work is 'unclassifiable'. He sees Conrad's fiction as 'spilling out of high literature into light reading and romance', and as 'floating uncertainly somewhere in between Proust and Robert Louis Stevenson' (Jameson, 206). Yet within that seemingly uncertain literary position Conrad provides us with a perspective on imperialism that challenges the optimism expressed in much of the literature of the nineteenth century and thus forges a new direction for imperial fiction. The 'ideal of conduct' to which Jim aspires, the self-delusions of Almayer and Willems, Lingard's belief in his own fictions, are all revealed through Conrad's early Malay fiction to be delusions. Such is the result of an over-reliance upon romance and upon the empty promises of an imperial nation that is increasingly coming face to face with evidence of its own fallibility. The optimism of the imperial romance, its supreme confidence in English superiority, is met and challenged by Conrad's dissenting voice. While he clearly endorses some of the values to be found in nineteenth-century literature, Conrad's scepticism registers a profound disquiet about trusting many of the long-held assumptions of the nineteenth century. Thus, what we find in his stories is that the promise of romantic adventure suggested by Millais's sailor's arm extending out into the exotic unknown is reduced to an enervating pessimism.

Images of the imperial romance

In a literary marketplace saturated with imperial romance it is perhaps not surprising to find that early critics were often puzzled by the fact that Conrad's Malay stories were not the formulaic adventures they had expected.[18] The setting is right: there are constant references to imperial gold; colourful Malays and Arabs fill the pages; and Conrad's European heroes are out in the East to seek their fortunes, attempting in the process to build glorious reputations. The visual impact of Conrad's Malaya is almost filmic.[19] Indeed early filmmakers were attracted to the visually exotic in Conrad's novels; but, as Gene Moore points out, they reduced the 'political or moral dimensions' to 'costume melodramas' (*Conrad on Film,* 10). All too often in Conrad films 'the colonial world has been reduced to a common repository of cultural tokens in which human values are seen only in terms of their power to reinforce traditional Western stereotypes about meek native servants, evil savages in the bush, or ceremonial dances and sacrifices' (*Conrad on Film*, 104–5). Nowhere is this more apparent than in Carol Reed's *Outcast of the Islands* (1952) and Richard Brooks's *Lord Jim* (1965), both of which ignore the cultural specificity of Conrad's Malaya.[20] These film-makers were following a tradition of visual representations of the Empire and its peoples as easily recognized stereotypes. Nineteenth-century imperial romances perpetuated such assumptions, and their accompanying illustrations served to reinforce these simple stereotypes (see for example plates 9 and 10).

It seems that only 'Typhoon' was illustrated in its first edition. Thomas J. Wise's bibliography reproduces the title page of the American edition published in 1902 and mentions six illustrations by Maurice Greiffenhagen, which presumably are the same ones that appear in the *Pall Mall Magazine* serialization.[21] Apart from these illustrations, advertisements in American newspapers, and illustrations in the French translations of Conrad's work by André Gide, the earliest visual representations of his fiction are the first films, which appear to be more influenced by the fiction and images of imperial romance than by Conrad's artistic vision.[22] It is not surprising that Conrad's first published books did not contain illustrations: his famous statement in the Preface to *The Nigger of the 'Narcissus'* (1897) that his task 'by the power of the written word' is 'before all, to make you *see*' (*NN*, 5) could be taken as a rejection of any visual representation of his literary art. This oft-quoted statement is, of course, open to multiple interpretations, but Conrad is at pains to express in this Preface that if fiction is to be art it must 'strenuously aspire to … the colour of painting' (*NN*, 4). Few, if any, writers of imperial romance had such an aesthetic ambition: their main purpose was to write best-selling literature. Patriotic loyalties and imperial zeal may have influenced them, but it is doubtful whether they had many artistic scruples, and illustrations thus increased the appeal of their work.

Jonathan Cott, quoting Gleeson White, says that 'it was not until the beginning of the nineteenth century that children's book illustrations … truly came into their own'. He goes on to say that the 1860s and 70s saw the blossoming of children's book illustration in England (Cott, vii). John Barr also cites the 1860s as a time when 'popular graphic artists had been commissioned to design *de luxe* gift-books intended for the drawing room rather than the nursery' (Barr, 69). This is particularly true of young children's books, but it also applies to the boys' imperial adventure books of the second half of the nineteenth century. The editions of Henty and Kingston that line my own bookshelves have elaborately decorated front covers (see plate 1 for example) and numerous black and white illustrations. Blackie editions with their colourful covers and gold lettering seem designed as gifts for young boys: many of my copies have inscriptions from fond aunts and uncles.

W. H. G. Kingston (1815–80) wrote imperial adventure stories that were often published by the Religious Tract Society, the SPCK (Society for Promoting Christian Knowledge), and the Sunday School Union.[23] These were morally didactic tales where, in the words of Patrick A. Dunae, the 'youthful argonauts were rather pious characters who tended to preach to their antagonists wherever they roamed' (Dunae, 107). Thus Kingston's books were 'wholesome' (Dunae, 106) and morally instructive with a strong religious message. The missionary spirit of converting 'heathen savages' to Christianity frequently informed these stories. For example, plate 10, from *Peter Biddulph* (1891) depicts two intrepid hunters looking aghast at the 'fantastic' dance of a group of Australian Aborigines. Such books were often given as school or Sunday school prizes, or donated to school libraries. My copy of *Ben Hadden* (1869)[24] for instance, bears a label revealing that it was donated to the Kettering Board Schools by the Kettering Industrial Co-operative Society. A copy of Kingston's *The Rival Crusoes* (1878) was awarded as a prize by the Christ Church Sunday School, Belper, in 1900, and *Michael Penguyne* (1873) was given to a young scholar by the rector of St Peter and St Paul, Uppingham, as late as 1919.

The plate section of this book contains numerous images from imperial romances and boys' imperial adventure books that serve as examples of the kind of visual stereotyping that took place in these novels. The exoticism of the Empire that had so enthralled the nineteenth-century imagination became schematized in the illustrations contained in the literature of imperial romance and adventure. Thus plate 12, from *Ben Hadden,* depicts the 'meek native' listening to the equally stereotyped English sea captain while the wide-eyed young Ben looks on. Plates 13 and 14, from Kingston's *In the Eastern Seas* (1879),[25] seek to represent the 'evil savages' while plate 16, from Buchan's *Prester John* (1910),[26] shows the 'native' indulging in 'ceremonial rituals'. Umslopogaas in plate 9, from *Allan Quatermain*, is the 'noble savage' protecting his English friends, ultimately at the cost of his own life. But it was not only the 'native' who was stereotyped: Quatermain, Curtis and Good are the archetypal English country gentlemen and intrepid explorers in plates 3 and 4. Plate 6 depicts Curtis and Good as grieving loyal friends at the noble Quatermain's deathbed. Henty's Dick Holland in *The Tiger of Mysore* (1895)[27] is seen in plate 15 as a plucky young imperial hero chivalrously rescuing a girl from an Indian harem while disguised in native dress. Melodramatic, sometimes colourful, and full of exotic detail these illustrations reinforce both the character-ization of the 'native' in the imperial romance and the perception of the English hero as a courageous, upright, chivalrous knight within the Empire. Native peoples, just as Moore observes concerning film repre-sentations, are drawn either as stereotypes of submissive servants or as barbaric savages.

Perhaps the lack of such exotic illustrations in his novels should have alerted Conrad's early reviewers to the fact that they were dealing with a very different type of fiction to that which they were expecting. After all it was not only children's imperial fiction that contained illustrations: adults' fiction like Rider Haggard's imperial romances were lavishly illustrated, as evidenced by the samples reproduced here. In *She* (1887)[28] and its sequels these drawings could even be quite risqué (see plate 7).[29] Works by boys' storywriters contained detailed drawings depicting key moments in the tale. In the case of Kingston these could be quite expensive colour plates. Illustrations contributed to the saleability of the books – although they did increase the price – and heightened the sensationalism of the stories.[30] Yet whereas boys' adventure books had embossed and highly pictorial hard covers, Conrad's book covers were plain, and even dust jackets were monotone and unadorned.[31]

The illustrations in the plate section help to define the type of sim-ple assumptions about England, the Empire, and its people that the imperial romance perpetuated. This was the type of attitude that Conrad was eager to distance himself from. For example, the portrayal of Rider Haggard's upper-class English gentlemen in plate 3 reflects a perceived order and stability at home, coupled with an elegant and luxurious lifestyle, exactly the existence to which Almayer and Willems aspire but never achieve. The evident 'superiority' of Haggard's heroes to their African surroundings in plate 4 is testimony to the 'superiority' of the English race. The pictures portray stereotypes of popular romance that are never in danger of the type of degeneracy to which Conrad's 'heroes' are prone. The illustrations therefore help to define the gulf between the overt optimism and confidence of the imperial romance and the subversive effect of Conrad's vision of white men in the tropics.

But these pictures also serve to define the tradition on which Conrad was drawing in his early Malay novels. Thus the bloodthirsty, headhunting Dyaks of plate 14 find strong resonances in Babalatchi's vision of himself as a 'true Orang Laut, living by rapine and plunder of coasts and ships' (*AF*, 52). The barbarity of Babalatchi's deeds is designed to shock the European reader into a full recognition of the 'otherness' of such a character. The Malay races are made distinct by Babalatchi's desires and the bloodlust of his past life. These are also the assumptions of the imperial romance about 'native savages'. The Dyaks of plate 14 celebrate over the severed head of an adversary: their scant attire, their bodies adorned with jewellery, and their Malay headgear contribute to the savagery of the scene. The sensational stories that Conrad sometimes drew upon when devising his Malay characters and his narratives of their lives are epitomized in such illustrations.

Conclusion: the Malay quartet

Joseph Conrad and the Imperial Romance is divided into six chapters. The genealogy of the English gentleman and how the notion of the English gentleman affected attitudes to women in the nineteenth century is the focus of Chapter 1, 'Making the Imperial Hero'. This discussion demonstrates how the stereotypical hero of the imperial romance emerged. The English public schools provided the Empire with its officers and administrators. Their attitudes towards the people they subjugated and the countries over which they presided were nurtured in the classrooms and on the playing fields of the Etons, Harrows, and Rugbys of England. The notion of 'breeding' and a fear of degeneracy were vital to the 'health' of the nation and to the power of the Empire. Those Englishmen out in the colonies had to be physical, moral, and psychological proof that the English were the supreme imperialists. It was the job of the public school to ensure that it provided such specimens of English 'perfection' for the Empire.

These issues of gentlemanly behaviour and English superiority are taken for granted in the imperial romance, but they are the very assumptions that Conrad challenges in his tales of empire. Almayer and Willems may be Dutch, but their delusions of reputation and a glorious future in Europe financed by imperial gold are in fact the fantasy destinies of the gentlemanly heroes of English imperial romance. Jim, with his schoolboy oaths and his preoccupations with codes of conduct, demonstrates what can go wrong when the dogma of the public school is put to the test. Thus Chapter 1 provides the basis for discussions about the imperial romance and about Conrad's Malay stories.

Chapter 2, 'The Possibilities of Romance', offers a detailed account of the imperial romance and the specific texts that will be discussed alongside Conrad's fiction. The imperial romance is extremely formulaic and generally very racist in its attitudes towards the peoples of the Empire. An outline of the formula of imperial romance is given in this chapter and the authors and works that will subsequently be referred to are introduced here. The chapter concludes by considering how Conrad subverts the notion of the Empire as the location of utopian dreams. Conrad's early fiction is a reversal of the typical formula of the imperial romance where gentlemanly heroes have action-packed adventures in the Empire before returning to Europe with their financial future secure. Conrad's protagonists may dream of such glory but their reality is a squalid life and a sordid death in the Far East. Even if Jim does manage to establish a sort of utopia, it is ephemeral: the 'real' world is always waiting to break in and destroy the idyll. This, then, leads into the main discussion of Conrad's Malay stories.

Three of the subsequent chapters, on *Almayer's Folly*, *An Outcast of the Islands*, and *Lord Jim* respectively, demonstrate Conrad's awareness of the imperial romance and reveal the strategies he employed to subvert the genre. The use of the tropes of the imperial romance is evident in some of the characterization and plot detail of Conrad's novels, showing that he was using the genre as well as subverting it. But imperial romance generally functions in his novels as the nineteenth-century dream against which Conrad's realism rebels. Therefore references to imperial romance work at two levels: they highlight the extent to which Conrad used its tropes to achieve narrative impetus and recognizable characters; but more significantly, they serve to emphasize the modernity of Conrad's conception of the Empire.

The book ends with a detailed discussion of *Lord Jim*, but prior to that is Chapter 5, ' "Karain": Constructing the Romantic Subject'. The short story 'Karain' represents Conrad's deliberate attempt to 'cash in' on the popular taste for exotic romance. Here he uses many of the formulaic elements detailed in Chapter 2 in order to produce a tale with commercial potential. In this respect, this chapter complements the other two by demonstrating that Conrad was quite capable of writing the type of fiction he often subverted. Indeed 'Karain' embodies the very exoticism of Millais's sailor; Karain's tale is precisely the kind of romantic adventure that the sailor seems to be recounting to the young Raleigh and his companion.

Joseph Conrad and the Imperial Romance thus uses issues of 'Englishness', gentlemanly conduct, stereotypes, and exoticism in the imperial romance as a means of engaging with Conrad's scepticism about nineteenth-century optimism. It concludes by positioning Conrad as a writer poised between the close of the nineteenth century and the dawn of the twentieth century. In providing a detailed analysis of *Lord Jim* in the context of imperial romance ground is covered that has previously been hinted at, but never fully explored. In the course of this discussion detailed attention is given to the early reception of Conrad's work and to some of his own responses to early reviews. The desire for imperial romance fiction can be seen in the comments of some reviewers indicating that Conrad had aroused the interest of those used to a diet of imperial romance. There may have been pressure on Conrad, for financial reasons, to write a more conventional type of popular fiction, but except perhaps in 'The Lagoon' and 'Karain' he never gave in to the temptation.

His early Malay fiction may challenge the consummate heroism and confident assumptions of English superiority found in nineteenth-century imperial romance; but at the same time Conrad reveals the romantic and conservative tendencies identified by Watts. Imperial romance, therefore, functions at various levels in Conrad's work; indeed it is much more significant to his purpose than has been previously recognized. After all, Conrad himself acknowledges the influence of the boys' adventure story on his work, whilst simultaneously distancing his writing from the genre. In a letter to William Blackwood, in May 1902, he includes Sir Arthur Quiller-Couch amongst those 'favourable critics' of 'Youth' who said, 'with a sort of surprise': 'This after all is a story for boys yet – – – – –'.[32] Conrad responds with this explanation: 'Exactly. Out of the material of a boys' story I've made *Youth* by the force of the idea expressed in accordance with a strict conception of my method' (*Letters* 2, 417). Conrad's 'method' includes a deliberate use and subversion of the romance. That strategy of subversion in his early work makes a significant contribution to Conrad's emergent modernist vision and thus helps to clarify his position, as Watts describes it, at 'the intersection of the late Victorian and the early modernist cultural phases'.

1
Making the Imperial Hero

The English gentleman is a central figure in the romance throughout the nineteenth century. The pages of Marryat's adventure romances for boys are littered with references to gentlemanly conduct: Mesty, in *Mr. Midshipman Easy* (1836)[1] always refers to Jack Easy as 'the young gentleman', and Mr. Oxbelly, Jack's second in command, who is himself 'honest and manly', believes that it is the first duty of every officer in the king's navy 'to show an example of courtesy and gentlemanly conduct in the execution of their duty' (*MME*, 312). Haggard's white heroes are all English gentlemen. At the opening of *King Solomon's Mines* Allan Quatermain declares, 'I was born a gentleman', and in answer to his own question, 'What is a gentleman?' he responds, 'a Royal Navy officer is', by virtue of 'God's winds that wash their hearts and blow the bitterness out of their minds and make them what men ought to be' (*KSM*, 4, 6–7). Indeed, *Allan Quatermain* is dedicated to Haggard's son:

I INSCRIBE THIS BOOK OF ADVENTURE
TO MY SON
ARTHUR JOHN RIDER HAGGARD
IN THE HOPE THAT IN DAYS TO COME
HE, AND MANY OTHER BOYS WHOM I SHALL NEVER KNOW, MAY
IN THE ACTS AND THOUGHTS OF ALLAN QUATERMAIN
AND HIS COMPANIONS, AS HEREIN RECORDED,
FIND SOMETHING TO HELP HIM AND THEM TO REACH
TO WHAT, WITH SIR HENRY CURTIS, I HOLD TO BE THE
HIGHEST RANK WHERETO WE CAN ATTAIN—
THE STATE AND DIGNITY OF ENGLISH GENTLEMEN[2]

Plate 3 clearly illustrates this 'state and dignity': Quatermain and company are pictured in the poses of upper-class English gentlemen smoking over an after-dinner glass of port in a sumptuous dining room. The starched high collars, dinner suits, and roaring log fire beneath an ornate mantelpiece all suggest English country gentlemen at ease with each other and their surroundings. In the frontispiece to that novel is a drawing of Quatermain purportedly from a 'picture in the possession of George Curtis, Esq.' (see plate 2) looking sad and dignified, sitting at his desk holding his pen, the epitome of the gentleman writer.[3]

The Longman editions of Haggard's novels are rich in illustrations of his heroes, but whatever their attire or their situation their poses are always manly and noble. Such is the assumption of the imperial romance about the men who seek their fortune in the Empire. When we come to Conrad, however, what constitutes the English gentleman is a much more debatable issue, but one that is pivotal to his concerns about the imperial adventurer. Gentleman Brown in *Lord Jim* and 'Gentleman' Jones in *Victory* (1915) both claim gentlemanly status and thus a kind of kinship with their respective adversaries, Jim and Heyst. Willems, as we shall see, briefly imagines himself a late nineteenth-century gentleman-husband as he tries to justify himself to his wife, Joanna. Most significant, however, is Jim's self-image as a gentleman: believing Marlow to be a gentleman, Jim asserts, 'I am—I am—a gentleman, too ...' (*LJ*, 131). But his jump from the *Patna* has already proven otherwise.

Perceptions of gentlemanly behaviour are central to the romance and therefore central also to my reading of Conrad within that genre. Thus, in order to understand what Conrad's characters, and indeed Conrad himself, understood by the term 'gentleman' we must trace how the revived idea of chivalry developed into what came to be recognized as gentlemanly behaviour in the romance and adventure fiction of the late nineteenth century. This will help to clarify the ideological foundations of the notion of the English gentleman and how he came to represent English manhood in imperial romances. For it is the ideal of behaviour promoted by this type of fiction that Conrad seeks to undermine through the actions and destinies of his imperial adventurers.

Chivalry and the nineteenth-century gentleman

In 1862 Tennyson wrote a dedication as preface to 'Idylls of the King'[4] for the late Prince Consort in which Albert is described as 'my king's ideal knight' (*IK*, 308). Of course the notion of a Christian knight was appropriate: the subject of the poem was the legend of King Arthur.

Tennyson was responding to one of the dominant images of his day: the English gentleman as a chivalric knight.[5] Chivalry, for some, became almost an obsession throughout the century. By providing a behavioural code for the gentlemen of England chivalric values came to represent much of the nineteenth-century's attitude not only to social behaviour but to the family and sexuality as well. Jeffrey Richards indicates how chivalry was adapted and applied to nineteenth-century concerns so that the gentleman became 'the embodiment of bravery, loyalty, courtesy, modesty, purity and honour and endowed with a sense of *noblesse oblige* towards women, children and social inferiors' (in Mangan and Walvin, 113).

The concern with medieval chivalry began early in the century. Kenelm Digby's *The Broad Stone of Honour* (1822) provided the foundations on which the nineteenth-century notion of the gentleman was built. The intention of the book, addressed to the 'Gentlemen of England', was, as Robin Gilmour says, the hope that 'they would learn from his compendium of medieval chivalric lore to see the responsibilities inherent in their privileges...' (Gilmour, 88). It was a manual for all social classes, but it was initially the aristocracy who espoused its ideals of gentlemanly behaviour. Archibald Montgomerie conceived the Eglinton Tournament in August 1839, for example, as a colourful and potent demonstration of the aristocracy's belief in the chivalric code. The event was an absurd fiasco, but it did nothing to dampen enthusiasm for the strict codes of honour embodied in the notion of chivalry.[6]

In 1822 the cult of medievalism informed notions of what it meant to be a gentleman. Mark Girouard outlines Digby's definition of chivalrous behaviour thus:

> The distinctive virtues of the chivalrous man, according to Digby, were belief and trust in God, generosity, high honour, independence, truthfulness, loyalty to friends and leaders, hardihood and contempt of luxury, courtesy, modesty, humanity, and respect for women... High honour included refusal to break a promise, tell a lie, act the spy or beg for mercy. Independence included refusal to push oneself, truthfulness included openness; gentlemen did not conceal their feelings, and always gave fair warning of their intentions. Loyalty to friends involved perfect confidence in them. (Girouard, 61–2)

This definition echoes through the character of Jim and his 'shadowy ideal of conduct' (*LJ*, 416): but shades of early nineteenth-century chivalry are shown by Conrad to be too insubstantial to sustain genuine lives when faced with the uncertainty and moral crises of the *fin de siècle*. Digby's brand of chivalry signals a yearning for a perceived, no doubt imaginary, earlier age of purity that mingled strength with gentleness and Christian morality. This was the medieval age, regarded by Digby as superior to the Homeric age because in it chivalry was necessarily linked to Christianity. Chivalry was a code of conduct for men of all classes. But it was much easier for the upper classes to adopt due to their education and public expectations; and significantly, medieval chivalry assumed a monarchy and a ruling class (see Girouard, 62).

In the middle of the nineteenth century these medieval notions of chivalry persisted, and Victoria and Albert thus represented the ideal expression of chivalry in monarchy. As queen, mother, and adoring wife, Victoria was promoted as an ideal of womanhood, worthy of the knight's devotion. Albert, her chivalric consort, was often portrayed in medieval armour.[7] In Tennyson's dedication Albert is a knight who 'reverenced his conscience as his/king;/Whose glory was, redressing human wrong;/Who spake no slander, no, nor listen'd/to it;/Who loved one only and who clave to her –'. Albert is further eulogized as 'Wearing the white flower of a blameless/life', and Tennyson challenges his reader to find 'A lovelier life, a more unstain'd than his?'. Just in case we missed the point, he is finally 'dubbed' by the poet 'Albert the Good' (*IK*, 308). It would be hard to find a more fitting example of Digby's ideal of knightly and gentlemanly behaviour than Tennyson's version of Albert. In the middle of the century such ideals went largely unchallenged in romantic literature; but notions of conscience, blamelessness, and unstained lives become problematic for the characters in Conrad's Malay fiction. For Jim they are the very ideals with which he bolsters his shattered reputation; they are, in the words of T. S. Eliot, the 'fragments' that Jim has 'shored against' his 'ruins'.[8]

Throughout the nineteenth century, chivalry was expressed in sport, in religious belief, in public schooling, in love, in war, in Empire, and, not least, in art and literature. It all amounted to a view of the English gentleman as essentially a chivalrous knight. Indeed for Digby the terms 'knight' and 'gentleman' were almost synonymous. The term 'gentleman' may seem rather quaint today, but in the middle of the last century the gentleman was instantly recognizable: always polite, even when being forceful, conservative of habit, immaculately dressed, deferential to women of all classes, scrupulously honest, and of course, a Christian. The notion of the English gentleman engages most writers of the time: it became part of the debate surrounding social mobility towards the middle of the century, and many writers, including Dickens, began to see contained within it vexed questions concerning birth, nature, and morality.[9]

Tom Brown's Schooldays (1857),[10] has, as its eponymous hero, a boy whose very name is suggestive of a 'plain' knight. Ruminating on his son's future, Squire Brown finally hits on his real reason for sending Tom off to Rugby: 'If he'll only turn out a brave, helpful, truth-telling Englishman, and a gentleman, and a Christian, that's all I want' (*TBS*, 64); and the novel charts Tom's progress towards that ideal. Tom is born into the gentry and it is therefore assumed that to be a gentleman is his birthright. This is also true of Mrs Craik's hero in *John Halifax, Gentleman* (1856)[11] who assumes the title of gentleman as his birthright because of the inscription by his father, 'Guy Halifax, gentleman', on the flyleaf of a Greek Testament, his only inherited possession; here the name, Guy Halifax, denotes a pure Anglo-Saxon male. Yet Mrs Craik's purpose is also to prove that John Halifax, through hard work, self-help, and a rigid code of Christian morality, earns the title of gentleman just as much as he may have inherited it.[12] The knightly gentleman is also central to the children's literature of the time: Marryat's young heroes combine the valour and purity of the knight with moral gentlemanly conduct to produce a model of behaviour for all English boys. Ballantyne's Jack, Ralph and Peterkin in *The Coral Island* are similarly chivalrous, emergent English gentlemen. They champion Avatea, a Polynesian girl, much as if she were an English lady (although she was a Christian and therefore worthy of their gallantry); 'heathen savages' are treated much less sympathetically. Nevertheless, being Polynesian, Avatea must marry within her race, and there is no suggestion of a union with one of her English champions. Besides, as Claudia Nelson argues, sexuality was not considered as a 'manly' issue in the mid-century.[13]

Knights and ladies

Chivalry assumed a deference towards women, but it also affected ideas about how women should behave: if the gentleman was essentially a chivalrous knight a no less idealistic model was required for his 'lady'. In *Sesame and Lilies* (1865) Ruskin wrote his impassioned plea to women: 'queens you must always be; queens to your lovers; queens to your husbands and your sons; queens of higher mystery to the world beyond, which bows itself, and will forever bow, before the myrtle crown, and the stainless sceptre, of womanhood' (Ruskin, 149). The man, says Ruskin, is 'always to be the wiser': he is the 'thinker, the ruler, the superior in knowledge and discretion, as in power' (Ruskin, 112). As we shall see, Willems briefly toys with this stereotype in his dealings with Joanna; and his arrogant distress when Aïssa veils herself against his wishes denotes his belief in male ideological dominance. What Willems misses in his self-delusive fiction is that in his dealings with women the man must be a chivalrous knight if the stereotype is to work: 'the first and necessary impulse of every truly taught and knightly heart is this of blind service to its lady ... and that in this rapturous obedience to the single love of his youth, is the sanctification of all man's strength, and the continuance of all his purposes' (Ruskin, 113–14).[14]

These attitudes to middle-class family and marriage are exemplified in such melodramatic novels as *John Halifax*. Ursula March is the ideal of womanhood for the young John, and later as wife and mother she provides the emotional balance to John's 'masculine' sense of right and wrong. Lady Caroline Brithwood, Ursula's wronged but adulterous cousin, is the catalyst for the debate between husband and wife: while John asserts the knightly ideal of woman's purity and refuses to have 'the least taint come near this wife of mine', Ursula urges pity and forgiveness because of Caroline's childlessness (*JH*, 289). John relents and allows Caroline into his home but maintains his duty as husband and father to preach on the 'impropriety' of her disobedience: 'Pardon me; but I think a wife is bound to the very last to obey in all things, not absolutely wrong, her husband's will' (*JH*, 292). Willems echoes this attitude in his thoughts about Joanna's wifely 'duties'. As Judith Rowbotham argues, it was 'firmly established in the minds of most English men and women that women were the emotional sex, just as men were the logical sex ... ' (Rowbotham, 43), a view that finds qualified expression in Marlow's attitude to women in *Heart of Darkness* and *Chance*.

Nineteenth-century constructions of the ideal relationship between man and woman were thus imaginatively recreated in the idea of the knight and his lady. The image even finds its way into *Lord Jim*, where Jim and Jewel come together 'like knight and maiden meeting to exchange vows amongst haunted ruins' (*LJ*, 312); in Heyst's rescue of Lena from the clutches of Stromberg in *Victory*; or in Captain Anthony's gentlemanly wooing of Flora de Barral in *Chance*. In the imperial romance the chivalric hero is a pivotal character: Jack, Ralph and Peterkin valiantly rescue Avatea from the 'savages' who are to roast her alive; Captain Good in *King Solomon's Mines* saves the hapless Foulata from the sacrificial knife and earns her undying devotion; Dick Holland in *The Tiger of Mysore* rescues the English girl, Annie, from a

Sultan's harem (see plate 15). It all amounts to a nineteenth-century construction of male power and feminine weakness.

At the centre of this knightly devotion to the lady was the notion of feminine purity: hence the 'good' queen, Nyleptha, in *Allan Quatermain*, is white while the 'wicked' queen, Sorais, is dark, vindictive, and sexually aggressive (see plate 5). The woman, as the object of devotion, represented unstained virtue; she should never be exposed to impurity or violence. Stein treats Jewel with 'chivalrous deference' as she walks by his side, her 'little hand' resting on his forearm (*LJ*, 350). Echoes of chivalric vows resound as Jewel declares Jim, 'false', and Stein counters with, 'Not false! True! true! true!' (*LJ*, 350). Even the renegade husband, Willems, fleetingly imagines his own 'chivalric' duty to his wife: 'Hang it all, there are sacred things in life, after all. The marriage tie was one of them, and he was not the man to break it' (*OI*, 26). Conrad's approach to his women characters is of course more complex than the knightly ideal of conduct laid down by Ruskin, but some of these nineteenth-century attitudes towards women are nevertheless embedded in his Malay novels.

Late nineteenth-century chivalry

Towards the latter end of the century the image of the gentleman-as-knight was enlisted in the cause of English racial and moral superiority. In 1891 W. E. Henley compiled his anthology of verse for boys, *Lyra Heroica*,[15] with the purpose to set forth, 'the beauty and the joy of living, the beauty and the blessedness of death, the glory of battle and adventure, the nobility of devotion—to a cause, an ideal, a passion even—the dignity of resistance, the sacred quality of patriotism' (*LH*, vii). Henley's anthology seeks to excite patriotic fervour through the image of the English gentleman and soldier as a knight. A typical example is Tennyson's 'The Heavy Brigade' where brave Englishmen whirl their sabres 'in circles of light!' (*LH*, 195) The 'fitness' of English rule in the Empire and the desirability of 'pure' Anglo-Saxon qualities are emphasized at a time when the Empire and the 'healthiness' of its English troops is increasingly being questioned.

Haggard's imperial romances, despite their overt sexuality and violence, cling to the mid-century ideal of the English gentleman as chivalric knight roaming the outposts of the Empire with proprietorial ease, as evidenced by the exploits of Quatermain, Curtis and Good. J. H. Shorthouse's popular sentimental medieval romance, *John Inglesant* (1881), is another example: the very name Inglesant suggests a saintly

Englishman. In *The Tiger of Mysore*, an imperial romance set in India, Dick Holland's mother urges her son never to countenance the bullying of younger boys: 'In the days of old, you know, the first duty of a true knight was to succour the oppressed, and I want you to be a true knight' (*TM*, 17). Of course Dick follows this advice and through his adventures proves his superiority to the native Indians.

These attitudes continued through popular fiction and poetry right up to the beginning of the 1914–18 war. Herbert Asquith's clerk, for example, in 'The Volunteer' yearns to have his lance broken in 'life's tournament'. He dies content 'to join the men of Agincourt' (in Black, 32). But the brutal experience of the war did much to dispel the myth of the glory and valour of the English gentleman and of the war experience itself. The verse of poets like Siegfried Sassoon soon lost its naive idealism and became infused with a bitter irony. In the brutal reality of war it became evident that gentlemanly behaviour could not guarantee victory on the battlefield. Many of the officers sent out to fight in the trenches were the products of a public school education that aimed to create imperial officers who were to prove English superiority throughout the Empire. The English public school thus played a crucial role in creating and perpetuating notions of the ideal gentleman and imperial officer.

Public schooling, athleticism, and empire

The values that a specialized public school training instilled in the young men who were to become imperial officers are exactly the values exhibited by the heroes of the imperial romance and boys' adventure stories, the 'light holiday literature' that inspires Jim's dreams of heroic adventure. The heroes of Marryat and Ballantyne are early examples who espouse the ideals of Christian manliness that the schools hoped to inculcate. But these young men had not been educated under the cult of athleticism that was to permeate the schools in the second half of the century. By the 1880s and 90s Rider Haggard's heroes were primarily specimens of physical prowess, ideal sons of England who could face African natives on the field of battle proving their superiority through fair play and physical fitness. Even the fatherless and penniless heroes of Henty and Kingston exhibit the reverence for fair play, patriotism, and 'stiff upper lip' determination that characterize the English public schoolboy of the late nineteenth century. Team spirit, athletic excellence, and 'playing the game' had become for most public schools the primary aim of education. Empire, as Boehmer points out, 'was a style and a boast; an eye-catching assemblage of hero cults, exhibitionism, rituals of self-glorification, and a general eagerness to 'Play Up, and Play the Game' (Boehmer, 32).[16] Nowhere was this more apparent than in the imperial romance.

The creation of Haggard's Leo Vincy or of Captain Good owe a great deal to what was perceived as the triumph of the public schools in creating the ideal English gentleman ready to go out and confront the native population of the Empire. Yet *Stalky & Co.* (1899) argues the need for a revision of public schooling in order to create a new type of imperial officer who displays the intelligence and initiative that Kipling perceived as vital for the stability of the Empire at the end of the century. When we come to Conrad's hero Jim, who is clearly influenced by public school ideals of male conduct, a grim suspicion of romantic idealism and the public school 'gentleman' is a central issue. The effect of public school education is thus essential to an understanding of what was happening in the literature of Empire and how it depicted English gentlemen at the end of the nineteenth century.

Jeffrey Richards cites the Rev. T. L. Papillon who summed up the spirit of the public school in the latter half of the nineteenth century. Papillon is dismayed by the lack of academic knowledge attained by public school boys but suggests that, nevertheless, the schoolboy 'brings away with him something beyond all price, a manly, straightforward character, a scorn of lying and meanness, habits of obedience and command, and fearless courage. Thus equipped, he goes into the world, and bears a man's part in subduing the earth, ruling its wild folk and building up the Empire' (Richards, 13). The essence of male education, then, was perceived as existing not in academic learning but in the creation of men of character, fit to rule the Empire. How all of this came about, and what the responses to this games ethic were, is a long story that has been exhaustively studied by many critics, notably J. A. Mangan. I want here to give a brief history of the cult of athleticism in the public schools and suggest how this was influenced late in the century by the perceived needs of the Empire.

Athleticism and discipline

Two ideas dominate any discussion of the public school ethos in the second half of the nineteenth century: Christian manliness and athleticism. From the mid-1800s onwards these two notions were used to focus the minds of young boys on what was perceived as being the purpose of their education: service to God, Queen, and Empire. The second half of the century brought dramatic changes to English public schools. In *Athleticism in the Victorian and Edwardian Public School*

(1981)[17] Mangan explains how the schools were transformed: Cotton at Marlborough, Thring at Uppingham, Vaughan at Harrow, Walford at Lancing, and Almond at Loretto all faced problems of discipline and behaviour. Independently of each other, these men created a cult of athleticism that was to influence the principles of public schooling well into the twentieth century. By importing masters who were specifically responsible for games activities Cotton was able to reform Marlborough: 'Through their efforts, wrote his wife after his death, "a civilised out-of-door life in the form of cricket, football and wholesome sports took the place of poaching, rat hunting and poultry stealing"' (*Athleticism*, 24).

As middle-class boys began to enter the public schools the old aristocratic values were reviewed in order to satisfy the demands of the rising bourgeoisie.[18] Richards outlines the ethic that had dominated the schools in the early years of the century: 'the public schools merely reflected the prevailing values of a dissolute aristocracy, whose world was one of hard drinking, ruinous gambling, horse racing, blood sports and prize fighting. The measure of a man was how much he could drink and how tough he was. It was an ethic that the aristocracy shared with the "rough" working class' (Richards, 9). The lawlessness that this type of behaviour expressed had to be controlled. Energies expended in immoral pastimes could be directed in positive ways that would produce those Christian gentlemen who would control the Empire. Richards points out that elite schooling 'gradually replaced noble birth as the identifying badge of the ruling class' (Richards, 10). The affluent middle and upper classes looked to the public school system to provide this education for their sons.

Playing the game: manly pursuits

Athleticism was one way in which reform was achieved. But it was not simply a method of regulating the boys' activities: the advocacy of physical excellence was linked to 'muscular Christianity', a term closely associated with Thomas Hughes and Charles Kingsley. A muscular Christian believed that, as God created our bodies and our minds, service to God required rigorous development of the body. Muscular Christianity was therefore particularly identified with physical 'manliness', a pivotal notion in Hughes' *Tom Brown's Schooldays*.[19] The young Tom, under Arnold's watchful eye, is carefully guided through adolescence to manhood, learning along the way how to become a manly Christian. Pure, honest, God-fearing, chivalrous, and patriotic, the Tom who emerges at the end of the book is the model student of Hughes's version of Rugby, an ideal future captain of Empire, and the very epitome of Lord Jim's ego ideal. Indeed Jim's 'shadowy ideal of conduct' owes its origins in large part to the values espoused by fictional heroes such as Tom Brown.

A large portion of Tom's education is devoted to understanding the virtues of team games. It is Cotton who, fictionalized as 'the young master', identifies the 'qualities' of cricket as a team game: '"The discipline and reliance on one another which it teaches is so valuable, I think," went on the master, "it ought to be such an unselfish game. It merges the individual in the eleven; he doesn't play that he may win, but that his side may"' (*TBS*, 315). This much-quoted statement contains those elements of democratic Christian patriotism that are the hallmarks of Hughes's ideals in education; at a time when women were still denied the vote such an education was significantly aimed at boys. His 'side' has more than one meaning: it is at once the side of Christianity, of the team, of the school or house, and also the 'side' of the country and the Empire. In Hughes's terms these considerations were interdependent. Learning loyalty to one's team was the first step towards learning loyalty to God and to country. As such the team game was a symbolic model for a muscular Christian.

The elevation of athleticism necessarily entailed diminishing the importance of academic excellence. J. R. de S. Honey notes how the inclination towards athleticism even affected the appointment of teachers: 'The culmination of this tendency was the appointment of men on games ability alone, illustrated by the story told in *The Contemporary Review* in 1900 of a university "blue" who on completing his century in the university cricket match received telegrams from five different headmasters with offers of posts' (Honey, 113). Brook, the hero of all right-minded boys and captain of the School-house football team in *Tom Brown's Schooldays*, is greeted with frantic cheers when he outlines his creed: 'I know I'd sooner win two School-house matches running than get the Balliol scholarship any day' (*TBS*, 108). The real Arnold may well have been appalled by Tom's ambition to acquire 'just as much Latin and Greek as will take [him] through Oxford respectably' (*TBS*, 277). After all, the classics were very important to public school education: they provided examples of athletic excellence in young men and models of superior behaviour; but Tom's aspiration is to be 'A1 at cricket and football'.[20] What is of primary importance to Tom Brown, and to Hughes, is to build character, and this is best achieved on the games field, not in the isolation of the study. Cricket was a particularly appropriate game to encourage a sense of loyalty and team work; with its dignity, reserve, and emphasis on rules of gentlemanly conduct it was the sport most fitting for the young men who were to present to the imperial subjects examples of English superiority.

In the second half of the nineteenth century games became compulsory in most public schools. Physical fitness amounted to purity and proof against degeneracy, introspection, and unmanliness, which too much immersion in the classics implied. Athleticism was elevated and intellectualism almost ignored: 'Investigators of the literature of public school life will look in vain for the hero as intellectual, dilettante or cosmopolitan. The heroes of the time were, in Kipling's words, "Gentlemen of England, cleanly bred". Their pleasures were wonderfully stoical, their virtues grounded in the physical' (*Athleticism*, 188).[21] This is true of Haggard's heroes and also of Henty's boys, who are never intellectual, but instead display physical prowess and courage; and, as we shall see in discussing *Lord Jim*, it is the ideal of conduct that Jim signally fails to live up to.

Training for empire

The cricket field came to represent the field of battle. It was perceived as excellent training for the young knights of Empire, like Tom Brown, who were to leave school and serve the Empire in India, Africa, and the colonies. Furthermore, these imperial servants had to be examples of pure-bred English manhood, not prone to the degenerative tendencies of cowardliness or laziness, so often attributed at this time to the 'native'. The imperial officers had to be able to resist the temptation of 'going native', of 'leaping ashore for a howl and a dance', as Marlow describes the temptation in *Heart of Darkness* (*HD*, 97).[22] Thus the opening pages of *Tom Brown's Schooldays* specifically identify the Brown family as staunchly Anglo-Saxon yeomen. Despite its autobiographical elements, in *Tom Brown's Schooldays* Hughes presents his hero as a representative Englishman: his name is clearly chosen to illustrate the point. The imperialist note is struck from the very beginning: 'For centuries in their quiet, dogged, homespun way, they have been subduing the earth in most English counties, and leaving their mark in American forests and Australian uplands' (*TBS*, 1). Ordinary Englishmen, the Browns, have validated the purity and superiority of the Anglo-Saxon race for centuries; Hughes thus gives the 'rightness' of the English imperial cause his absolute approval. Tom's education at Rugby is designed to continue the historical supremacy of England by making him 'fit' for imperial service. This is quite clear in the final cricket match, which proves the worth of the boys' education. The young master, equating the Doctor with an imperial ruler, presses the point home: '"What a sight it is," broke in the master, "the Doctor as a ruler! Perhaps ours is the only little corner of the British Empire which is thoroughly, wisely, and strongly ruled just now"' (*TBS*, 316). Thoroughness, wisdom, and strength are the qualities that make England a justified imperial power. Hughes, as Richards asserts, had struck the right chords for his nineteenth-century readers.

It was partly for this reason that Dean Farrar's *Eric, or Little by Little* (1861) was often reviled. Empire required its young men to be emotionally reserved and physically and mentally fit, the Roman ideal of manhood. With its sentimental friendships and deathbed scenes *Eric* elevated emotionalism and denied the value of team games by making pride in athleticism the cause of its hero's moral demise. This, of course, was at odds with popular opinion concerning 'fit' education for the boys who were to administer the Empire. Mangan outlines how the Empire relied upon public school educated officers:

> For many Victorians and Edwardians there was an obvious link between the development of endurance, toughness and courage on English playing fields and pioneering in Australia, preaching in Africa and soldiering in Burma. And though the association between playing field and battle field may have been too tightly made, it did make some sense. The ferocity of keenly-contested house matches helped create a hardened imperial officer class naively eager for colonial wars. With Britain's vast empire offering as James Morris has observed, 'a more or less perpetual battlefield', the public schools with superogatory [*sic*] zeal, sent forth a constant flow of athletic, young warriors. (*Athleticism*, 138)[23]

By the end of the century, however, anti-imperialism, a late nineteenth-century notion of decadence, and aestheticism were perceived as a threat to the healthiness of the nation and the Empire. Kipling published *Stalky & Co.* in 1899, reacting to the 1890s with wisdom and hindsight. It was a time of national doubt and fear about the future of the country and the Empire. His young heroes dismiss the cult of athleticism and house and school loyalty in favour of a much more complex system of loyalty and self-development designed to stabilize the imperial army. The book was, in a sense, an attack upon on the simplistic moulding of boys' characters into the stereotypes of imperial soldiers produced by Tom Brown's Rugby, while at the same time ridiculing the sentimentalism of Dean Farrar ('Eriking' is used as term of derision in *Stalky & Co.*). Although he felt that the Empire required pure-bred Englishmen, Kipling's criteria for educating them were less dependent on stereotypes. Stalky is an individual, and his instinctive skills are what Kipling sees as vital to the Empire. Just as later in *Kim* (1901)[24] it is the individual spirit that must be nurtured and brought into service, Stalky's rebelliousness is channelled into positive defence of his country's interests in India in the last chapter, 'Slaves of the Lamp'. Neither is intellectualism seen as a threat to manliness: Beetle is, after all, a largely autobiographical creation and very much interested in academic pursuits.

With the Empire beginning to disintegrate and the threat of war closer to home many writers and critics were urging racial purity and wholesomeness, which they perceived as necessary in order to combat the current 'malaise' of 'degeneracy'. This idea is central to Conrad's preoccupations in *Lord Jim* and particularly relevant to Jim's impulsive jump from the *Patna* down to the level of the degenerate crew. In considering Conrad's Malay fiction it is necessary to explore attitudes towards racial purity and English superiority. These are the issues to which I will now turn.

Racial superiority and degeneracy

The case for English superiority

In the last twenty years or so of the nineteenth century imperialism gripped the public imagination in England. Empire was proof of English moral and racial superiority over all other races in the world.[25] It was vital to English self-esteem that the colonized nations be seen as being administered by men who exhibited the wholesome Christian manliness and physical strength and purity that it was assumed characterized the English race at home and abroad. The elite of the Empire, the captains and rulers, was thus drawn from the public schools where these men had already proven their wholesomeness on the games field.

The Social-Darwinian argument was used to assert the rightness of English rule over Africa, India, and the colonies. It was a common assumption that the English ruled the colonies by right of being specially gifted to do so, an argument given historical grounding by Sir Frederick Lugard:

> As Roman imperialism laid the foundation of modern civilization and led the wild barbarians of these islands [Britain] along the path of progress, so in Africa today we are repaying the debt, and bringing to the dark places of the earth – the abode of barbarism

and cruelty – the torch of culture and progress...we hold these
countries because it is the genius of our race to colonize, to trade
and to govern. (See Mangan, *The Games Ethic and Imperilaism*, 102)[26]

This is essentially a paternalistic approach: the Africans were children,
under-developed and in need of parental guidance. It was England's
'duty' to educate and nurture them.[27] Edward Said makes this very point
concerning Kipling's representation of the 1857 Indian Mutiny in *Kim*:

And when Kipling has the old soldier describe the British counter-
revolt – with its horrendous reprisals by white men bent on 'moral'
action – as 'calling' the Indian mutineers 'to strict account', we
have left the world of history and entered the world of imperialist
polemic, in which the native is naturally a delinquent, the
white man a stern but moral parent and judge. (*Culture and
Imperialism*, 178)

It was a convenient argument, allowing those who fostered it to ignore
the commercial benefits that England gained from her paternalistic
care of Africa.[28] But there are deeper and more ominous implications
concerning the popular conceptions of what it meant to be English;
assumptions concerning English superiority were deeply rooted. The
Anglo-Saxon race, as described by Hughes in *Tom Brown's Schooldays*,
were pure and undegenerate 'sons of the soil'. By contrast, the French,
for example, were decadent, and English naval victories had proven
French 'inferiority'. When it came to the colonized nations the view of
the Africans and Indians as children implied an inferior moral, cultural, and political development. Biological research had even led some
to assert that Africans were inferior because of the shape of their skulls
and the alleged size of their brains. This absurd notion was also
applied, by some, to argue the inferiority of women.[29]

Such assumptions of English racial superiority are evident in the literature of Empire from Defoe's *Robinson Crusoe* through Marryat and
Ballantyne to Kingston, Henty, and Haggard. What distinguishes late
nineteenth-century writers from those writing in the mid-century, however, is how racial superiority is portrayed. Earlier writers of Empire rested
the case for English superiority largely upon the notion of Christianity.
The Christian races, notably the English, were perceived as morally and
culturally above the native peoples of the colonies, and the English were
regarded as morally superior to the other colonizing countries. Although
they also believed in their physical superiority it was not until Darwin's

Origin of Species in 1859 that actual 'scientific proof' was available. Subsequent Social-Darwinist tenets provided the ideological framework to support the argument for English racial superiority: the English were a 'fit' race and the fittest survived. The expansion and retention of the Empire was seen as testimony to this. But 'fitness' in the Darwinist sense meant that natural selection ensured the survival of those best adapted to their environment; thus there is a slippage between Darwin's theories and the late nineteenth-century notion of being 'fit' for Empire which required racial purity and a distinctly English morality.

James Walvin observes that athleticism provided evidence that Britain was 'the world's pre-eminent power': 'Moreover, that global pre-eminence was to be found in the personal and collective qualities of her people. If Britain was the world's leading power, it was because her people were superior' (in Mangan and Walvin, 251).[30] The middle and upper classes of the public schools were, by virtue of their education, training, and social position those considered most 'fit' to govern the Empire, in the racial, physical and psychological senses. During the last twenty or so years of the nineteenth century, when empire was at its height and England the most powerful imperial nation, the main concern was with the stability and continuance of the Empire. After all, empire had become a symbol of national superiority. The perceived *fin de siècle* 'disease' of degeneracy threatened not only the health of the nation but also England's capacity to hold on to the Empire itself.

Empire, degeneracy, and the service ethic

Said defines the terms 'imperialism' and 'colonialism' for his own purposes, as 'the practice, the theory, and the attitudes of a dominating metropolitan centre ruling a distant territory; "colonialism", which is almost a consequence of imperialism, is the implanting of settlements on a distant territory' (*Culture and Imperialism*, 8). Perhaps this is an oversimplification of imperialism, but how the notion of 'the dominating metropolitan centre' relates to English imperialism is important. Domination entails subjugation of a people by a race that is in some sense stronger. For British imperialism this implied the superiority of the English race, the specifically Anglo-Saxon race. This in turn is inseparable from the late nineteenth-century notion of degeneracy. Degeneracy was seen as a threat from various quarters, but it had a special relevance to the Empire. For that 'superiority' with which the English justified their imperial impulse was constantly in need of affirmation: there were threats from within as well as from without.

As early as 1852, Sir Henry Yule in writing his poem 'The Birkenhead' tried to play down the Chartist threat to the established aristocracy identifying the heroes of the disaster as 'weavers from the stocking-frame' and 'Boys from the plough'. He invited his reader to 'thank/Heaven for those undegenerate sons who sank/Aboard the Birkenhead in Simon's Bay' (*LH*, 215–16). Half a century later the question of degeneracy was an even more burning issue. While registering his discontent with the public schools of the time, H. B. Gray put the needs of Empire foremost in his scheme for education: the upper classes would govern and 'the integrity and permanence of the Empire [would] depend largely on the characters of those who [would] compose this tide of emigration' (Gray, 47–8). The character of the men who were to run the Empire was crucial: they had to have an English background in education. Even other nationalities within Britain were barely acceptable: 'Those from Irish, Scottish, Welsh and Dominion universities who "gate-crashed" the Service were few in number, often extremely well qualified, both academically and athletically, and perhaps more to the point, the majority (17 out of 24) came from public schools!' (*Games Ethic*, 90). An English public school education was thus regarded as a safeguard against degeneracy.

The undegenerate ex-public schoolboy is a familiar character in the literature of Empire. Rider Haggard's heroes are exemplary specimens of upper-class physical excellence. Leo Vincy in *She* is a 'sturdy young Englishman' and 'one of the most English-looking men [Holly] ever saw': 'He is very tall and broad-chested, and yet not awkward, as so many big men are, and his head is set upon him in such a fashion as to give him a proud and vigorous air, which was well described by his Amahagger name of 'Lion' (*S*, 207). Leo's golden 'mane' testifies to his Anglo-Saxon heritage, for although he is half-Greek he has inherited none of the 'slippery manner of the modern Greek'. Sir Henry Curtis and Captain Good in *King Solomon's Mines* are similar specimens of physical superiority. The African king and warrior Infadoos openly acknowledges Curtis's superior military and physical prowess: 'I have lived a long life among warriors, and have known many a brave one, yet have I never seen a man like unto thee' (*KSM*, 251). In Haggard's fiction and the imperial romance in general, the English race is superior, and the public school has created these men.

Conrad and empire

So far I discussed the development and implementation of ideas concerning the continuance of the Empire and the education of those sent out to govern it. One final point needs to be made in order to illustrate how this debate provides a context for a discussion of Conrad. Baden-Powell frequently used the example of the disintegration of the Roman Empire to indicate the need for efficiency in England's governance of the British Empire, as John Springhall observes:

> He believed that the threat of national decadence was evident in both the supposed physical deterioration of the British race and in the lack of enthusiasm for Empire ... It is hardly surprising that the decline and fall of the Roman Empire should have been adopted as one of his more favourite analogies. One remedy to save Britain from the fate of Rome was encapsulated in the concept of national efficiency, which was among the most influential intellectual concepts in Edwardian governing circles. (Springhall, 57)

This has a direct bearing on Conrad's concept of English imperialism in *Heart of Darkness* where Marlow compares the efficiency of the English colonies to that of the Romans. Said makes this point:

> Such people conquered and did little else. By contrast, 'what saves us is efficiency – the devotion to efficiency', unlike the Romans, who relied on brute force, which is scarcely more than 'an accident arising from the weakness of others'. ... In his account of his great river journey, Marlow extends the point to mark a distinction between Belgian rapacity and (by implication) British rationality in the conduct of imperialism. (*Culture and Imperialism*, 81–2)

But the Romans did demonstrate high degrees of efficiency in their heating and water systems, and their sewerage and communications systems; all of which were models for nineteenth-century England. If we accept Said's interpretation of Conrad's point, however, there is a clear connection between Marlow's argument for the redemptive qualities of English imperialism and Baden-Powell's imperial purposes with the Boy Scouts. When Marlow says of the colours on the imperial map, 'There was a vast amount of red—good to see at any time, because one knows that some real work is done in there', he is implying English efficiency and superiority in imperial rule (*HD*, 55). For Marlow, and probably for Conrad, the Roman Empire 'was just robbery with violence, aggravated murder on a great scale, and men going at it blind' (*HD*, 50). But the English had their vision, Marlow's redemptive idea: 'something you can set up, and bow down before, and offer a sacrifice to ....' (*HD*, 51).

Baden-Powell's use of the analogy of the Roman Empire was by no means unique.[31] Both men responded to a current desire to justify the English presence in the Empire. Where Marlow differs, and perhaps where he provokes so much debate, is that he is aware of the moral complexity of imperialism: 'The conquest of the earth, which mostly means the taking it away from those who have a different complexion or slightly flatter noses than ourselves, is not a pretty thing when you look into it too much. What redeems it is the idea only' (*HD*, 50–1) Maybe Marlow himself did look into it too much and, not liking what he saw, retreated to the safe distance of the redemptive idea. This is a favourite quotation for Said: he uses it as a frontispiece to *Culture and Imperialism* and cites it in *Orientalism* (1978). Perhaps Said is so interested in Marlow's statement because it highlights the problem of how to deal with Conrad and his concept of Empire. It is not good enough simply to label Conrad a racist and an imperial apologist and leave it at that. Andrew Michael Roberts has indicated the complexity of responding to Conrad's imperialism in the years after Achebe's attack on *Heart of Darkness*.[32] Any examination of Conrad's imperial texts must address this issue and in Roberts's words 'the ideological underpinnings' of the texts. The elements of romance and adventure in Conrad's work are no exception: late nineteenth-century attitudes towards the Empire, its peoples, and its administrators can be indentified through the tropes of imperial romance that Conrad uses and subverts. In examining *Almayer's Folly*, *An Outcast of the Islands*, 'Karain', and *Lord Jim* through the genre of the romance and adventure fiction of the nineteenth century it is vital to have a clear understanding of what concerns surrounded the Empire in the 1890s and how these concerns were apparent in the romance, and in Conrad's work.

2
The Possibilities of Romance

The romance: to 'half-shut' one's eyes

In 1884 during his good-natured debate with Henry James on the nature of 'high art' Robert Louis Stevenson made claims for the superiority of the romance over realism. He claimed that truth was 'a word of very debatable propriety' and that art cannot 'compete with life': 'What, then, is the object, what the method, of an art, and what the source of its power? The whole secret is that no art does "compete with life". Man's one method, whether he reasons or creates, is to half-shut his eyes against the dazzle and confusion of reality' ('A Humble Remonstrance' 158–9).[1] Whilst Stevenson was making a broader statement about the nature of fiction itself his comment has interesting implications if we apply it specifically to the late nineteenth-century romance. To 'half-shut' one's eyes against reality means necessarily to be selective about what one writes. Although this applies to all forms of fiction, including realism, the nature of what is selected, and what is left out, helps to identify the genre.[2] In the imperial romances of the late nineteenth century the selection of ideas contained in the novels usually reflects current values, and opinions about empire. What is left out of the text is often omitted because it would undermine the imperial cause; this makes for a deeply conservative type of literature.

Novelists writing imperial romances and boys' adventure stories invariably 'half-shut' their eyes to the less palatable issues of imperialism. Thus we find Rider Haggard and Henty writing books that glorify the English experience in the Empire whilst ignoring or idealizing the effects of imperialism on the colonized population. In doing so they reinforced racial attitudes and provided comforting affirmation of English imperialism and superiority. Boehmer points out that for a Victorian writer to 'resist the prevailing representations of Empire would have meant resisting the very self-perceptions on which late nineteenth-century society grounded itself' (Boehmer, 44). For writers of imperial fiction 'the dazzle and confusion of reality' mentioned by Stevenson was left out in the interests of patriotism and creating best-sellers for a market hungry for fictional adventures that would reinforce its own 'self-perceptions' and presumptions about the Empire.

The formula of the imperial romance

In the final decades of the nineteenth century, amidst fears of degeneracy in the Empire, the imperial romance asserted English racial superiority while transporting its readers to the exotic lands of Africa, India, or the Far East. It presented idealized visions of the past and romanticized versions of the present. For this reason, as White argues, it was an essentially nostalgic fiction that 'yearned for an imagined golden moment in the nation's past, now endangered or lost completely, and at the same time argued for present outlooks and future courses of action that the fiction itself made especially attractive and justifiable' (White, 62). Heroes of fiction are, as Mike Storry and Peter Childs suggest, 'strong characters in whom British readers are invited to invest their hopes and values' (in Storry and Childs, 18). Among such heroes Storry and Childs include Allan Quatermain. The hero of imperial romance thus exemplified the qualities of gentlemanly conduct, Christian morality, patriotism, and the pure Anglo-Saxon racial attributes that were the desired outcome of a public school education. In short, the hero of the imperial romance was England's ideal imperial son: through his adventures he proved his superiority and that of his race; his ultimate triumph was an enactment of a nineteenth-century England's will to imperial dominance.

The success of Haggard's novels affirms what many of his contemporary readers wanted to hear about the Empire. His first bestseller, *King Solomon's Mines*, was written in response to his brother's challenge to 'write anything half so good' as *Treasure Island*, and was completed in just ten weeks. In one year alone it sold thirty-one thousand copies, bringing Haggard royalties of £750 and far outstripping the sales and profitability of Stevenson's popular novel.[3] His next two imperial romances, *Allan Quatermain* and *She*, were equally successful. As D. S. Higgins observes: 'Among the many letters of congratulations Haggard received from admirers and cranks was one from a thirteen-year-old boy, who had been sent a copy of *Allan Quatermain* because Haggard knew his aunt, Lady Lisle':

> Thank you so much for sending me *Allan Quatermain* … it was so good of you. I like "A.Q." better than *King Solomon's Mines*; it is more amusing. I hope you will write a great many more books. I remain, Yours truly, Winston S. Churchill. (Higgins, 117)

Children and adults alike relished these tales of exotic imperial adventure, in part because they deny the creeping doubts surrounding the Empire and English 'fitness' that were already in evidence when Haggard began his writing career. Curtis's closing statements in *Allan Quatermain* even serve as an invective against modern society and confirm White's contention that the romance yearns for an earlier golden age. Curtis avers that 'gunpowder, telegraphs, steam, daily newspapers, universal suffrage, &c., &c.,' have been the cause of much 'evil' (*AQ*, 276), and vows to keep the rest of the world out of Zu-Vendis, the idyllic African kingdom he discovers. Curtis expresses a yearning for a pastoral past, a pre-industrial age, perceived as simpler and more noble. Haggard's message was popular with those who still idealized the British imperial cause; but there were dissenters even so. In August 1887, writing under the name of 'Gavin Ogilvy' for the *British Weekly*, J. M. Barrie delivered this condemnation: '*Allan Quatermain* tells the adventures of three worthless old men, who go to Africa and slay there thousands of human beings. (They are responsible for the deaths of not less than 50,000.) It would have been a nobler part to stay at home and hire themselves out to butchers' (Higgins, 117). Nevertheless, Haggard continued to write best-selling romance well into the twentieth century: the formula clearly worked.

For Haggard and others, imperial romances and adventure novels proved so successful that their creators became very wealthy. The formula was straightforward, relying on simple assumptions about empire and the English imperial endeavour, augmented with stereotypical characters: hence the pure English heroes of Haggard, Henty, and Kingston. The 'native' generally falls into two categories: the 'noble savage', like Umslopogaas (plate 9), or the atavistic 'native' (plate 10) who refuses to be 'civilized'. So Haggard's Umslopogaas and Ignosi are superb warriors in the tradition of the 'noble savage'; evil, ugly creatures like Gagool, or sensuous beauties like Ayesha suggest the dangers lurking in the 'dark continent' and a prehistory with preternatural undertones. By linking Africa's ancient history to these witch-like women Haggard suggests a dangerous female power (in Ayesha's case, sexual power: see plate 7) in the continent itself.[4] In Henty's India heroes like Clive struggle to establish British territory in the face of rebellious Indians. His boy heroes discover manhood and resourcefulness in the Empire whilst acquiring untold riches plundered from the annexed lands. Gorgeous and exotic, dripping with riches, Henty's India is transformed into a British colony through the exertions of English military commanders and patriotic boy heroes.

A faithful friend like Marryat's Masterman Ready, Stevenson's Alan Breck, and Haggard's Allan Quatermain usually accompanies the hero of imperial romance. This friend often comes to be regarded as a surrogate father, such as we see in plate 12 where the English captain is flanked by his young protégé.[5] Sir Henry Curtis avers, 'I loved Quatermain as dearly as though he were my own father', and he would 'never have dreamed of allowing [his] marriage to interfere with that affection' (*AQ*, 274). The friend often carries veiled hints of a one-time outlaw existence, promising a reassuring competence in the face of danger. Thus Stevenson's Alan Breck is 'a condemned rebel, and a deserter, and a man of the French King's' (*Catriona*, 71). The hero is safe under his care: he acts as parent, teacher, and moral and physical guardian steering his protégé through the perils of a hostile world. Marlow, of course, in his involvement with Jim's destiny, mirrors this stereotype, as does Lingard in his dealings with Almayer and Willems.

Violence, betrayal, and intrigue dog the footsteps of the typical romance and adventure hero and his companion. In the boys' fiction of Ballantyne, Kingston, and Henty the hero's moral fibre is tested: he deals with hordes of painted 'savages', bloodthirsty pirates, or resentful 'natives', such as we see in plates 13 and 14. This hero always emerges victorious, asserting his racial superiority, the potency of Christian morality, and the soundness of the English imperial venture. As Jefferson Hunter says, in adventure fiction imperialism 'filled the theater of action with natives who would have to be variously pacified, exploited, educated, or enfranchised, and on the horizon it set competitors coming abroad quickly for their own share of the exploiting and educating' (Jefferson Hunter, 100). Treasure or a promise of wealth either precipitates the action, as in *Treasure Island* and *King Solomon's Mines*, or wealth is acquired as a result of the hero's adventures, as in Henty's fiction. The hero returns home wealthy and wiser, and marries an English girl: Marryat's William Seagrave reaches the relative civilization of Sydney and becomes happily married, having inherited his father's estate; Ouida's Bertie Cecil in *Under Two Flags* (1867)[6] returns from the

French Foreign Legion to claim his inheritance and marry a beautiful Englishwoman; Dick Holland in *The Tiger of Mysore* marries the English girl he rescued from a harem, whilst masquerading as an Indian prince (see plate 15). The racial purity of the family and the stability of the English class structure are assured by marriage to pure-bred, middle- and upper-class English girls.

This fictional world is simplified and reassuring, and it relies on distinct stereotypical identities: 'Exotic lands held out to Englishmen the promise of lost simplicities; abroad, away from England and its problems, they could find undiscovered territory, physical danger, cleaner choices between courage and cowardice, signs of identity to be taken in at a glance (to Marlow and Conrad, Lord Jim is immediately "one of us"), and welcome rituals of discipline' (Jefferson Hunter, 83). Thus Bertie Cecil is always recognized as an English gentleman: Cigarette, the French girl-soldier who loves him, discerns his nobility in his 'figure of a superb cavalry rider' and his white hands; she calls him *'Beau lion'* (*UTF*, 207). The Colonel of Chasseurs describes Cecil's glance as that of a *grand seigneur*, a fine gentleman (*UTF*, 214).

After his death Quatermain is described by Sir Henry Curtis as, 'the ablest man, the truest gentleman, the firmest friend, the finest sportsman, and, I believe, the best shot in all Africa' (*AQ*, 275): in short, the ideal hero of romance and adventure. Indeed, Quatermain is so revered by Curtis that he is forgiven his jealousy of Nyleptha, the white African queen whom Curtis marries, because 'it is, after all, but one little weakness, which makes no great show among so many and such lovable [*sic*] virtues' (*AQ*, 274). Unlike the complex human relationships and moral dilemmas of the realist novel, and of Conrad's early fiction, the romance relies on simple male loyalties and idealized love. Thus in Quatermain's deathbed scene depicted in plate 6 the draperies, the dignified poses of Curtis, Good, and Nyleptha, and the classic profile of the dying man constitute an image of noble suffering and dignified grief. The figures are deliberately reminiscent of classical Greek statuary. The picture conjures the image of a noble death of the sort Jim imagines for himself. Placed in opposition to Almayer's wretched demise or Willems's murder at the hands of Aïssa, this picture exemplifies the simplified world of romance and adventure; death in the imperial settings of Conrad's novels still resembles the degrading reality of Emma Bovary's gruesome death throes and ghastly corpse.[7] Of course Haggard's romances are often very tongue-in-cheek and the accompanying illustrations reflect this; but, nevertheless, the satirical approach to his heroes does little to mask the slaughter of Africans that Barrie objected to, or the assumption that wealth could be appropriated blamelessly from the African continent.[8]

The native subject of imperial romance and adventure is a simple soul, trusting the superior moral, political, and cultural power attributed to the white hero. If the hero has a 'native' friend that friend is adopted by virtue of his or her status as a 'noble savage': hence Umslopogaas in *Allan Quatermain* (see plate 9), Mesty in *Mr. Midshipman Easy*, Avatea in *The Coral Island*, and Pertaub in *The Tiger of Mysore*. However, these friends are always inferior to their white companions. As White says, the relationship between Mesty and Jack 'depends for its success on its inequality; "they" are still easy to distinguish from "us." To everyone's satisfaction, racial lines are maintained and class lines are restored' (White, 69). These friendships established between the English hero and a 'native sidekick' became an 'unquestioned commonplace' (Boehmer, 47). Resentful natives, by contrast, were stereotyped as ugly degenerates, like Gagool in *King Solomon's Mines*, or the murderous yellow-haired chief in *The Coral Island*, scheming and manipulative, snakes in paradise to be destroyed before an English utopian colony can be established. Haggard's Africa, Henty's India, and Kingston's Pacific islands are populated with colourful, one-dimensional stereotypes, either trusting examples of 'native' inferiority, or wicked fiends threatening chaos and anarchy like the head-hunting Dyaks of plate 14, or the painted Aborigines of plate 10. The Empire was thus the stage upon which the English imperial adventurer acted his part as the representative of a superior, pure, Anglo-Saxon race against the backdrop of exotic lands teeming with inferior savages.

This is the formula of a fiction that propelled its readers into imaginary worlds where the complex issues of late nineteenth-century life could be forgotten. It is the basis of the 'course of light holiday literature' that inspires Jim's romantic ego-ideal (*LJ*, 5); Almayer's dream of a splendid future recalls the ideal ending of a fictional romance; Willems's self-image as the imperial adventurer resounds with the promises of imperial romance; and the story of Karain, with his myth-like kingdom and his romantic quest, is Conrad's deliberate attempt to evoke the nineteenth-century popular imperial romance. Reactionary in its values and attitudes towards the Empire, the imperial romance sought to underpin that belief in white superiority which characterizes the assumptions of the European heroes of Conrad's early Malay fiction.

Literature set in the Empire emerged long before the 1880s and 90s. The real starting point is probably *The Tempest*. In *Robinson Crusoe*

(1719) the fictionalized adventures of Alexander Selkirk hold clear colonial implications. In *Masterman Ready* the middle-class English Seagrave family is similarly shipwrecked and attempts to create a colonial paradise out of the island on which they are marooned. Ballantyne's young heroes in *The Coral Island* are public schoolboys exporting English Christian morality and gentlemanly ethics to the South Seas. Kingston is even more didactic in his stories: books like *Ben Hadden* celebrated English Protestantism and missionary work in the Pacific islands.

Ben Hadden, *Masterman Ready*, and *The Coral Island* are essentially children's stories aiming to teach young people, boys in particular, how to maintain a righteous existence in the face of adversity. Ben Hadden's motto, for example, drilled into him by his father, is 'Do right whatever comes of it'. Christian virtues and the Protestant ethic of hard work are made the foundations upon which male 'character' is built and fortunes are made.[9] Masterman Ready explains to young William Seagrave how they will survive through careful farming and God's benevolence: 'We shall soon be well stocked and live in plenty. Every year, if it please God, we shall be richer' (*MR*, 112). In the exotic and relatively little known South Seas the universal rightness of English Christian morality is proven. Thus Ralph Rover in *The Coral Island* declares: 'God bless and prosper the missionaries till they get a footing in every island of the sea!' (*CI*, 224). This type of literature is not simply good clean boyish fun: the moral and racial assumptions contained within it indicate the dominant concerns of the age in which it is written. Thus the aim of writers like Marryat, Ballantyne, and Kingston, writing for children in the mid-nineteenth century, was to make young readers aware of their Christian responsibilities both at home and within the Empire.

G. A. Henty: imperial adventure, materialism, and racism for boys

The decline in religious themes in children's literature of Empire in the second half of the century coincided with a rise in the desire for economic wealth and also reflects the decline in religious belief. Henty's novels echo this change in approach to the Empire. Dunae says that Henty's phenomenally popular boys' books 'reflect the secular ideals and the materialistic spirit which came to characterize late Victorian imperialism' (Dunae, 110).[10] Earlier nineteenth-century imperialist writers submerged the 'vulgar' materialist pursuits of Empire beneath religious doctrine: the purpose of English presence in the Empire was to convert the 'savages' to Christianity. Later in the century boys' novelists embraced the idea of plundering the Empire for personal gain. Thus Henty's Dick Holland comes to India with little material wealth; by the time he returns to England the Indian continent has made him a very rich young man. Remaining in the Empire is rarely an option, for as Roy Turnbaugh observes, Henty's Empire was 'a kind of theatre for aggression, rather than...a place to settle and spend one's life' (Turnbaugh, 735).

Henty's Empire is not restricted to India: as early as 1868 he had portrayed South America as a land of plenty for the enterprising English gentleman. In *Out on the Pampas* the Hardy family – their name suggests their durability – emigrate to Argentina and tame the land, as well as the native population, make a fortune out of colonizing the wilderness with their cattle ranch, and return home to enjoy the spoils of their adventure. Argentina is regarded as nothing more than a place in which to create wealth that is to be transported back to England. At the end of the novel Mr Hardy, with astonishing confidence in his colonial investment, calculates the profit to be made out of their estate over the next ten years. This estate is finally sold off, and the profit equips the family to lead the leisurely life of landed English gentry. The native population of Argentina is only significant in the sense that it poses a threat to the Hardy's interests: they drive off the cattle, thus destabilizing the family's economy. There is never any question of the right of the English colonizers to acquire Argentine land, and no motive is given for the attacks. It is simply assumed that the 'Indians' are 'savages'. To go deeper into their motivation would be to unearth the unpalatable possibility that these people might resent the acquisition of their land by the colonists.

As the Hardy boys launch their attack on the 'Indians' who have taken their cattle, their father fills them with patriotic fervour for the pursuit: 'Now boys, hurrah for old England!' (*OP*, 151). The Argentinians are regarded as little more than animals: at first sight they are simply a 'black mass of something' (*OP*, 142). Later they are identified with cattle: 'The lump seemed to be about the same size that our cattle do when they are close together' (*OP*, 144). Later still a herd of cattle is actually mistaken for the 'Indians' (*OP*, 167). The tendency to describe the 'Indians' as subhuman occurs again when they 'rushed from their huts like swarms of bees' (*OP*, 285). When several men wounded in the fighting are tended by the family who inflicted the injury they 'maintained during the whole time the stolid apathy of their race' (*OP*, 212).

It does not occur to the Hardys that their taciturnity might be due to a resentment of the people who had harmed them; it is much more comforting to ascribe it to inferior racial characteristics. Only once does Henty bother to give a detailed description of the Argentinians and then it is in order to prove their inferiority:

> The Indians of the South American Pampas and Sierras are a very inferior race to the noble-looking Comanches and Apaches of the North American Prairies. They are generally short, wiry men, with long black hair. They have flat faces, with high cheek-bones. Their complexion is a dark copper colour, and they are generally extremely ugly. (*OP*, 213)[11]

The Comanches and Apaches are superior to the South Americans by virtue of their English physical characteristics.

The overriding assumption in Henty's literature is of English 'fitness' to rule the Empire or acquire land in the New World. When Dick Holland in *The Tiger of Mysore* tries to disguise himself, his uncle, the Rajah Mortiz, cautions him on how to behave: 'You must remember that your motions are quicker and more energetic than are those of the people here' (*TM*, 176). Not only are Indians portrayed as physically sluggish and apathetic, intellectually they are inferior: Dick, watching a display of ram-baiting, is bored by the proceedings while the Indians, clearly identified with the barbarity of the event, are engrossed and excited (*TM*, 203). When Dick rescues Tippoo's harem from a rampaging tiger, his Indian friend, Pertaub, praises his quick reactions and courage, evidence of his 'English qualities': 'The English sahib is very young, and yet to him comes in a moment what is the best thing to be done. He does not stop to think of the danger; while all others stand in consternation he acts, and slays the tiger before one of them has so much as moved from his place' (*TM*, 209).

The English perform feats of outstanding military skill throughout the novel. The Hardys' ability to slaughter countless Argentinians with only a few guns is matched by the English army's ability to squash rebellion in *The Tiger of Mysore*.[12] The governor of one province describes the English as 'terrible soldiers' who have the strangest ability to 'make the natives under them fight as bravely as they do themselves': 'The English brought up guns where it was thought no guns could be taken; they knocked the defences to pieces; and, after winning their way to the top, in one day captured this fort and that on the hill yonder. It seems miraculous' (*TM*, 231). Imperial rule in Henty's novels is thus constantly justified by English physical and military superiority. The argument is given greater force by the frequent Indian voices admiring 'English qualities'. Pertaub perceives a racial difference that justifies the English take-over of India: 'This is how it is that the English have become lords of so wide a territory. They are quick: while we hesitate and spend great time in making up our minds to do any-thing, they decide and act in a moment; they are always ready, we are always slow; they see the point where a blow has to be struck, they make straight to it and strike' (*TM*, 209). Mortiz, foresees a time when the 'English will be the rulers of all India' (*TM*, 296). The embracing of English rule by Indians is designed to sanction the English presence in India and to point to the stability of the Empire at a time when that stability was under threat within the Empire itself.

The Tiger of Mysore is set in the early 1800s, when the British Empire was just being established in India. The fact that Mortiz welcomes a future English government glosses over the fact that by the time Henty was writing in the late nineteenth century many Indians were not so accommodating. The Indian Mutiny of 1858 had resulted in the British government taking control of India from the East India Company, but it also indicated the desire of many Indians for complete independence. The establishment of the India Congress Party in 1885 provided a focus for Indian nationalist feeling. Thus, by making his Indian characters rec-ognize the superiority of the English and denigrate their own race, Henty emphasizes the desirability of English control of India.

The native population welcomes English morality and political sys-tems. Mortiz accepts English rule because it has improved the lot of the people: 'I saw how great the English were, how steadily they extended their dominions, and how vastly better off were our people under their sway than they were in the days when every rajah made war against his neighbour, and the land was never at rest' (*TM*, 51). Peace and sta-bility, then, are seen as a consequence of English rule; and of course, that was to a large extent true, a point to be taken up when discussing *An Outcast* and Lingard's paternalistic attitude to 'his' Malays. Mortiz expresses a very English way of justifying imperialism. Ironically though, this supposed harmony is unconsciously undermined when Dick admires the European feel of Madras, or the Madras he sees:

> 'It is not like a hotel, mother,' Dick remarked as they drew up; 'it is more like a gentleman's house, standing in its own park.'
> 'Almost all the European houses are built so here, Dick, and it is much more pleasant than when they are packed together.'

'Much nicer,' Dick agreed. 'If each house has a lot of ground like this, the place must cover a tremendous extent of country.'

'It does, Dick; but as everyone keeps horses and carriages that does not matter much. Blacktown, as they call the native town, stands quite apart from the European quarter.' (*TM*, 45)

Mrs Holland's final statement is ominous: the native population might prove dangerous if they were to live too close. The clean spaciousness of the European dwellings implies an unhealthy opposite in the Indian dwellings. English values have been transported to the Empire, but this is a privilege to be enjoyed only by the whites. Boehmer explains the social history behind this segregation:

At the time when Social Darwinist ideas were popular, it was generally believed that consort with dark peoples compromised white selfhood and threatened race purity. Especially in the second half of the nineteenth century, the post-Mutiny period, colonizers strove to maintain a strict divide between themselves and the local population. No matter how hard those who had been colonized might try to Europeanize themselves, colonial society whether in India or elsewhere was built upon this fundamental separation. (Boehmer, 68)

Underlying all of this is the racial tension that would cause so much instability in colonial India.

Henty's novels are firmly in the reactionary tradition of boys' romance and adventure fiction in the late nineteenth century. They extol the perceived virtues of Englishness and espouse unashamedly jingoistic attitudes, making outrageous racist statements and accepting unreservedly the superiority of English middle- and upper-class values. Furthermore Henty's boy heroes are typical products of the English education system: athletic gentlemen, specifically nurtured to be knights of Empire. Dick patronizingly points out to Annie, the girl he will eventually marry, the training and endurance that creates good English soldiers:

That is a fist, Annie. You see, it is hard enough to knock a fellow down, though it does not very often do that; but it hurts him a bit without doing him any harm, except that it may black his eyes or puff up his face for a day or two – and no boy minds that. It accustoms one to bear pain, and is a splendid thing for teaching a boy to keep his temper, and I believe it is one reason why the English make such good soldiers. (*TM*, 279)

The stability of the Empire, its provision of wealth, and English moral and military 'fitness' were central to Henty's boys' fiction; he largely shut his eyes to the ethical questions of imperialism. Many of the boys who read Henty were destined to become captains of Empire, and his novels were designed to instil the confidence and racial arrogance necessary to maintain English rule. Henty was not concerned with India for Indians; as Mark Naidis observes, 'Henty's idea of India had to do with British colonial life' (Naidis, 56).

Imperial romance for adults

Ouida's *Under Two Flags* is an imperial romance for adults and young people. It concerns an extravagant, but essentially honourable young man who exiles himself to French colonial Africa in order to save a married woman from scandal.[13] The book is a celebration of English *sang-froid* and gentlemanly behaviour. Cecil is the archetypal aristocratic English gentleman: he is brave, and physically powerful; his saintly loyalty to his friends and fellow soldiers earns him an unbelievable degree of fidelity in colleagues and enemies alike. They loved him:

> [W]ith a rough, ardent, dog-like love, when they found that his last crust in a long march would always be divided; that the most desperate service of danger was always volunteered for by him; that no severity of personal chastisement ever made him clear himself of a false charge at a comrade's expense; and all his *décompte* went in giving a veteran a stoup of wine, or a sick conscript a tempting meal, or a prisoner of Beylick some food through the grating, scaled, too, at risk of life and limb. (*UTF*, 268)

Such complacency about the nobility of the English character is typical of nineteenth-century romantic literature. Moreover, any suggestion of degeneracy in the aristocracy is an aberration rather than a threatening trend.[14] The happy ending amounts to an affirmation of conservative upper-class English values. Cecil returns to the tranquil English countryside and the security of marriage to a good woman as the reward for suffering exile in violent imperial Africa and proving himself a purebred English gentleman. In 'the forest wealth of Royallieu' (*UTF*, 607) there is no suggestion of the poverty and deprivation that Dickens saw in the inner cities.

Romance and adventure novels of this type were conceived in an atmosphere of general confidence about empire and English moral and physical health. Religious belief was still perceived as being widespread and 'the angel in the house' had not yet spread her wings enough to cause serious unease about the role of women. By the closing decades of the century, however, questions about the role of women had become more pressing; writers were voicing their religious scepticism; there was considerable concern about the state of the inner cities and what was perceived as the degeneration of the race; and serious worries about the legitimacy and the efficiency of English rule in the Empire were emerging. Much of the romance literature of the time responds to those worries. Wendy Katz observes that a 'dynamic relationship exists between late-nineteenth-century imperialism and the literary climate of Great Britain, the development of romance literature being the most striking by-product of this relationship' (Katz, 4). The exploits of Haggard's adventurers in Africa exemplify that dynamism.

In contrast to the concerns of the naturalist writers about the squalid living conditions of the working class, writers of romance, notably Haggard, were producing novels that continued to assert the superiority of the English middle and upper classes.[15] Haggard's was a reactionary literature using the Empire to validate its assumptions about the English character. Writing in the *Contemporary Review* in 1887, Haggard identifies 'the paths and calm retreats of pure imagination' as the theme for his fiction. He claims for his 'humble tale' a 'harmless moral', and looks to a future when naturalism 'has had its day' and what he calls 'the Society novel' will be 'utterly played out'. Then, he says, 'the kindly race of men' will enjoy 'those works of fancy which appeal, not to a class, or a nation, or even to an age, but to all time and humanity at large' (*Contemporary Review,* 180). One wonders if Haggard includes native Africans in his definition of humanity; if so he condemns his novels by his own definition. Haggard was fictionalizing then widely held attitudes and making a fortune in the process. He was capable of portraying Africans sympathetically, as in *Nada the Lily* (1892),[16] but even here the heroes and heroines espouse European values, and the villains are 'savages'. Nada is beautiful, but it is strongly suggested that the European strain in her blood accounts for her uncanny beauty. She is called 'the Lily' because her skin is unusually white: the racial implications are inescapable.[17] Moreover, as Edward Boyd observes in his Introduction to the novel, the character who lends the book 'more than a merely narrative significance' is a white man:

He is a symbol, the white colonist who is there symbolically at the beginning of it all and who is still there, with an even more meaningful symbolism perhaps, when it is all over with the great Zulu nation destroyed, shattered and dispersed. *Nada the Lily* is really about that white man. The book is an almost perfect projection of the nineteenth century colonial mind, with all its conflicting and coexistent attitudes. (*NL*, 15)

Quatermain may occasionally voice opinions that seem strangely in favour of racial equality, but when it comes to miscegenation he is unequivocal: the death of Foulata in *King Solomon's Mines* is 'a fortunate occurrence', saving Good from undesirable 'complications'. Foulata herself is given the last word on the 'impossibility' of such a union when she says, 'Can the sun mate with the darkness, or the white with the black?' (*KSM*, 333). As Katz points out, Haggard 'was an ideological presence, part of his period's popular culture; and he contributed to a certain state of mind' (Katz, 4). That state of mind took for granted English greatness, English imperialism, and English racial superiority. It also assumed that unions across racial boundaries were a threat to the purity of the English race. Marriage to sensuous 'native' beauties like Foulata was to be avoided at all costs. Yet Nada is almost certainly the granddaughter of a Portuguese ironmonger and a Swazi woman, dimly suggesting the fact that 'native' women were indeed used for sex in the Empire even if this rarely resulted in marriage.[18] Nada's beauty is, after all, 'the beauty of the white people' (*NL*, 71), and significantly she too dies at the end of the novel, leaving no children to carry on the legacy of that forbidden union.

Conrad's dystopia

In the context of a study of Rider Haggard and his novels Katz states that 'Conrad seems to have felt that the heroic tradition was at an end', and that his concern was with 'the failures of conventional heroism' (Katz, 60).[19] In the imperial romance 'conventional heroism' finds its fullest expression. By contrast, Conrad's early Malay tales unveil the vanity and powerlessness underlying the liberal assumptions of those who wish to 'civilize' the Empire, amongst whom Haggard would count himself. Like Barrie, Conrad reviled Haggard's romances, finding them, according to Edward Garnett, 'too horrible for words'; he particularly objected to Captain Good (Garnett, xiii). It would thus be reasonable to assume that, being familiar with Haggard's fiction, Conrad was not unaware of its implications for his own work.

The romance tends ultimately to present a utopian perspective on the imperial endeavour. Whether it be Henty's vision of an exotic India made 'civilized' under English rule, or Haggard's fictional Zu-Vendis where Quatermain, Curtis, and Good establish an ideal pastoral community in the heart of Africa, the narrative offers escape from a late nineteenth-century England where the 'tranquil waterway' of the Thames 'seemed to lead into the heart of an immense darkness' (*HD*, 162). Conrad's Malaya, however, is a present dystopia from which escape is never possible because it defines the conditions of personal existence in the *fin de siècle*. Setting his tales of individual isolation and misery in an exotic East that had traditionally been the location of the ideal romantic experience, Conrad denies the possibility of refuge from the disturbing realities of late nineteenth-century life. If Conrad's Eastern forests initially resemble the idyllic natural worlds of the imperial romance it is only in order that he may subvert the idyll and emphasize instead the grim facts of decay, death, and ineffectuality beneath the gorgeous surface. Only in 'Karain' does Conrad present an exotic paradise, and even then a deep anxiety about England's inner cities being troubled and alienated jungles surfaces as the story closes.

White examines how 'Haggard's fiction subverted genre expectations by questioning home values' and suggests that the reluctance of Haggard's heroes to 'remain in England and their refusal to return sound a new note' (White, 93, 97).[20] Quatermain, like Haggard himself, is uncomfortable with life as an English country squire and 'the new commercial middle classes' (White, 93). Quatermain longs for the type of clean adventure and simple values only to be found in the undiscovered corners of Haggard's fictional Africa. Time and again he leaves his comfortable country retreat for the rigours of African adventure, eventually dying among the white African race of Zu-Vendis. White contends that Haggard's 'fiction helped to make the genre that had always defended the status quo capable of subverting it', by demonstrating an implicit criticism of English life (White, 99).

Reviewing White's book, Felix Driver argues that the experiences of Mungo Park, Henry Stanley, and David Livingstone suggest that Quatermain's attitude was not as 'unconventional' as White would have us believe. He claims that a reading of Conrad and Haggard 'alongside contemporary writings on anthropology and geography would enable their work to be situated within wider concerns about evolution and race', thus revealing further subversive voices (Driver, 107–9). Whilst Driver is no doubt correct in calling for a broader context for the imperial theme in the work of Conrad and Haggard, White's study and the present discussion are concerned with examining the presentation of romance and adventure through the *fiction* of Empire. Apart from the dropping of religious themes around the mid-century, this is a fiction that remained more or less static in its representation of the imperial subject and the adventurers' attitudes to the Empire and its people during most of the nineteenth century. Driver's note of caution is a valid one, but to stray into the territory of anthropological and geographical investigation at this point would be to obscure the focal argument, which is that Conrad was using, manipulating, and subverting the romance and adventure genre in fiction.

Albert Guerard suggests that, 'A glance at the South Sea Yarns of Stevenson, which immediately preceded *Almayer's Folly*, indicates in what sense Conrad "brought seriousness" to the exotic novel of adventure. It also reminds us of what Conrad's early readers must have expected and not found' (Guerard, 88). Yet Stevenson's South Sea yarns themselves indicate the emergence of a more complex and sceptical approach to Eastern exoticism. In fact 'The Beach of Falesá' and *The Ebb-Tide* demonstrate how far from the adventure tale Stevenson had moved. That shift continued with Conrad: beneath the exotic surface of his narratives Conrad uses, manipulates, and subverts a popular genre that lionized its heroes and assumed English racial superiority. Conrad's early Malay fiction is deeply sceptical of the claims made by the imperial romance. Whether they are utopian visions, or the clean adventure and consummate heroism of the imperial romance, ideals in Conrad's fiction are demythologized. They are the foolish dreams of men and women who must ultimately face the limitations placed on experience by their own natures, by the fallibility of others, and by the fact of an indifferent universe. This theme is central to the experience of Willems in *An Outcast*, and of Jim in *Lord Jim*; and in his first novel, *Almayer's Folly*, Conrad explores how the conflict between romantic idealism and reality is a major contributor to the disillusionment and decline of his central character, Almayer.

3
Almayer's Folly: When Romance Collides with Reality

The literary context: subversive voices

In a letter to T. Fisher Unwin in March 1895, Conrad speaks of 'Letters by every post' coming from 'North and west and south and east' demanding news of the publication date of *Almayer's Folly* (*Letters 1*, 206). Perhaps these people were anxious to get hold of another imperial adventure in the style of Henty or Haggard; if so, they were rewarded for their wait with a very different kind of novel. When *Almayer's Folly* appeared in April 1895 some reviewers were disappointed by its failure to live up to their romantic expectations as the reviews in Sherry's *Conrad: The Critical Heritage*[1] show. The anonymous reviewer for *World* on 15 May found it 'as dull as it well could be' (*CH*, 51); and the reviewer for *Nation* on 17 October begins a lamentable piece by complaining that a novel 'in which the only white man of importance is a Dutch Trader, while all the women are Malays or half castes, does not promise much entertainment' (*CH*, 60). Even some favourable reviews mistook *Almayer's Folly* for a romance: the *Guardian*'s reviewer thought it a 'most charming' romance (*CH*, 57); James Ashcroft Noble, writing for *Academy* on 15 June, felt the Malay Archipelago 'an unfamiliar background for romance' (*CH*, 54);[2] and the *Spectator*'s reviewer famously declared that Conrad 'might become the Kipling of the Malay Archipelago' (*CH*, 61). What many reviewers failed to understand, however, is that *Almayer's Folly* is a novel that challenges the assumptions of the romance rather than perpetuating them; it is ultimately a realist tale whose preoccupation with subverting the imperial romance signals the first step in Conrad's progress towards literary modernism.

The elements of romance and adventure in *Almayer's Folly* were recognized by the reviewer for the *Athenaeum* on 25 May 1895: it is a 'story of the loves and hates, the intrigues and counter plots of Dutch, Malay, and Arab traders on "an Eastern river"' (*CH*, 52). Ian Watt identifies the 'many standard adventure story motifs', which include a secret upriver channel, a notebook hinting at treasure, pirates, gunrunning, political intrigue, and a romantic hero, Dain Maroola. Watt cites the threat to Dain's life and the fact that he is saved by 'two of the most plausible but time-hallowed devices of fiction; first that of mistaken identity—the false clue of Dain's ring on the drowned corpse; and second that of the heroine's dauntless self-sacrifice—the scene where Nina interposes herself between her lover and her irate father's revolver' (Watt, 47). In fact these 'devices' are even more emblematic of romance and adventure fiction than of fiction in general; the ring in particular looks forward to the talisman in 'Karain' and that other ring which allows Jim to enter the romance world of Patusan.[3] Further to this we have the imperial adventurer, Almayer, and his surrogate father, Lingard. These are familiar motifs, but, as Watt states, *Almayer's Folly* does not fall into the adventure story mould for long (Watt, 47). We can recognize the motifs and the superficial resemblance of some of the characters to those of the popular genre, but what actually happens in the novel has very little to do with romance. If in boys' adventure fiction closure involves a return to 'civilization' then Conrad's story of Kaspar Almayer has one obvious deviation from the popular formula: Almayer remains and dies in his Eastern backwater. Indeed there is no indication that Almayer had ever been to Europe, let alone Amsterdam. His family home is 'the parental bungalow' in Java, and his dreams of glory in Amsterdam are no doubt fuelled by his mother's tales of her life there as 'the daughter of a cigar dealer' (*AF*, 5).[4]

Immediately before *Almayer's Folly*, in 'The Beach of Falesá', Stevenson similarly shifts the direction of his fiction by leaving his hero marooned on a South Pacific island. Wiltshire's recognition of his duty to his Polynesian wife and children is presented with a good-natured ruefulness more reminiscent of the realist tale than the romance.[5] While Stevenson was by no means the advocate of imperialism that Haggard was, the two writers shared a scepticism about interfering with native cultures that, when registered in their fiction, reveals a radically new perspective. White observes that Stevenson's observations about the detrimental effects of white intrusions in the South Seas echo Haggard's concerns about Africa.[6] Stevenson's essay 'In the South Seas' expresses his concerns about 'the white man's often fatal influence on those island people through disease and domination', and he observed that 'the groups among whom the fewest changes were imposed survived the most successfully' (White, 92).

Conrad's attitude to 'native' affairs is rarely so liberal: indeed some would argue that in *Heart of Darkness* his concern is less for the effect of imperialism on the African than for the dangers presented to Europeans if they get too close to a primitive culture and are tempted to reveal their own inherent savagery. Nevertheless, the dissenting voice of Stevenson finds some sympathy in Conrad's early work. If the romance and adventure fiction of the later Stevenson challenged some basic beliefs about imperialized subjects, Conrad went further by questioning the essential values espoused by the romance and adventure genre itself. This intention is most self-conscious in *Lord Jim*, but in *Almayer's Folly* Conrad certainly draws on the imperial romance in order to generate interest, but more significantly, to point to the futility of an existence based upon romantic idealism.

The appeal of the East: capturing an audience, subverting a genre

In the 'Author's Note' to *Almayer's Folly*, written in 1895 but not included until the 1921 *Collected Edition*, Conrad outlines the popular perception of 'that literature which preys on strange people and prowls in far-off countries'. 'The critic and the judge,' says Conrad, 'seems to think that in those distant lands all joy is a yell and a war dance, all pathos is a howl and a ghastly grin of filed teeth, and that the solution of all problems is found in the barrel of a revolver or on the point of an assegai' (*AF*, vii). He challenges this notion by claiming 'a bond between us and that humanity so far away' (*AF*, viii). The stereotype of the romance, Conrad asserts, is not his subject: 'I am content to sympathize with common mortals, no matter where they live; in houses or in tents, in the streets under a fog, or in the forests behind the dark line of dismal mangroves that fringe the vast solitude of the sea' (*AF*, viii). As Heliéna Krenn observes, the omission of the 'Author's Note' from early editions of *Almayer's Folly* had far-reaching consequences. An awareness of Conrad's beliefs as expressed in the 'Author's Note' could have 'spared him and his readers many frustrating experiences and saved him from the suspicion of racist tendencies' (Krenn, 8).[7]

Nevertheless, it seems highly likely that Conrad used the romantic appeal of the Malay Archipelago and its people to improve his prospects of publication and secure an interest in his first book. On 4 October 1894, in a letter to Marguerite Poradowska, Conrad states that 'the mere fact of publication is of great importance. Every week some dozens of novels appear—and it is truly difficult to get oneself into print' (*Letters 1*, 178).[8] One way of easing this difficulty was to draw on the current demand for exotic romance. Conrad's choice of pseudonym, 'Kamudi', which he defines as 'a Malay word meaning rudder', could well be an attempt to trade on the saleability of the exotic (*Letters 1*, 170). His concern that Poradowska would find *Almayer's Folly* 'mawkish' may reflect Conrad's awareness of the story's resistance to the popular formula (*Letters 1*, 156).[9]

As ever, Conrad was desperate for money: he took twenty pounds for the manuscript rather than risk a share in the profits (*Letters 1*, 180). But Conrad was a novice and probably also accepted the money because he had no bargaining power as yet. Certainly he felt insecure about life as a novelist: before the book was accepted by Unwin he was still anticipating returning to sea.[10] *Almayer's Folly* may be the 'work of art' H. G. Wells claimed it to be (*CH*, 53), but artistic worth was no guarantee of sales or even publication. George Gissing makes that quite clear in Edwin Reardon's struggles to remain a writer of integrity in *New Grub Street* (1891). Offering twenty pounds for the manuscript of *Almayer's Folly*, Unwin warned Conrad: 'you are unknown and your book will appeal to a very limited public' (*Letters 1*, 180).[11] It thus seems highly likely that part of the reason for Conrad's choice of Sambir for the location of *Almayer's Folly* was generated by the need to capitalize on the current taste for the exotic.[12] As the reviewer for the *Daily News*, 25 April 1895, pointed out: 'No novelist has yet annexed the island of Borneo' (*CH*, 47). Ballantyne's South Seas, Henty's India, and Haggard's Africa were well known romance territory; Conrad moves to a new location that still carries suggestions of the exoticism of the popular romance.

His childhood reading provided Conrad with intimate knowledge of the romance genre, and given his comments on Captain Good, he was clearly aware of the success of popular contemporary writers like Haggard.[13] The first two paragraphs in his 'Author's Note' to *Almayer's Folly* also seem to refer to the popular imperial romance. Zdzislaw Najder cites Conrad's need for a background that was unfamiliar to his English readers and which would give his 'imagination relative freedom': 'the Malay Archipelago had considerable advantages: the surroundings and customs were exotic; they were made interesting by complicated national, political, and religious interrelations, and the conflicts of different civilizations and competing colonial powers' (*Joseph Conrad: a Chronicle*, 101). Laurence Graver dismisses *An Outcast of the*

Islands claiming that little can be done to 'redeem the saga of the lamentable Willems': 'If a reader wants Conrad in his early Malayan phase, *Almayer's Folly* offers adequate proportions of tangled vegetation and tormented castaways to satisfy a taste for the picturesque' (Graver, 58).

Sambir is indeed unfamiliar and exotic: it is hot, tropical, and sleepy; palm trees tower on the skyline, and the distant sea rushes to Celebes and Macassar; the Malays sleep in huts on mats or hammocks behind rattan blinds; they cook rice in iron pots around campfires, wear sarongs, strange headgear, and carry a dagger, the kriss; there is talk of tribal warfare, of volcanoes, and tropical storms. The exoticism of Eastern life is immediately suggested to the Western reader. Before the end of the first chapter, however, the promise of the popular formula is undercut; the picturesque quickly becomes the prosaic. Life in Sambir is as sordid as life in an English city. Beneath the exotic veneer lie dirt and squalor: red stains on the floor indicate the local habit of chewing betel nut (unpleasant to the European); in the debilitating heat mosquitoes swarm on the veranda, and broken bottles litter the ground. An atmosphere of decay and neglect surrounds Almayer's campong, suggestive of something more sombre, inert, and degenerate than anything to be found in the imperial romance. After all, in direct conflict with assumptions that European colonizers impose cleanliness and order on the picturesque but haphazard domestic arrangements of the East, it is a European, Kaspar Almayer, who corrupts his exotic environment.

Coconuts, bananas, fresh water, and a plentiful supply of wild pigs are available to the hero of adventure stories. In *The Coral Island* and *Masterman Ready* an ordered, agrarian life is created in the midst of natural tropical bounty. The Mackenzie family in *Allan Quatermain*, make themselves a 'little England' in an African landscape – a moat surrounds an English country garden, overlooked by an English church, symbolic of the inexorable march of Christianity into the 'dark places' of the world. Stranded on a deserted island with the Seagrave family, Masterman Ready informs the young William that they 'ought to make a little garden, and sow the seeds which your father brought from England with him' (*MR*, 112). Implicitly, the natural world of romance and adventure offers utopian possibilities for white Christian adventurers: it is at their disposal, friendly and abundant in its supplies. Nature in Sambir is indifferent to human lives. No tropical bounty is evident in Almayer's campong: the staple diet is rice and that not always plentiful, presumably due to the failure of Almayer's trading ventures. Unlike the escapism of imperial romance, Almayer's world is governed by forces that dominate the real world: trade and finance. Sambir is no

tropical Eden: it is a place of narrow ditches where stagnant water over-
flows from the river and suffocating smoke exudes from the campfires.
Rather than healthy tropical lushness, the breezes bring 'from the
woods opposite a faint and sickly perfume as of decaying flowers'
(*AF*, 16). European attention to cleanliness and order is absent here.
Almayer's existence in Sambir belies the popular imperial romance
message that the East is a place where utopian idylls can be created
by white Protestant labour. The dirt and decay of his campong are
evidence of Almayer's powerlessness, his inability to tame his exotic
surroundings and establish a European order. Almayer's miserable establishment thus undercuts the unquestioned and unrealistic assumptions
of colonialism.

As we have seen in the example of Henty's *The Tiger of Mysore*, white
settlers in the imperial romance keep their dwellings separate from
those of the 'natives'. Such fiction suggests a return to Eden, and yet,
paradoxically, this exotic paradise is perpetually other: in *Allan
Quatermain* Mackenzie's moat marks a boundary between himself and
the real Africa. There is a sense of contradiction here: in the apparent
desire for the exotic is mingled a fear of its otherness, as expressed by
the refusal to be assimilated into it. The barriers that Europeans erect
between their homes and the exotic landscape they colonize at once
signal their determined presence there and their consciousness as out-
siders within the Empire. By contrast, Almayer's home, a statement of
his European heritage, in fact creates no boundaries: it becomes the
space within which whites and Malays cohabit and its domestic
arrangements are distinctly Malay. Almayer lives in squalor: when his
Sulu wife systematically dismantles his initial efforts towards sartorial
comfort he abandons any attempt to impose European order on his
domestic circumstances. The dilapidated state of Almayer's house bears
testimony to the fact that 'whiteness' is no proof against degeneration
into squalor or 'going native'.

As Jacques Berthoud observes, Conrad dissociates himself from the
exotic romance 'on the grounds of its exploitative insensitivity—of the
unreality of its exoticism and the reductiveness of its treatment of
human beings': 'His Indonesia will not be like Rider Haggard's Africa—
a place offering no resistance to the fantasies of ignorance and desire'
(*AF* [Oxford World's Classics], xiii). Conrad signals this opposition to
the romance in the 'Author's Note' where the 'nature of the evidence',
by which he means the imperial romance, is 'misleading': 'I am speaking here of men and women—not of the charming and graceful phantoms that move about in our mud and smoke and are softly luminous

with the radiance of all our virtues; that are possessed of all refine-
ments, of all sensibilities, of all wisdom—but being only phantoms,
possess no heart' (*AF*, vii–viii). At the centre of Conrad's story of 'real'
men and women is Kaspar Almayer, a real man who dreams of an
unreal life. With the collision of reality and romance in *Almayer's Folly*
Conrad announces a theme that will become one of the central concerns of his Malay novels: the fragility of lives based upon romantic
ideals.

Dreams of imperial gold

The imperial romance takes the actual experience of empire and
dresses it up as romantic fiction so that it becomes the location of easily procured riches. It assumes the Empire to be the location of limitless wealth easily acquired by 'plucky' young adventurers. In actuality
many adventurers in the Empire did become fabulously rich, making
the dream of imperial gold so compelling for writers of adventure fiction and their readers alike. Boehmer cites Charlie Marryat in Henty's
With Clive in India (1884) who observes that 'everyone who went to
India made fortunes' (Boehmer, 37). In the romance of empire wealth
is accrued almost effortlessly, as with Dick Holland who moves through
Henty's India picking up priceless jewels as gifts from grateful Indian
princes; or the wealth comes in the form of treasure scooped up by
heroes who have proven their 'manly' worth, as in *King Solomon's Mines*.

This myth of imperial wealth clearly preoccupies Almayer. But the
gold at the centre of his thoughts is never realized; he never leaves the
East, and the whole notion of gold acquires a vulgar quality. Lingard
bullies Almayer into marrying his adopted daughter with the suggestion of great wealth: 'Nobody will see the colour of your wife's skin.
The dollars are too thick for that, I tell you!' (*AF*, 10); and Almayer con-
templates the convenient disappearance of his wife once the fortune is
secured. The imperial romance is invoked by Almayer's dream of
'splendid future' only to be quickly undermined by his coarse ruminations and Lingard's crude promises. For, as Krenn states, 'In Conrad's
fiction trust in wealth that is obtained by means other than honest
work and courage is a symptom of decadence' (Krenn, 20). Juliet
McLauchlan argues that Conrad's disdain of the pursuit of wealth is
even more pronounced. Among the prominent Conradian themes she
includes 'the futility of seeking happiness through material wealth or
through adherence to the non-values of supposed "civilization"'
(McLauchlan, 113). This is a point most clearly developed in *Nostromo*

(1904), but it finds full enough expression in *Almayer's Folly* to require serious attention.

Almayer's story has the superficial impetus of the popular formula: in his white imperial uniform he left Java 'with a light heart' and 'ready to conquer the world' (*AF*, 5), like the hopeful young Peter Biddulph of plate 11. Almost: Peter Biddulph sets sail from England; Almayer has never been in Europe. In the narrative present of the novel, Almayer yearns for deliverance from the very scene of the promised adventure. Excusing his lack of fortune on the pretext that 'Circumstances had been against him' (*AF*, 11), Almayer misses the fact that a true conqueror of the world would never depend on circumstance. Even for the hero of romance 'circumstance' is not enough: success requires character and positive action. Romance and reality are thus the opposing poles of the novel. The brooding atmosphere of the novel's opening undermines the romantic suggestiveness of the plot. We are told twice that Almayer is dreaming: dreams centred on gold, made more vivid by the 'glowing gold tinge on the waters of the Pantai' (*AF*, 3). But this is in stark opposition to the 'shrill voice' of his wife, 'the unpleasant realities of the present hour', and 'the bitterness of toil and strife' that mark Almayer's existence in Sambir (*AF*, 3). Allan Simmons argues that Almayer's delusions are further emphasized through the way in which his dreams are qualified by Nina's 'mixed blood' and by Dain's continued absence. This, says Simmons, 'removes the first link in the associative chain – "glowing gold" → gold → dream realized – which the narrative has encouraged. We are just into the second page of the novel and Almayer's dream is already being undermined' (*Conradian* 14:1 and 2, 12). This, then, is a narrative that mocks the illusions of romance through the evident folly of Almayer's belief in its possibilities, and through the narrative strategies that regularly subvert his naive dreams.

Lingard: mythic hero and dream-maker

The boastful assurances of Lingard supply the basis of Almayer's self-delusive dreams. Almayer believes in Lingard's boasts without recognizing that they are exaggerations of reality. The excesses of the imperial romance genre are ironized in Lingard's tales of wealth and power, so that he too becomes a very particular part of Conrad's subversion of the romance tradition. Lingard is initially presented as a romantic figure, 'he whom the Malays, honest or dishonest, quiet fishermen or desperate cut-throats, recognized as "the Rajah-Laut"—the King of the Sea' (*AF*, 7). He has earned this Malay title and as such seems to be a romantic hero deserving of 'native' adulation, like Quatermain, Curtis, and Good. In a distinct echo of the imperial romance tradition where the hero's tools of trade symbolize his reputation, Lingard owns a brig called *Flash,* a boat as legendary as its master, recalling Hawkeye's rifle, *Killdeer,* and Umslopogaas's axe, *Slaughterer.* He battles with pirates, deals in gunpowder and rifles; he has adopted a girl, captured from a pirate boat; he disappears on mysterious adventures and is 'unaffected by any amount of liquor' (*AF*, 8). Most interesting of all, at least for Almayer, is that Lingard seems to have money, lots of it.

At first this swashbuckling sea captain appears to have stepped out of the pages of a novel by Marryat or Stevenson. One is reminded of Masterman Ready, and of Alan Breck and Long John Silver. Lingard seems to have all the characteristics of the conventional 'older man' of romance fiction. In plate 12 a stereotypical sea captain sits cross-legged on the ground in conciliatory fashion while his protégé looks on in awe and admiration. Lingard's ego ideal as father figure to Almayer and benevolent patriarch to 'his Malays' is the elusive ideal of imperial romance, of Kingston's, Henty's, and Haggard's fiction, the idealized father figure that we see in plate 12. An ironic version of this stereotype is invoked in Conrad's characterization of the flawed and blinkered Lingard. Yet Conrad manages to sustain both the romance and the anti-romance simultaneously through Lingard: this romantic swashbuckling sea captain appears to hold the key to Almayer's 'glorious' future while at the same time being deeply implicated in his downfall.

The Lingard / Almayer relationship has a basis in real life, as Norman Sherry carefully documents.[14] The history of the 'real' Lingard provided Conrad with the basis for his fictional Captain Tom. Watts calls William Lingard the 'genitor of Tom Lingard': he was a 'formidable sea-rover who fought pirates and knew the coastal waters better than any other European' (Watts, 26). In Tom Lingard Conrad combines the daring deeds of William Lingard, his generosity, his tendency to acquire protégés, his explorations, and his wealth, with the romantic image of the tall sea captain of boys' adventure fiction: a red-faced and white-bearded patriarch, with a deep booming voice and penchant for recounting his exploits to any willing to listen. He thus created a character that appears to conform to the stereotype. Initially Lingard seems to have been fashioned from the same mould as Marryat's Masterman Ready. Ready had been 'more than fifty years at sea':

> His face was browned from long exposure, and there were deep furrows on his cheeks, but he was still a hale and active man. He had served many years on board a man-of-war, and had been in every climate: he had many strange stories to tell, and he might be believed even when his stories were strange, for he would not tell an untruth. (*MR*, 13)

Mr Seagrave regards Ready as an 'excellent old man': 'What a heart of oak is hid under that rugged bark!' (*MR*, 67). In 'Tales of the Sea' Conrad freely acknowledges the influence of Marryat and Fenimore Cooper in his choice of seafaring career (*NLL*, 56). But Lingard moves beyond the bold, honest, and reliable stereotype and becomes the means of subverting notions of altruistic heroism.

Lingard is a powerful presence inspiring the type of trust the young boy displays in plate 12. He fuels Almayer's dream, first prompted by his mother's tales of the 'lost glories' of Amsterdam. 'Crowning all' is Almayer's fantasy where 'in the far future gleamed like a fairy palace the big mansion in Amsterdam, that earthly palace of his dreams, where made king amongst men by old Lingard's money, he would pass the evening of his days in inexpressible splendour' (*AF*, 10). The language of the 'fairy-tale' points to the dream-like nature of Almayer's ambitions and the hollowness of Lingard's promises. Childlike, Almayer adopts almost verbatim some of Lingard's more fanciful projections. Almayer imagines Nina accompanying him to Europe in a clear echo of Lingard's prophecy years earlier: 'Nobody would think of her mixed blood in the presence of her great beauty and of his immense wealth' (*AF*, 3). Deluding himself again, Almayer believes that his imaginary gold will obscure Nina's racial difference; and significantly his wife is absent from these future plans.

In actuality the Lingard of *Almayer's Folly* has feet of clay. He is not the infallible, wealthy benefactor of Almayer's dreams and Lingard's own ego-ideal; rather, he has as many problems with reality as does his protégé. Almayer accepts Lingard's patronage, is even persuaded to call the old man 'father', and believes in the promises of a glorious future. But, unable to realize his own fantasies, Lingard abandons his partner and 'son-in-law' to disappear somewhere in Europe, his remarkable reputation in ruins. Lingard is no Alan Breck or Allan Quatermain possessed of boundless fidelity. The friendship, after all, proves not to be as romantic as it first appeared: Lingard 'adopted' Almayer to provide a husband for his adopted daughter, thus discharging his responsibilities. For Almayer, Lingard was a means to an end: he marries the Sulu girl to get his hands on Lingard's money. No romance hero would ever marry a 'native', however desperate for money he was. As exemplified by the case of Good and Foulata in *King Solomon's Mines*, the imperial romance reinforces the colonial paradigm: Haggard uses Foulata to make the point that miscegenation is regarded as undesirable. Altruism and romantic loyalty exist only in fiction: the father/son relationship, the treasure, the return to 'civilization', all the familiar motifs of the popular adventure story are exposed in *Almayer's Folly* as foolish day-dreams obscuring the fact that in the real world, where Almayer has never actively worked with others in a spirit of solidarity, he must forge his own destiny alone.

The dream/reality division in the novel is expressed through the narrative's direct contact with the perceptions and fantasies of the characters. A kind of *Bovary*ism is at work here. Indeed, in *Joseph Conrad: Betrayal and Identity*,[15] Robert Hampson asserts that 'Kaspar Almayer is Conrad's version of Emma Bovary' (*Betrayal*, 30). Emma Bovary loses contact with reality by identifying with the romance of the sentimental novel; Almayer's foolishness is defined through the opposition between his dreams of imperial wealth and the reality of his situation. This is true also of Lingard: his larger than life reputation as pirate, gunrunner, and general romantic adventurer is at odds with the narrative present of the story. While to Almayer the discussions between Lingard and Vinck sound like 'a battle of the gods', the narrator, with corrosive irony, describes them as 'two mastiffs fighting over a marrowy bone' (*AF*, 8). Contradictory perceptions like these undermine Lingard's self-aggrandizing manner and Almayer's credulous acceptance of his assurance that 'There will be millions, Kaspar! Millions I say!' (*AF*, 10).[16] Such exaggeration on Lingard's part confirms the unreliability of his boasts: one wonders who he is trying to convince, his interlocutors or himself? The promise of limitless wealth has strong resonances of the illusory world of imperial romance, of the fictional riches of the mines of King Solomon.

Here, then, is a clear collision between romance and reality: the fast-moving, retrospective narration of the Lingard/Almayer relationship is told within a frame narrative that is ironic and sombre. Our suspicions concerning Lingard's capabilities are aroused by the fact that his story contains numerous tropes of the imperial romance genre that are at odds with the psychological detail and disillusionment evident in the frame narrative. Almayer is torn from his reverie by the call to eat a plate of rice, hardly the glorious feast befitting a wealthy imperial adventurer. The memory of the pseudo-romance of his past adventure with Lingard terminates when Almayer is 'recalled to the realities of life by the care necessary to prevent a fall on the uneven ground where the stones, decaying planks, and half-sawn beams were piled up in inextricable confusion' (*AF*, 12). Unlike his fantasy world in Amsterdam, Almayer's actual environment is littered with obstacles: the debris of his attempts to recreate an elegant European dwelling are strewn at his feet and cause him to pick his way through the 'confusion' he has himself created.

Dain: the romantic hero

In his Bovary-like dreams Almayer constructs fantasies that hinge upon the heroes of his imagination. His desperate prayer, 'All this was nearly within his reach. Let only Dain return!' (*AF*, 4), reveals the extent of Almayer's reliance on Dain and introduces the Balinese prince as a potent force within the dream framework of Almayer's ambitions. In the opening stages of the novel Dain functions at the level of romance. He is an exotic Eastern prince, a 'noble savage', and a romantic hero:

> Nina, hesitating on the threshold, saw an erect lithe figure of medium height with a breadth of shoulder suggesting great power. Under the folds of a blue turban, whose fringed ends hung gracefully over the left shoulder, was a face full of determination and expressing a reckless good-humour, not devoid, however, of some dignity. The squareness of lower jaw, the full red lips, the mobile nostrils, and the proud carriage of the head gave the impression of a being half-savage, untamed, perhaps cruel, and corrected the liquid softness of the almost feminine eye, that general characteristic of the race. (*AF*, 55)

He has the courage, charisma, temper, and serene grace of a romantic hero. One is reminded of Uncas in *The Last of the Mohicans* (1826)[17] who had 'no concealment to his dark, glancing, fearless eye, alike terrible and calm; the bold outline of his high, haughty features, pure in their native red' (*LM*, 62). Dain combines nobility and exoticism with an aura of wealth, power, and gorgeous beauty:

> The crude light of the lamp shone on the gold embroidery of his black silk jacket, broke in a thousand sparkling rays on the jewelled

hilt of his kriss protruding from under the many folds of the red sarong gathered into a sash around his waist, and played on the precious stones of the many rings on his dark fingers. (*AF*, 54–5)

Confronting Dain, the embodiment of her mother's tales of 'savage glories', Nina felt 'a hitherto unknown feeling of shyness, mixed with alarm and some delight, enter and penetrate her whole being' (*AF*, 55). The narrative focus shifts from Almayer to the sexual attraction between Dain and Nina and the sense of conventional romance is heightened. Into the drab and depressing atmosphere of Almayer's campong comes a virile Oriental male, a living expression of Eastern splendour: the turban, the kriss, the colourful silks all speak of the exoticism of the East graphically depicted in Dick Holland's costume in plate 15. This is a conscious evocation of the imperial romance on Conrad's part.

Speaking of 'Orientalist' writing in the nineteenth century and of Flaubert in particular, Edward Said argues that the Orient offered sexual experiences unavailable in Europe. The East promises 'a different type of sexuality, perhaps more libertine, and less guilt-ridden' (*Orientalism*, 190).[18] The irony is, of course, that the 'libertine' lovemaking in *Almayer's Folly* is initiated as much by Nina, the half-European, as it is by Dain, the exotic Oriental. In her 'outward and visible sign of all she felt for the man' Nina threw 'her arms around Dain's neck and pressed her lips to his in a long and burning kiss' (*AF*, 72). Dain is surprised and fascinated by this action which is, as Berthoud says, 'so transgressive of Indonesian traditions of feminine decorum'.[19] Dain, says Berthoud, is attracted to Nina because she 'represents the seduction of emancipated femininity', and because she is European; by choosing Dain, Nina opts for the 'Indonesian in her' (*AF* [OUP edn], xxiii). Something more complex is at work here than the assumptions about Oriental sexuality to be found in the imperial romance. In Dain's surprise at Nina's forwardness, assumptions of Eastern 'libertine' lovemaking are overturned. Conrad's awareness of Indonesian culture reverses the expectations of the imperial romance where the licentious Eastern male affronts the European woman, or the sensuous 'native' female tempts the hero with her blatant sexuality. Furthermore, White notes how through Mrs Almayer's contempt for her husband, Conrad questions the idea that dark races are attracted to white races but not the other way round (White, 127).

The taboo surrounding miscegenation in the Empire found in the imperial romance fails to restrain Conrad's heroes. The deaths of the

African women, Foulata and Ustane, in Haggard's fiction ensure the racial purity of his heroes and their offspring. Sexual relations between Conrad's characters cross racial boundaries. While the unions of men like Almayer and Willems with Malay women indicates their moral bankruptcy (both men marry on the promise of a large inheritance as a bribe to compromise their racial scruples), their wives come to despise the incompetence and ineffectuality of their white husbands. Through the complex sexual and marital relationships evident in *Almayer's Folly* Conrad's assertion in the 'Author's Note' that he is 'speaking of men and women' is borne out: his characters resist the easy stereotyping of the 'native' of imperial romance. Yet we should not miss the fact that Almayer's marriage to a 'native' woman is a symptom of his degeneracy, prefiguring Willems's disastrous relationships. Perhaps a hint of the racism of the imperial romance is still in evidence, despite Conrad's claims to the contrary.

For Mrs Almayer Dain is a 'great Rajah'; for Nina he is an arousing presence; but for Almayer, he is a savage representative of an inferior race. Believing the drowned corpse is Dain's, Almayer's emotions centre upon himself, not the crushed body of the man before him: 'A dead Malay; he had seen many dead Malays without any emotion; and now he felt inclined to weep, but it was over the fate of a white man he knew; a man that fell over a deep precipice and did not die' (*AF*, 99). Having no concern for the individual, Almayer stereotypes this 'native', believing he can manipulate Dain to serve his own ends. As Brantlinger notes, 'native sidekicks' are common in imperial literature: 'Mesty is to Midshipman Jack Easy as Friday is to Robinson Crusoe, Chingachcook to Natty Bumppo, and Umslopogaas to Allan Quatermain: the noble savage in partnership with the conquering hero (*Rule of Darkness*, 58). Thus Almayer imagines himself a conquering hero aided by a loyal and admiring 'native'. The fact is though, that had Dain not seen Nina 'he would have probably refused to engage himself and his men in the projected expedition to Gunong Mas—the mountain of gold' (*AF*, 82). Dain is working out his own destiny with Nina, proving his human impulses to be as powerful as those of any white man. He may seem romantically large, but he too is only human, prone to failure, the loss of the gunpowder, and driven as much by his physical desires as any other man. Clear-cut allegiances and daring deeds proving the loyalty and dependability of the romantic hero belong in the domain of adventure fiction. This myth describes the parameters of Almayer's imagination and thus reveals the limitations placed on romantic adventure and heroism at the *fin de siècle*. The faith that Almayer places in Dain proves as misguided and naive as his faith in Lingard.

Berthoud suggests that 'in romance the projects of others are not taken seriously: "others" are never finally "themselves". *Almayer's Folly*, a deeply realist text, works on different conditions. One could say that it has no protagonist, in the sense that all its characters, even the most insignificant, are presented as the protagonists of their own lives' (*AF* [OUP edn], xxii). This is evident in the character of Dain Maroola, who arrives in the book like a romantic hero, bringing potential for vigour and action to the torpor of Almayer's existence. But Dain rises out of a tradition of romantic imperial literature only to confound popular notions of the native. Berthoud makes the point that Dain's characterization as more than a 'figure out of adventure romance', is due to the necessity for him to conform to the realism of the text and the complex web of interrelations and dependencies that govern action and experience within the novel (*AF* [OUP edn], xxi). Dain as the 'protagonist of his own life' is far more than the exotic 'native' stereotype he seems to be on his entry into the novel.

The enchanted princess and her lover

Nina Almayer, like an enchanted princess, is trapped by her father's dreams, with Dain as the prince coming carry her off.[20] His arrival awakens Nina from her entranced existence into an awareness of her physical self and the potential for escape from the torpor of Sambir. While Almayer retreats into the illusions of dreams, Nina emerges from her trance-like state into a world of realizable possibilities. To the local people she is distant and aloof, a mysterious and exotic figure: 'They got used to the silent figure moving in their midst calm and white-robed, a being from another world and incomprehensible to them' (*AF*, 38). She is the focus of the dreams and desires of others: Dain falls passionately in love with her; Reshid desires her; Lingard transfers his affections from her mother to Nina. For Almayer, Nina is the only being he has ever loved. Even the young Dutch naval officer is momentarily affected by her presence, until he remembers that she is 'after all a half-caste girl', which causes him to 'pluck up heart and look at Nina sideways' (*AF*, 126).

Nina's long black hair is significant of her Sulu blood, but also carries sensuous overtones of the mystery and allure common to romantic hero-ines. In American romance one thinks of Poe's Ligeia or Hawthorne's Zenobia. The type is most clearly defined in Haggard's exotic and sensuous Ayesha (plate 7), who, 'with a little coquettish movement', turns herself to Holly and Leo, 'holding up one arm, so as to reveal all its loveliness and the rich hair of raven blackness that streamed in soft ripples down the snowy robes, almost to her sandalled feet' (*S*, 140). Ayesha has an irresistible sexuality as indicated by plate 7 where she provocatively removes her veils to reveal her naked body. Holly speaks of her 'tinted face' and of her 'broad and noble brow, on which the hair grew low' (*S*, 153). Similar feminine sexual allure and Eastern physical characteristics are ascribed to Nina: 'She stood there all in white, straight, flexible, graceful, unconscious of herself, her low but broad forehead crowned by a mass of long black hair that fell in heavy tresses over her shoulders, and made her pale olive complexion look paler still by the contrast of its coal-black hue' (*AF*, 17). Nina's white robe symbolizes sexual purity, but the mass of black hair hints at sensuality, and, combined with the olive complexion, signals her mixed race.[21]

Dain's gaze, like that of Leo and Holly towards Ayesha, is compelled by the vision of feminine beauty before him. In chivalric Eastern fashion, he pays homage, bending low, 'elevating his joined hands above his head in a sign of respect' (*AF*, 54). Nina, confused, responds with becoming Malay modesty, drawing 'the lower part of the curtain across her face, leaving a half-rounded cheek, a stray tress, and one eye exposed, wherewith to contemplate the gorgeous and bold being' (*AF*, 55). We are immediately alerted to the sexual attraction of each for the other. Yet, had Almayer not been obsessed by gold he, too, would have noticed the signs. The lovers' gestures speak of their shared Malay heritage: in an early warning that she will reject white civilization and embrace Malay culture, Nina 'instinctively' veils her face in accordance with the custom of her mother's people. Almayer's imaginative model of the world does not afford Nina an independent life of her own: an extension of his ego, Almayer assumes Nina shares his dreams and prejudices; it never occurs to him that she could be attracted to a Malay, even if he is a Balinese prince.

The first encounter of Nina and Dain is a sensuous, romantic, and symbolic moment, reminiscent of imperial romance; but imperial romance rarely foregrounds the sexual relations of 'natives'. The quest for treasure that precipitates such literature, unites the heroes, and secures closure becomes a divisive obsession in *Almayer's Folly*. The close thematic ties between romantic love, adventure, and wealth that characterize the imperial romance are severed in Conrad's tale so that each character pursues his or her own individual desire causing ultimate disunity and disillusionment instead of the utopian ending of the romantic fiction of Empire. Thus, rather than being one occurrence in the series of events that lead to the resolution of the hero's ordeals, the meeting of Dain and Nina marks another break in the 'associative chain' identified by Simmons.

The love affair is formulaic: beautiful lovers, moonlight trysts, threats of death or separation, and a possessive father causing a crisis of loyalties. The jealous 'other woman' appears, in the form of Taminah, the slave girl, also sexually aroused by Dain's presence. But Mrs Almayer, with merciless cynicism, is determined that Nina will understand the true conditions of her status as a Malay wife:

> 'There will be other women,' she repeated firmly; 'I tell you that, because you are half white, and may forget that he is a great chief, and that such things must be. Hide your anger, and do not let him see on your face the pain that will eat your heart…As long as he looks upon many women your power will last, but should there be one, one only with whom he seems to forget you, then—' (*AF*, 153)

'Then,' says Mrs Almayer, 'to that woman, Nina, show no mercy' (*AF*, 154).[22] Nina's romantic illusion of enduring marital harmony is fractured when confronted by the wisdom of her mother, which springs from genuine experience. Unlike the imperial romance writer who makes each event move the narrative predictably towards the expected triumphant ending, Conrad counters his characters' dreams and aspirations with painful checks and balances, reminders that the struggle to survive in the real world often involves unpalatable choices and an abandonment of naive ideals.

Earlier, as Nina and Dain float along the river in an ecstasy of love, Conrad brings the jungle into sharp focus:

> [A]ll around them in a ring of luxuriant vegetation bathed in the warm air charged with strong and harsh perfumes, the intense work of tropical nature went on: plants shooting upward, entwined, interlaced in inextricable confusion, climbing madly and brutally over each other in the terrible silence of a desperate struggle towards the life-giving sunshine above—as if struck with sudden horror at the seething mass of corruption below, at the death and decay from which they sprang. (*AF*, 71)

The brutal world of nature undercuts the dream world of the lovers. Watt analyses this passage in Darwinian terms, detailing how the natural cycle of birth and decay 'violently subverts the conventional assumptions of popular romance' (Watt, 45). The lovers drifting in their 'little nutshells' and showered with perfumed red blossoms from above are unaware of the 'seething mass of corruption below'; Conrad brings it vividly before us, reminding us again of the struggle for survival. While the lovers are associated with the gorgeous tropical blossoms, they cannot be wholly dissociated from the 'death and decay from which they sprang'; the romantic glamour of tropical nature is the offspring of rotting vegetation. This anticipates Mrs Almayer's advice to Nina to 'strike with a steady hand' (*AF*, 154); but it also anticipates the decline and death that will engulf Almayer as a result of the lovers' escape. In the world of Conrad's protagonists action has effects that ripple out into other lives. The consequences of Nina and Dain's flight are manifold: Almayer and Taminah wither and die; Mrs Almayer seeks refuge under the roof of her erstwhile lover, Lakamba; the Rajah of Bali acquires a grandson, and so on. Nina is a survivor while Almayer is not. She acts with courage and conviction. Moreover, she has been alerted to the turmoil that can afflict sexual relations. Nina embraces the 'real' world of strife and struggle; Almayer dies seeking the illusory promises of romance.

While Nina learns the hard facts of life and love from her mother, Dain examines the nature of love itself. Waiting for her in Bulangi's clearing, Dain 'could look into the depths of his passionate love, see its strength and its weakness, and felt afraid' (*AF*, 168). Passion robs Dain of his manly courage. Conrad gently mocks his Balinese hero who, like a romantic schoolboy, fantasizes about dying a hero's death with the blood of his enemies 'spurting before his eyes': 'Carried away by his excitement, he snatched the kriss hidden in his sarong, and, drawing a long breath, rushed forward, struck at the empty air, and fell on his face' (*AF*, 168). Such is not the fate of a genuine hero of romance; Dain renounces heroism for female love. In Conrad's fiction love means life, but also an emasculating surrender to woman. Mrs Almayer has already hinted at the perceived danger of woman's seductive power when she tells Nina, 'Do not let him look too long in your eyes, nor lay his head on your knees without reminding him that men should fight before they rest' (*AF*, 152).

Haggard's Holly blames woman's sexual power for over half the ills of the world: 'Curses on the fatal curiosity that is ever prompting man to draw the veil from woman, and curses on the natural impulse that begets it! It is the cause of half—ay, and more than half—of our misfortunes' (*S*, 132). As Rebecca Stott says, the 'loss of self and of certitude in an unexplored universe is precisely the dilemma of the Conradian hero who, threatened with "the shadowy embrace" of both the jungle and the native woman, experiences a dissolution of the self' (Stott, 161).

Conrad will develop this theme more fully in *An Outcast*, but in Dain's horror at the 'doubt of his own bravery' there are clear signals of the perceived dangers of the 'shadowy embrace'. This becomes evident in Nina's representation as a seductress:

> She drew back her head and fastened her eyes on his in one of those long looks that are a woman's most terrible weapon; a look that is more stirring than the closest touch, and more dangerous than the thrust of a dagger, because it also whips the soul out of the body, but leaves the body alive and helpless, to be swayed here and there by the capricious tempests of passion and desire; a look that enwraps the whole body, and that penetrates into the innermost recesses of the being, bringing terrible defeat in the delirious uplifting of accomplished conquest. (*AF*, 171)

Nina, momentarily, becomes the embodiment of the threat to male potency posed by feminine sexuality. Indeed, the paranoia evident in such purple prose echoes some of the more misogynist passages in Haggard where women are associated with snakes and spiders. Ayesha's 'snake-like grace' (*S*, 140) as suggested in plate 7, finds a counterpart in Conrad's drawing (plate 8) where the woman's blatant exoticism is linked to her intimacy with the snake to create an image at once erotic and disturbing.

During their lovemaking Dain talks of the sea and 'its hidden meaning that no living man has penetrated yet' and how its depths are 'for ever the same, cold and cruel, and full of the wisdom of destroyed life'. A few moments later his real meaning becomes clear: 'The sea, O Nina, is like a woman's heart' (*AF*, 174). What seemed to be a fairy tale love affair is a mature relationship laced with the sexual anxieties about the emasculating power of women so typical of late nineteenth-century romance. This is a different view of femininity from that expressed by Hardy in Tess, Eustacia Vye, or even Sue Bridehead. Nina is stereotyped in a way that could never happen to a heroine in Hardy's fiction. Or rather, if it did it would be through the misguided perceptions of a character such as Angel Clare. Lovemaking in Conrad's Eastern forests hovers perilously close to the dubious assumptions and values of the romance of empire.

Yet despite its resonances of imperial romance, *Almayer's Folly* is the antithesis of that genre. Conrad's protagonists repeatedly resist the stereotypes they seem to represent. Speaking of Dain and Nina in terms of Conrad's realism, Berthoud says that 'the novel does not forget that these two-souls-that-are-one are socially constituted' (*AF* [OUP edn], xxii).

Dain's recognition of Nina's 'otherness' is clear when he becomes 'conscious of something in her he could not understand': 'He felt something invisible that stood between them, something that would let him approach her so far, but no farther. No desire, no longing, no effort of will or length of life could destroy this vague feeling of their difference' (*AF*, 187). Their difference is the difference between man and woman, but, significantly, it is also the cultural divide between Malay and European. Nina, a blend of both races, is comprehensible to neither. Thus Dain appeals to Almayer to help solve the mystery of her tears: 'My Ranee smiles when looking at the man she loves. It is the white woman that is crying now' (*AF*, 188). Conrad now confounds the easy stereotyping of the Oriental woman in the romance by presenting us with a character who conforms to neither the Oriental nor the European stereotype. This woman is herself, half-Sulu, half-Dutch, and behaves accordingly. Furthermore, as Hampson indicates, Almayer himself forgets Nina's mixed race, the fact that 'she is as much a part of her mother as of him' and thus 'must necessarily share some of her mother's nature' (*Betrayal*, 12).

At the climax of the story the three characters battle for possession of each other on the edge of the tropical forest. The lovers triumph because Almayer could not bear the thought of Nina being found with a 'savage'. Almayer's final vision of them is of beautiful, romantic creatures: 'He looked at the man's brown shoulders, at the red sarong round his waist; at the tall, slender, dazzling white figure he supported. He looked at the white dress, at the falling masses of the long black hair' (*AF*, 194). As they disappear into the sun and over the horizon in a yellow-sailed prau which 'shone brilliantly for a fleeting minute on the blue of the open sea' (*AF*, 195), the novel seems to point a romantic closure. At the novel's end Babalatchi tells of the 'news from Bali last moon', of how a 'grandson is born to the old Rajah, and there is great rejoicing' (*AF*, 206). The last word on Nina and her Balinese prince seems to confirm the fairy-tale ending.

Yet not quite so: the conflicting visions of the book do not allow for such easy assumptions. When Mrs Almayer warns Nina that there will be 'other women' she speaks with the knowledge of the customs of her race. But we do not have only Mrs Almayer's word for it: in Bulangi's clearing Almayer unknowingly concurs with his wife, adding weight to her warning, when he pleads with Nina to stay:

> Do you know what you are doing? Do you know what is waiting for you if you follow that man? Have you no pity for yourself? Do you

know that you shall be first his plaything and then a scorned slave, a drudge, and a servant of some new fancy of that man? (*AF*, 177–8)

Bearing in mind his wife's advice to Nina, Almayer's outburst is more than the malicious product of the mind of a racist European: he speaks with the voice of one who has lived long enough in the tropics to know the people and their customs. He aligns himself with the mature wisdom of Nina's mother. The romantic atmosphere of Nina's departure is thus disturbed by the unsettling suggestion that the fairy-tale ending is only one perception within a story of multiple and conflicting perspectives. The warnings of Almayer and his wife reach beyond the book's ending and suggest a future strife that subverts, or at least questions, an apparently romantic love story.

Babalatchi and Mrs Almayer: 'native' degenerates

Although Sherry argues convincingly that Conrad relied, in part at least, upon travel writing for his creation of Babalatchi (he cites, in particular, Jadee, in Sherard Osborn's *My Journal in Malayan Waters*) it is for the biographical detail and penchant for story-telling that these works were used (*Eastern World*, 165–9). Babalatchi in fact, owes a great deal to the villain of romance, bestial and deformed degenerate types like Stevenson's Mr Hyde or Blind Pew. The 'native' villain in the imperial romance comes in for even harsher treatment. Fenimore Cooper's Magua is 'repulsive'. Gagool in *King Solomon's Mines* is a monkey whose yellow and wrinkled scalp 'moved and contracted like the hood of a cobra' (*KSM*, 158). The evil and predatory Ayesha shrivels up until she is 'no larger than a big ape, and hideous—ah, too hideous for words!' (*S*, 287). The Marquesan chief Mow-Mow in Melville's *Typee* (1846) is grossly ugly: 'His cheek had been pierced by the point of a spear, and the wound imparted a still more frightful expression to his hideously tattooed face, already deformed by the loss of an eye' (*Typee*, 313).

Babalatchi is slippery and manipulative, perfectly prepared to poison Almayer should Lakamba require it. The loyal henchman of a scheming master, Babalatchi is deformed and ugly: 'In truth he was perfectly repulsive, possessing only one eye and a pock-marked face, with nose and lips horribly disfigured by the smallpox' (*AF*, 38). Perhaps a veiled hint at syphilis is in evidence here. Babalatchi's licentiousness is suggested in his desire to acquire the slave girl, Taminah: 'Decidedly he would offer fifty dollars more to that thief Bulangi. The girl pleased him' (*AF*, 134). Suggestions of Mrs Almayer's liaison with Lakamba are given further substance by Babalatchi's intimate conversations with her. The nature of their talk is slyly hinted at: 'What the subject of their discourses was might have been guessed from the subsequent domestic scenes by Almayer's hearthstone' (*AF*, 38); secret assignations with Lakamba are no doubt the outcome.

Babalatchi is variously described by the ironic titles of Lakamba's 'prime minister, harbour master, financial adviser, and general factotum', and a 'gentleman—of Sulu origin' (*AF*, 38); in brief, a scheming scoundrel and one-time pirate. His 'unofficial costume, composed of a piece of pink calico round his waist' (*AF*, 38), somewhat after the fashion of the Dyaks in plate 13, indicates a self-confident disregard for his appearance and hints at a sordid sexuality. There are moments, however, when Babalatchi's ruminations touch upon the common lot of human beings:

> The ruler was growing old, and Babalatchi, aware of an uneasy feeling at the pit of his stomach, put both hands there with a suddenly vivid and sad perception of the fact that he himself was growing old too; that the time of reckless daring was past for both of them, and that they had to seek refuge in prudent cunning. (*AF*, 86)

Certainly the 'prudent cunning' carries the suggestion that Orientals are naturally vicious and untrustworthy, but Babaltchi's recognition of his own mortality takes him beyond the flat stereotype of imperial romance. The Babalatchi of *Almayer's Folly* rarely reveals himself as more than a manipulative native; in *An Outcast* we discover more of his genealogy and his bitterness towards white imperialists. But the brief insights into his inner life betoken an intention on Conrad's part of a realism that demands a more heterogeneous characterization than that afforded the simple 'native' villains of fiction. This intention, indeed, becomes more evident in Mrs Almayer.

Babalatchi is linked with Mrs Almayer through their common Sulu origin and their connections with Lakamba. But they are also both cast in roles of sordid 'native' degenerates working to undermine the white hero's enterprises. Mrs Almayer's witch-like appearance anticipates that other downtrodden wife, Joanna Willems. With her shrill voice, claw-like hand, and long straggly hair, she squats over a boiling cauldron much as one of the hags in *Macbeth*. She spits, snarls, and shrieks like an animal. Almayer regards with dread her separation from Nina, imagining his wife as a 'savage tigress deprived of her young' (*AF*, 26–7). But, after two days of wailing she returns to 'her former mode of life, chewing betel-nut, and sitting all day amongst her women in stupefied idleness' (*AF*, 27).

This sense of a subhuman creature is evident in her 'burning the furniture and tearing down the pretty curtains in her unreasoning hate of those signs of civilization' while Almayer meditates upon the 'best way of getting rid of her' as though she were some troublesome dog (*AF*, 26). As Berthoud points out, this appears to be a 'gratuitous act on the part of Mrs Almayer, until one realizes that it is a gesture of cultural vandalism'.[23] Here we begin to see that even Conrad's minor characters reveal depths and complexities of motivation at odds with the stereotype. Mrs Almayer's 'cultural vandalism' is aimed at a civilization that tried to 'tame' her, and singularly failed to do so. Her quiet acquiescence in Lingard's educational project was based on her expectation of becoming his 'wife, counsellor, and guide' (*AF*, 22). When this dream is thwarted by her marriage to Almayer she is understandably dismayed. Her daughter taken from her, Mrs Almayer 'aged very rapidly', and she is relegated to a 'river-side hut in the compound where she dwelt in perfect seclusion' (*AF*, 27). Once her physical attraction has waned Almayer finds no further use for her; his upbraiding of her over Lakamba is probably more the result of his European desire to 'keep up appearances' than sexual jealousy. The assumptions of racial, cultural, and religious superiority of those who determine Mrs Almayer's fate (notably she is given no name of her own), also determine her violent rejection of European values. Mrs Almayer is as much a victim as she is, apparently, a 'villain'. Indeed, despite Almayer's protestations of white superiority, he is no more virtuous than his wife: while she sits in 'stupefied idleness' chewing betel-nut, he drinks himself into a stupor. In the end Mrs Almayer is triumphant: she acquires the dowry, a chest full of silver, and the protection of Lakamba. Almayer has only the empty 'Folly'.

For all the superficial characterization of this woman as a savage, a slatternly hag, even a latter-day female Caliban, in that she 'learned the new language very easily, yet understood but little of the new faith the good sisters taught her' (*AF*, 22), she is more resourceful and has more social consciousness than her white husband. The fact that she tore down the curtains 'to make sarongs for the slave-girls' and burnt the furniture 'to cook the family rice' (*AF*, 91), not only belies the 'stupefied idleness', but also implies a greater awareness of her responsibilities than her husband displays. Her motherly advice to Nina, her eagerness for her daughter's departure (she will presumably never see Nina again) indicate a wisdom and an unselfish parental concern that are beyond the capabilities of her egoist husband. As Nina leaves her mother cannot suppress her sense of loss:

> Mrs. Almayer rose with a deep sigh, while two tears wandered slowly down her withered cheeks. She wiped them off quickly with a wisp of her grey hair as if ashamed of herself, but could not stifle another loud sigh, for her heart was heavy and she suffered much, being unused to tender emotions. (*AF*, 154)

Her unfamiliarity with 'tender emotions' is a reminder of her 'savage' nature, but also indicates the hardships of life as Almayer's wife: those 'tender emotions' have been stifled in order to survive.

Mrs Almayer is as much the product of the blunders of the well-intentioned Lingard, and the prejudices of Almayer, as she is of Malay culture. Her function is thus more than formulaic. Through Mrs Almayer's position in the story as a victim of Lingard's misguided generosity and Almayer's greed, we gain a critical perspective on the white characters that is rarely available in the imperial romance. Conventional assumptions concerning the inherent rightness of the imperial venture and its beneficial effects for the imperial subjects are challenged in Conrad's tale through the sad plight of all its protagonists. Watt sees the minor Malay characters of *Almayer's Folly* as successful insofar as they are 'flat' because 'the plot does not require them to have a real or developing inner life': 'Romance, adventure, and melodrama are alike in requiring only that the individual performers be easily recognisable' (Watt, 62). But Conrad was concerned that we recognize these people as human beings with whom we have a 'bond'. Mrs Almayer first appears in the novel as a stereotype: the savage 'native' woman motivated by malice towards the hero, a Malay Gagool. But this initial characterization is undermined by the subsequent revelation of her history and her dreams. Her essential humanity is revealed to us, and Conrad's promise in his 'Author's Note' to 'sympathize with common mortals' is made good.

Towards a modernist dilemma

In an introduction to *The Coral Island*, Margaret Jeffrey notes how J. M. Barrie stated that 'to be born is to be wrecked on an island' (*CI*,16). The isolation of Ballantyne's boys on their island never reduces them to despair or hopelessness; theirs is a physical isolation from 'white civilisation' that is remedied at the story's end. Barrie's statement carries the darker implication that the condition of human kind is one of isolation. A contemporary of Conrad's who began his writing career in 1888, Barrie touches on a theme more relevant to *Almayer's Folly* than *The Coral Island*. In Barrie's vision we sense a foreboding of what lies beneath the opulent surface of Edwardian Britain, and this is much closer to Conrad's *fin de siècle* scepticism than it is to Ballantyne's mid-nineteenth-century adventure tale.

By the time Conrad's narrative reaches the point where he is piling graves of sand over Nina's footprints it has long been clear that Almayer is no adventure hero. A soul 'wrecked on an island' with no means of escape, Almayer is closer to the modernist protagonist confronting the crisis of an existence where nothing is enduring and nothing is finally the truth. In Almayer's world the sand continually shifts beneath his feet. In a chaotic and indifferent universe the only stable world is the illusory world of dreams into which Almayer retreats. Simple loyalties, stereotypical identities, and an easy passage into genteel European society, loaded with imperial gold, are the fantasies with which Almayer fends off the fact of his isolation and failure. The world of romantic dreams is one in which good fortune prevails, and where heroes structure their destinies according to their desires.

Romance thus becomes the counterpoint to reality in the novel through Almayer's decision to deny his actual condition and rely instead, like Emma Bovary, on the illusion of dreams. In a letter to Cunninghame Graham of 31 January 1898, Conrad insists that it is the lot of human kind to seek refuge in illusions in order to avoid the essential pain of existence:

> What makes mankind tragic is not that they are the victims of nature, it is that they are conscious of it. To be part of the animal kingdom under the conditions of this earth is very well—but as soon as you know of your slavery the pain, the anger, the strife—the tragedy begins. We can't return to nature, since we can't change our place in it. Our refuge is in stupidity, in drunken[n]ess of all kinds, in lies, in beliefs, in murder, thieving, reforming—in negation, in contempt—each man according to the promptings of his particular devil. (*Letters 2*, 30)

As Daphna Erdinast-Vulcan puts it, the 'collapse of the myths which had postulated the existence of God, the transcendental authority of the moral order, the privileged position of man within the natural scheme, and the teleological nature of human existence, has turned us into victims of our own consciousness' (Erdinast-Vulcan, 2). Our consciousness, our reason, those faculties that above all else distinguish us from the beast, are the very cause of our despair. When the myths of romantic dreams fail to sustain him opium becomes Almayer's 'particular devil', his refuge from consciousness and despair.

Conrad transforms the promises of the romance and adventure novel into a sombre meditation on the frailty and isolation of the individual. As David Thorburn says, the conventional adventure hero escapes 'the confines of the ordinary world' and 'escapes also from his human limitations', but Conrad's hero escapes into 'an unfamiliar universe only to be confronted with the fact of his error and weakness, with the sure and terrible limitations of his humanity, and with his need for other men' (Thorburn, 145). Babalatchi's realization that adventure is a thing of the past and that the present is a time for 'prudent cunning' is not just the malevolent brooding of a minor character: it is an interpretation of reality, a recognition of the limitations placed on human endeavour, that Almayer is incapable of making.

Abdulla, his long-time adversary, is also brought to a sad acceptance of fading possibilities as he looks down on Almayer's corpse. There is in his old heart 'a feeling of regret for that thing gone out of his life. He was leaving fast behind him friendships, and enmities, successes, and disappointments—all that makes up a life; and before him was only the end' (*AF*, 208). Death, as Abdulla realizes, is the only enduring certainty. The noble and classic poses of mourning struck by Curtis, Good, and Nyleptha in plate 6 are the melodramatic postures of imperial romance. Almayer's is a sordid, degraded end, overlooked by his old enemy, the Arab Abdulla. No high-minded epitaph such as Curtis affords Quatermain is spoken over Almayer's prostrate form. Abdulla's thoughts are sad, but he is sad 'for that thing gone out of his life'. In the end no one mourns Almayer, and the thoughts of the onlookers are only of themselves.

4
An Outcast of the Islands: Echoes of Romance

Conrad appears to have chosen the title of his second novel expressly for the purpose of attracting an audience used to a diet of romance and adventure fiction; it is even more in that tradition than his original title, *Two Vagabonds*.[1] Unwin had lost money on *Almayer's Folly*, a fact that must have troubled Conrad, still contemplating a life at sea. On 10 March 1896, just after *An Outcast of the Islands* was published Conrad wrote to Karol Zagórski saying that having refused a command writing was his only source of income: 'I know what I can do. It is therefore only a question of earning money—' (*Letters 1*, 266). Wise notes that in a 'copy of the First Edition of *An Outcast of the Islands* Mr. Conrad has written: "Before beginning this book I hesitated whether I should go on writing or not. Edward Garnett's remark 'you have the temperament, you have the style—why not write?' tipped the scale"' (Wise, 9).

Like *Almayer's Folly*, the novel was hailed by early reviewers, including H. G. Wells, as a romance. Conrad was, for the first time, compared by many with Stevenson, and also Melville, and his name coupled again with that of Kipling.[2] In fact the novel does read more like Stevenson's *The Ebb-Tide* or 'The Beach of Falesá', which, as Brantlinger says, 'marks the end of the innocent, heroic adventurousness of Marryat and early Victorian imperialism' (*Rule of Darkness*, 41). The reviewer for the *Daily Chronicle* on 16 March 1896 says that Willems's degradation is charted 'with a power and an insight that are truly Stevensonian' (*CH*, 64). But again Conrad disappointed those reviewers who were hoping for unalloyed exotic adventure. On 18 April 1896 the *National Observer*'s reviewer declared *An Outcast* 'undeniably dull':

It is like one of Mr. Stevenson's South Sea stories, grown miraculously long and miraculously tedious. There is no crispness about it and the action is not quick enough, a serious charge to make against a book of adventure. Even schoolboys will probably have some difficulty in getting through it and we fear adults will find it impossible. (*CH*, 70)

Conrad's 'diffuseness', noted by many commentators, had not yet alerted them to the fact that while locating his fiction in the exotic landscapes of the traditional imperial romance, his focus is on altogether different matters.

The imperial hero manqué

Willems is corrupt from the outset; the only characteristic he has in common with the typical hero of imperial romance is his whiteness; he is not even English. The hallmark of the white imperial hero, moral uprightness, is significantly absent:

> When he stepped off the straight and narrow path of his peculiar honesty, it was with an inward assertion of unflinching resolve to fall back again into the monotonous but safe stride of virtue as soon as his little excursion into the wayside quagmires had produced the desired effect. (*OI*, 3)

The 'unflinching resolve' anticipates Jim's vision of himself as an 'unflinching' romantic hero; but the idiom of imperial romance receives ironic treatment in Conrad's narratives. Treading a straight and narrow path is a common cliché, a prerequisite for the imperial adventurer.[3] The temptation to stray is a familiar one for Conrad's protagonists: Jim jumps; Nostromo steals; Kurtz 'goes native'; each chooses to take the wrong road, a road that leads to destruction. Conrad's heroes may imagine themselves to be romantically heroic, but the choices they make are indicative of their fallibility. Heroic status, such as Willems fantasizes about, is the illusion of fiction, an insubstantial dream posed against the limitations of individual character. Through his characters' self-delusions Conrad invokes the formulaic hero; through their actions he questions the possibility of heroism.

Willems has not even the debatable appeal of a character like Jim. He is Dutch; and within the Conradian scheme of things to be Dutch is to be decidedly not 'one of us'. His honesty is 'peculiar', begging the question of whether Willems ever was virtuous. White observes that from the 'opening sentence we know that the "he" can refer to no ordinary hero' (White, 137). While he congratulates himself on his privileged position, presenting his grubby domestic circumstances as evidence of his own glory, Willems reveals the hollowness of his self-image and the extent of his conceit. That he will 'tyrannize good-humouredly over his half-caste wife', or 'notice with tender contempt his pale yellow child', and 'patronize loftily his dark-skinned brother-in-law' (*OI*, 3), suggests Willems's sense of superiority; but Conrad's irony cuts through the sham romance of his hero's imagination to reveal a self-aggrandizing fool beneath the pretentious surface.

Willems regards himself as an imperial hero: in contrast to the 'half-caste' wife, the 'pale yellow' child, and the 'dark-skinned' brother-in-law, he is the 'successful white man' to whose 'shrine' these dependants offer 'coarse incense' (*OI*, 4). As Hampson notes, while others seem to accept Willems's self-image, 'the ironic overtones of such label-like phrases as "the successful white man", at the same time, subtly problematise that self-image' (*Betrayal*, 33). Like the imperial benefactor of boys' adventure fiction, Willems believes he commands the 'loquacious love' of 'those degenerate descendants of Portuguese conquerors': 'They lived now by the grace of his will. This was power. Willems loved it' (*OI*, 5). He imagines that he descended amongst them like Haggard's white imperialists Quatermain, Curtis, and Good who announce to their African hosts in *King Solomon's Mines* that they 'come from the Stars' (*KSM*, 154).[4] Conrad's irony undercuts his hero's narrative: he fails to recognize that in 'descending amongst them' he has become one of them. In imperial romance white adventurers, masquerading as gods, bring peace, stability, and prosperity to 'native' peoples. Willems's intervention in local affairs sparks off political unrest and highlights his inadequacy, his conceit, and his own degeneracy.

Believing his race to be proof of his superiority, Willems boasts of his success and cleverness in the bars and billiard rooms. But with biting irony Conrad records how the 'Chinaman' marker regards his utterances as 'the buzzing monotony of the unintelligible stream of words poured out by the white man' (*OI*, 6). Willems's philosophy is sacred to him, almost a religion, whereas it is in reality amoral and corrupt: 'The wise, the strong, the respected, have no scruples. Where there are scruples there can be no power. On that text he preached often to the young men. It was his doctrine, and he, himself, was a shining example of its truth' (*OI*, 8). His immense arrogance is born out of assumptions of white imperial potency. Willems glosses over the fact that he is already a criminal, that the 'sheer pluck' with which he won his reputation as a trader was employed in bribery, corruption, opium deals, and illegal gunpowder sales. The notion of 'sheer pluck' evokes the boy hero of romance and adventure: there is even a novel by Henty called *By Sheer Pluck* (1884). In this context, however, the expression comments ironically upon Willems's self-image.[5] The theft of Hudig's money is 'a very small matter', but Hudig sees it otherwise (*OI*, 11). In his delusions of wealth and power Willems exaggerates his own potential: 'A man of his stamp could carry off anything, do anything, aspire to anything' (*OI*, 9). Yet, as Mrs Vink observes, 'a man of his stamp' beats his wife.

Willems is no Quatermain, mourned by Sir Henry Curtis as a character 'as near perfection as any it has ever been my lot to encounter', and who had only two faults, one of which was 'excessive modesty' (*AQ*, 273–4). Nor is he one of Henty's plucky, upright Dicks or Neds. Yet woven into Conrad's tale of degeneracy and betrayal are unmistakable echoes of romance and adventure. Willems enjoys embellishing his history with the fact that 'he came east fourteen years ago—a cabin boy' (*OI*, 7). The boy heroes of Henty and Kingston leave the genteel poverty of their English homes for adventure and wealth in the East, as in the picture of the young hopeful of plate 11. Kingston's Ben Hadden, a cabin boy himself, discovers that the harmony and management of a ship depend on 'prompt and exact obedience to all laws and orders' (*BH*, 51). He 'soon learned all about a ship' and was as 'active and intelligent and daring as any of the boys in the ship' (*BH*, 54).

Lingard's first encounter with Willems even reads like boys' adventure fiction:

> He roused up his sleeping boat-crew and stood waiting for them to get ready, when he felt a tug at his coat and a thin voice said, very distinctly—
>
> 'English captain.'
>
> Lingard turned round quickly, and what seemed to be a very lean boy jumped back with commendable activity.
>
> 'Who are you? Where did you spring from?' asked Lingard, in startled surprise.
>
> From a safe distance the boy pointed towards a cargo lighter moored to the quay. (*OI*, 15)

And so Lingard takes Willems under his wing:

> 'There's not much of you for seventeen. Are you hungry?'
> 'A little.'

'Will you come with me, in that brig there?'

The boy moved without a word towards the boat and scrambled into the bows.

'Knows his place,' muttered Lingard to himself as he stepped heavily into the stern sheets and took up the yoke lines. 'Give way there.'

The Malay boat crew lay back together, and the gig sprang away from the quay heading towards the brig's riding light.

Such was the beginning of Willems' career. (*OI*, 16)

Like the boy in plate 12, Willems has acquired a benevolent father figure. But the opening chapter has already revealed the sordid outcome of this auspicious beginning. Furthermore, this account of his meeting with Lingard leaves out the fact that Willems has just deserted ship. Running barefoot along the decks of the *Kosmopoliet IV* and 'objurgating his immediate surroundings with blasphemous lips' (*OI*, 14), Willems's idea of heroism is to jump ship.

Conrad's method here for subverting Willems's heroic pretensions is to bring his narrative tantalizingly close to popular adventure fiction and then to undermine the expectations he has raised. Thus Lingard learns the whole of Willems's 'commonplace story' in half an hour. It is almost an exact reversal of the history of a typical Henty hero: Henty's boys are usually fatherless, with a loving mother and doting sisters to provide for. Their home background is poor but clean, and morally sound. Dick Holland's mother is sensible and loving. When her husband fails to return from India 'Mrs. Holland at once gave up her house and moved into a smaller one'. She is possessed of 'strong common-sense and firmness of character' (*TM*, 16). Willems is motherless: his 'shabby' and 'disconsolate' father shows foreign skippers around the seedy haunts of Rotterdam, returning 'sick with too much smoking and drinking', while his numerous brothers and sisters run wild. His credentials as a would-be hero are dealt the final crushing blow with the revelation that he 'was hopelessly at variance with the spirit of the sea': 'He had an instinctive contempt for the honest simplicity of that work which led to nothing he cared for' (*OI*, 17).

As Hampson observes, Willems operates through 'perverted forms of sea-virtue': '"Work" and "duty" appear as "the tasks of restitution" and "the duty of not being found out." Courage appears as "that courage that will not scale heights, yet will wade bravely through the mud—if there be no other road"' (*Betrayal*, 35). Courage, work, and duty: the necessary qualities of any would-be imperial hero, are, in Willems's case corrupted; his idea of courage, in fact, hovers perilously close to cowardice. No Ben Hadden, Willems rejects life at sea in favour of the life of 'those longshore quill-drivers' amongst whom, according to Lingard, he gets himself 'so crooked'. The sea is the only 'place for an honest man', says Lingard, but Willems 'never would; didn't think there was enough money in it' (*OI*, 41–2). For Lingard, and for Conrad, the discipline of life at sea offers healthy action, the subsuming of the self into the ship's community, and a safe alternative to the corrupting influence of trade and life on shore. Lingard echoes the words of Conrad's chief mate, Mr. B—, in *The Mirror of the Sea* (1906): 'Ports are no good—ships rot, men go to the devil!' (*MS*, 128). In 'Well Done' Conrad extols the virtues of a seafaring life. The tradition of 'sea-craft', he says, is an 'occupation in which men have to depend on each other. It raises them, so to speak, above the frailties of their dead selves' (*NLL*, 183). Willems becomes 'crooked' because he refuses the conditions of sea-life that the hero of adventure embraces. Even the spoilt and work-shy Harvey Cheyne of Kipling's *Captains Courageous* (1896) becomes an accomplished seaman: by the end of his time on the *We're Here* Harvey 'felt like the most ancient of mariners' (*Captains Courageous*, 278). The popular formula has been inverted in *An Outcast*: instead of rising above his 'frailties', Willems gives in to them.

Marriage, race, and ego

Willems's marriage to Joanna echoes Almayer's marriage. This relation-ship with a woman of 'mixed race' produces a sickly child, evidence that liaisons with 'native' women compromises racial purity. Again we cannot escape the fact that some of the nineteenth-century's more conservative attitudes towards race underpin Conrad's narratives. While his treatment of Willems may be ironic there lingers beneath the surface of his story the disturbing suggestion that Conrad actually endorses the notion of racial purity; and Willems's attempts to put a respectable gloss on that relationship thus appear even more pathetic.

Believing himself married to a submissive and obedient wife, Willems thinks he commands loyalty and respect as a husband. He casts himself as a nineteenth century male stereotype, like John Halifax in Mrs Craik's novel. Halifax is 'what all fathers should be—the truest representative here on earth of that father in heaven, who is at once justice, wisdom, and perfect love' (*JH*, 287). But Willems is no John Halifax, and he is certainly no gentleman. Picturing the revela-tion of his disgrace to his wife, Joanna, he fantasizes about his own power as the provider and husband while revealing an inability to

regard Joanna as anything but an extension of his own ego, a possession at best, a burden at worst:

> No doubt she will cry, she will lament, she will be helpless and
> frightened and passive as ever. And he would have to drag that limp
> weight on and on through the darkness of a spoiled life. Horrible!
> Of course he could not abandon her and the child to certain misery
> or possible starvation. The wife and child of Willems. Willems the
> successful, the smart; Willems the conf.... Pah! (*OI*, 24)

It is a curious blend of belief in male power and blatant egotism.

Ideal husbands in nineteenth-century romance honour and respect
their wives; but then the wife in such literature is a 'pure' example of
English femininity. The 'wife of Willems' is, according to her husband,
a 'dismal woman with startled eyes and dolorously drooping mouth'
(*OI*, 9).[6] Willems's 'passive' and 'obedient' wife is a sadly bedraggled
spectacle: 'She trailed through life in that red-dressing gown, with its
row of dirty blue bows down the front, stained, and hooked on awry; a
torn flounce at the bottom following her like a snake as she moved
languidly about, with her hair negligently caught up, and a tangled
wisp straggling untidily down her back' (*OI*, 25). With her 'lean throat',
'obtrusive collarbone', her 'thin arm' and 'bony hand clasping the
child', she is one step removed from the 'doubled-up crone' that Aïssa
becomes at the novel's end. Such is the luxurious existence of the wife
of the successful Willems. Yet he loftily outlines the gratitude due to
him as a faithful, model husband:

> She had years of glory as Willems' wife, and years of comfort, of
> loyal care, and of such tenderness as she deserved. He had guarded
> her carefully from any bodily hurt; and of other suffering he had no
> conception. The assertion of his superiority was only another bene-
> fit conferred on her. All this was a matter of course, but he told her
> all this so as to bring vividly before her the greatness of her loss.
> (*OI*, 25–6)

This is hollow rhetoric: while it smacks of the literary tradition
of chivalric love and mid-nineteenth-century ideals of marriage,
under-lying it is a characteristic narrative irony. Joanna received 'such
tenderness as she deserved': the patronizing arrogance of this statement
reveals Willems as a cruel and heartless egoist – such is Joanna's 'loss'.

Assuming responsibility for their future lives, Willems' words have
the emptiness of the stereotype: 'You have the money I left at home

this morning, Joanna?' he asked. 'We will want it all now'. These words made him feel that 'he was a fine fellow' (*OI*, 26). Willems assumes Joanna's acquiescence in his self-made fiction because she is a woman and his wife. But his delusions of grand romantic gestures are short-lived as Joanna, no doubt recalling the beatings, the neglect, and the tyranny meted out by her 'model' husband spurns him: 'You are less than dirt, you that have wiped your feet on me. I have waited for this. I am not afraid now' (*OI*, 27). She will not and does not conform to the passive role he creates for her.

While Willems clings to his illusory identity, Joanna and her family define his actual condition with venomous clarity. Joanna calls him a 'man from nowhere; a vagabond!' Leonard says, 'You are a savage. Not at all like we, whites' (*OI*, 28).[7] Both characters deny him the status of civilized European, a status that requires commitment to values to which Willems can only pay lip service. This is at variance with the literature of Empire. For, as White comments, the discourse of imperial fiction 'has not before revealed the representatives of European empires as having such easily corrupted and divided natures' (White, 140). The suggestions of Willems's domestic violence and the revelation of the Da Souza family's fear of, and disgust at, his behaviour cut through Willems's ego ideal as the nineteenth-century gentleman-husband. These 'degenerate descendants of Portuguese conquerors' whom he had imagined to worship him, in fact regard Willems himself as a moral degenerate. Thus we have an inversion of the standard stereotypes in imperial fiction where 'humble natives' worship the white man. Leonard tears at the veil of Willems' self-delusion but makes no impression because of Willems's over-reaching conceit. Furthermore, as John Stape observes, Willems 'refuses to ground himself, to set down roots in a cultural and social matrix', and ultimately 'his dream of a self capable of existing outside ordinary norms serves only to isolate him' (*OI* [World's Classics edn], x).

When Ignosi, the African king in *King Solomon's Mines*, accepts that Quatermain cannot remain in Kukuanaland he is acknowledging their racial difference: 'I do perceive that now as ever thy words are wise and full of reason, Macumazahn; that which flies in the air loves not to run along the ground; the white man loves not to live on the level of the black or to house among his kraals' (*KSM*, 339).[8] The non-Malay and non-Arab characters in Conrad's novel exhibit similar attitudes to those found in the literature of Empire. They measure worth in terms of race, vying with each other for moral superiority over the native people. Superiority is measured by each in terms of their distance from

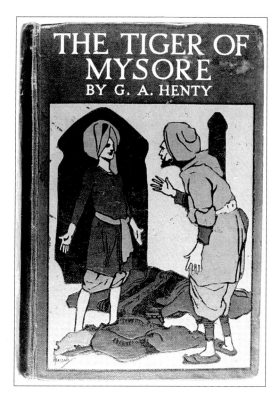

1 Hard cover of G. A. Henty,
The Tiger of Mysore (London:
Blackie and Son Limited, n.d.)

2 'From the picture in the possession of
George Curtis Esq.' Frontispiece to
H. Rider Haggard, *Allan Quatermain*
(London: Longmans, Green and Co.,
1901).

3 '"It's a big order," said Sir Henry, reflectively.' From H. Rider Haggard, *Allan Quatermain* (London: Longmans, Green and Co., 1901). Facing p.10.

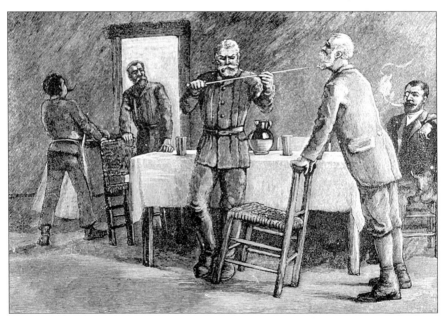

4 'We all examined it, and shook our heads.' From H. Rider Haggard, *Allan Quatermain* (London: Longmans, Green and Co., 1901). Facing p.36.

5 'The Sister Queens.' From H. Rider Haggard, *Allan Quatermain* (London: Longmans, Green and Co., 1901). Facing p.140.

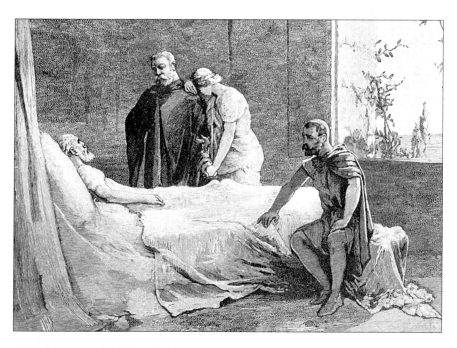

6 'God Bless You All.' From H.Rider Haggard, *Allan Quatermain* (Longmans, Green and Co., 1901). Facing p.274.

7 'Ayesha Unveils.' From H. Rider Haggard, *She* (London: Longmans, Green and Co., 1918). Facing p.152.

8 A drawing by Conrad of a woman with a serpent. A copy is held by the New York Public Library on which is written: 'This sketch must have been done between the years of 1892–1894. They came into my possession at my marriage in 1896. Jessie Conrad.' Reproduced in Cedric Watts, *A Preface to Conrad* (Harlow: Longman, 1982), p.99.

9 'How Umslopogaas Held the Stair.' From H. Rider Haggard, *Allan Quatermain* (Longmans, Green and Co., 1901). Facing p.254.

0 'Dancing About in the Most Fantastic Manner.' Frontispiece to W. H. G. Kingston, *Peter Biddulph* (London: The Sunday School Union, n.d.).

11 'Farewell.' From W. H. G.
Kingston, *Peter Biddulph*
(London: The Sunday
School Union, n.d.), p.31.

12 Frontispiece to W. H. G.
Kingston, *Ben Hadden*
(London: The Religious
Tract Society, n.d.).

13 'We were dragged up to him.' Frontispiece to W. H. G. Kingston, *In the Eastern Seas* (London: Thomas Nelson and Sons, n.d.).

4 'A Dyak waved his head in triumph in the air.' From W. H. G. Kingston, *In the Eastern Seas* (London: Thomas Nelson and Sons, n.d.). Facing p.470.

15 'The White Slave-Girl Thanks
Dick For Saving Her Life.' From
G. A. Henty, *The Tiger of Mysore*
(London: Blackie and Sons,
n.d.). Facing p.244.

16 '"In the name of God," came
the voice, "I deliver to the
heir of John the Snake of
John."' From John Buchan,
Prester John (London: Thomas
Nelson and Sons, Ltd., n.d.).
Facing p.192.

the 'native'. When Willems returns to Almayer's campong dishevelled, in a sarong, and shouting, Almayer is outraged: 'Do you think yourself in the forest with your... your friends? This is a civilized man's house. A white man's. Understand?' (*OI*, 88). Yet moments later Almayer reveals his own lack of restraint when, with absurdly childish malice, he exhorts Nina to call Willems 'pig'. By denying Willems's status as a 'white', branding him a 'savage', and identifying himself and Joanna as 'white', Leonard claims their superiority. The native people also make their claims to superiority. At the climax of the novel, Aïssa, Willems's half-Arab half-Malay lover, reveals her contempt for Joanna. She is 'A Sirani woman. A woman of a people despised by all' (*OI*, 358).[9] The simple 'us and them' model of the imperial romance is thus muddied in this tale of moral delinquency. Conrad's specificity about the different groupings of native people implies a complex social order in the imperial East that is rarely, if ever, found in the imperial romance.

This is a story of one man's descent into moral chaos. Heroism, adventure, wealth: these tropes characterize the destinies of the heroes of Kingston, Henty, and Haggard. In *An Outcast* the promise of wealth and reputation that the East appears to offer is a fantasy of Willems's own making. As Said points out, speaking specifically of *Lord Jim*, the ideal which Conrad's heroes imagine for themselves becomes progressively clearer as they move away from it: 'Only in the domains of intention and fantasy to which Conrad's heroes have a fatal attraction can there be a completion for schemes of the kind Jim devises for himself; but such a place is apprehendable only during the constantly progressing narrative of his doom and failure' (*The World, The Text and the Critic*, 105). While in his imagination Willems fabricates a glorious, expansive future for himself, his actual progress is downward and inward. Willems descends into the depths of the Malay forest in a relentless retreat from the world of commerce and fame to which he aspires until his only companions are his rejected lover, Aïssa, and the shrivelled old serving woman. In this unromantic isolation he becomes the antithesis of the imperial hero. Willems's sordid death inverts the formula of imperial romance: the triumphant return to Europe and a virginal bride is denied him; instead he is carried back to Sambir, a half-clothed corpse, shot by his 'native' lover. Lakamba's clearing is Willems's private hell; his body is returned, not to Europe but to the place from which he yearned to escape, Sambir. He is confined forever to look down upon the scene of his disgrace from his grave on the hill across the Pantai. Even in death Willems is bitterly cursed by Almayer who wishes him to 'smart' in a place where there is 'no mercy' for him;

a far cry from the noble death and glowing epitaph afforded to the imperial hero Quatermain by his countryman Curtis (see plate 6).

Lingard's fictions

Willems is a victim of his own delusions; but he is also, like Almayer, a victim of Lingard's misguided benevolence. Lingard's role as father figure in *Almayer's Folly* is repeated in *An Outcast* through his 'adoption' of Willems. We also learn more of Lingard's history and his legendary brig, *Flash*: 'They came north together—both young—out of an Australian port, and after a very few years there was not a white man in the islands, from Palembang to Ternate, from Ombawa to Palawan, that did not know Captain Tom and his lucky craft' (*OI*, 13). The exotic locations in which he is recognized positions Lingard as a romantic figure. Conrad may also have had in mind Sir James Brooke, the Rajah of Sarawak, when he created the character of Lingard. John Gordan mentions the 'romance of the man' and points to the similarities with Lingard: 'Like Brooke, Lingard, too, was an English adventurer who made himself a great power in a native state—Sambir. And both men were addressed by their Malay admirers as Rajah Laut, or King of the Sea' (Gordan, 618). Rumours of Lingard's daring exploits also recall Brooke's actual suppression of Malay and Dyak pirates: 'by his successful recklessness in several encounters with pirates, [he] established the terror of his name' (*OI*, 14). The emblem of Lingard's success is the fact that the locals dropped 'the ceremonious "Captain Lingard"' and began to address him 'half seriously as Rajah Laut—The King of the Sea' (*OI*, 14).

So far so good: Lingard looks set to re-enact the romantic role of his fictional predecessors and the imperial success of Brooke. Early reviewers warmed to the Lingard of *An Outcast*: James Payne in the *Illustrated London News* of 4 April 1896 saw him as 'a noble character' (*CH*, 67); the reviewer for the *Spectator* on 30 May 1896 described him as a character 'conceived on the colossal scale of primitive romance' who 'looms through the lurid atmosphere of crime and sensuality like a legendary type of rugged, incorruptible manhood' (*CH*, 78). But Conrad adds various qualifiers to his description of Lingard and his glorious reputation that undermine these definitions: his title, 'Rajah Laut', is conferred only 'half seriously'; we learn of his 'fierce aspect, his loud voice, his fearless eyes', but also of his 'stupidly guileless heart', and his 'absurd faith in himself' (*OI*, 13). Although he began by being feared for his violent temper he was soon found out, 'and the word went round that Captain Tom's fury was less dangerous than many a man's smile' (*OI*, 13–14). Lingard needs flattery, as Peter Knox-Shaw points out: 'the generosity which is his most remarkable trait often masks a compulsive need for applause, and furthermore…his habit of having his own way leads him to place a premium on deference among his acquaintance and friends' (Knox-Shaw, 130). Such is not the character of the true romantic hero: one of Quatermain's most striking features is his 'modesty', a quality Lingard singularly lacks. Thus Conrad swiftly subverts the romantic type he invokes. In the end Lingard is a pale and fallible reflection of the manly adventurers of imperial fiction: the real-life James Brooke was far more colourful and effective.

Paternalism and exploitation

Lingard persists in what Vernon Young calls his 'misguided chivalry' (Young, 525). He recognizes in Willems something of himself as a young man; in return Willems schemes to supplant Lingard and acquire his wealth. The romance and suggestions of success accruing to Lingard are the fantasies that fuel Willems's greedy ambitions, and Lingard blinds himself to his protégé's treacherous intentions. In rescuing Willems from the quay in Samarang Lingard sowed the seeds of his own destruction. While Lingard describes him as 'that clever young fellow', regarding him 'with innocent pride in his honest eyes' (*OI*, 17), Willems is plotting with Hudig to betray him.[10] The simple loyalties of the romance genre, in fact the loyalty that Lingard with his 'stupidly guileless heart' expects, are the fictions with which Conrad's characters delude themselves. In this story of betrayal and self-deception loyalty is given only to the self. Lingard foolishly believes in his own supremacy as 'father' and in Willems's undivided loyalty. But these are the simple assumptions of the fictions of romance and adventure; they are values and role models that Conrad empties of meaning. Despite Willems's moral disintegration, Lingard cannot abandon his role as surrogate father. Calling Willems 'my boy', he whisks him away to Sambir, giving the impression that, parent-like, he will make everything all right. Willems will be the beneficiary of Lingard's imperial power and wealth, the 'son' who will inherit the estate.

Filled with fantasies of power and reputation, Lingard casts himself in the role of benevolent imperial ruler, very much in the style of James Brooke. 'D'ye see, I have them all in my pocket. The rajah is an old friend of mine. My word is law—and I am the only trader', he confidently asserts (*OI*, 43). John McClure asks why the simple-hearted Lingard should admire a character as dissolute as Willems: 'The first suggestion is that Lingard's virtues blind him to Willems's faults, but as the story unfolds another answer emerges: Lingard manifests most of these faults himself. The role he has created for himself at Sambir closely resembles that of Willems at Maccassar; the most significant difference is one of scale' (McClure, 109). Lingard's delusions of power and reputation are in fact reminiscent of Willems's fantasy as benefactor of the Da Souza family. Sambir is Lingard's imperial utopia:

> You see, Willems, I brought prosperity to that place. I composed their quarrels, and saw them grow under my eyes. There's peace and happiness there. I am more master there than his Dutch Excellency down in Batavia ever will be when some day a lazy man-of-war blunders at last against the river. (*OI*, 45)

This is Lingard's fiction, the fiction of the Empire. We are reminded of the many voices in Henty's novels affirming the beneficial effect of English rule in India, and contributing to the idea that imperialism brought 'light' to the 'dark places' of the world. It was the guise under which the Europeans invaded Africa and the East. Lingard, however, is motivated by more than an altruistic sense of imperial paternalism. His sense of possession is the key to his motivation: it is *his* river and *his* secret. Even before he outlines his utopian fantasy of Sambir and his benevolent rule he hints at the wealth available there with gleeful rapacity: 'Keep mum about my river when you get amongst the traders again. There's many would give their ears for the knowledge of it. I'll tell you something: that's where I get all my guttah and rattans. Simply inexhaustible, my boy' (*OI*, 43). It is in Lingard's own interest to keep the local population happy. The multi-layered discourses of imperialism are thus revealed. While the paternal eye of the white imperialist watches indulgently over its subjects it also watches over the systematic exploitation of the land's resources. This is familiar territory for imperial romance. Henty's Indian characters affirm the political, moral, and financial benefits of English rule and his boy heroes, apparently, effect nothing but good as they roam the Empire amassing fabulous riches.

Lingard, like Henty's boys and Haggard's heroes, believes in the beneficial effects of his rule, and Conrad gives qualified approval to his imperial venture:

> His deep-seated and immovable conviction that only he—he, Lingard—knew what was good for them was characteristic of him,

and, after all, not so very far wrong. He would make them happy whether or no, he said, and he meant it. His trade brought prosperity to the young state, and the fear of his heavy hand secured its internal peace for many years. (*OI*, 200)

Bringing political stability to African or Eastern states is the prerogative of the white adventurer. Thus, as Quatermain, Curtis, and Good leave Kukuanaland they exhort Ignosi to 'rule justly, to respect the law, and to put none to death without a cause. So shalt thou prosper' (*KSM*, 338). Ignosi, under the influence of the English gentlemen, has restored order to a land where anarchy and tyranny prevailed. Brian Street notes that Haggard acknowledged 'the harmful aspects of contact' but ultimately believed in the beneficial influence of white invasion: 'Thus, whenever his characters have an inland "paradise", it is always under the improving influences of someone with Western ideals' (Street, 123). Lingard believes that he performs the same function for his 'little corner of the world' (*OI*, 200). There are undertones here of James Brooke: Steven Runciman comments that Brooke felt that too much association of native peoples with Europeans did them 'nothing but harm; he had himself remarked in India that the English-speaking Indians were the most unreliable and corrupt. He had no illusions about the native character. The Malays were given the epithet of treacherous, the Hindostanis lazy' (Runciman, 49–50).

Despite his paternalistic care, Lingard regards Malays as treacherous, but protects his little empire from incursions by other races. Like Brooke, and like Haggard's heroes, Lingard wishes to perpetuate the peaceful 'innocence' of the native life over which he jealously watches: he determines to keep out the traders to preserve his monopoly, but also the 'verminous breed' of Arabs with 'their lies and their intrigues' (*OI*, 45). Sambir is for Lingard an Arcadia 'which he loved to think all his own':

He looked proudly upon his work. With every passing year he loved more the land, the people, the muddy river that, if he could help it, would carry no other craft but the *Flash* on its unclean and friendly surface. As he slowly warped his vessel up-stream he would scan with knowing looks the riverside clearings, and pronounce solemn judgement upon the prospects of the season's rice-crop. He knew every settler on the banks between the sea and Sambir; he knew their wives, their children; he knew every individual of the multi-coloured groups that, standing on the flimsy platforms of tiny reed dwellings built over the water, waved their hands and shouted shrilly: 'O! Kapal layer! Haï!' while the *Flash* swept slowly through the populated reach … (*OI*, 200–1)

Lingard's ruminations evoke such images as we see in plate 12 where peaceful 'natives' in an exotic utopia discourse with a benevolent sea captain. But Conrad probes Lingard's subconscious to reveal the egotism of the man: 'His river! By it he was not only rich—he was interesting. This secret of his which made him different to the other traders of those seas gave intimate satisfaction to that desire for singularity which he shared with the rest of mankind, without being aware of its presence within his breast' (*OI*, 202). The simple tale of the imperial adventurer becoming wealthy and powerful, using his superior intelligence for the benefit of the Empire becomes in Conrad's hands the story of the immense vanity of humankind.

Lingard achieves none of the glory associated with the Rajah Brooke. Despite attacks on his methods from Parliament in England, Brooke maintained his control of Sarawak and passed his Empire on to his nephew. Unlike Brooke, Lingard is unable to hold on to his interests. Willems and Almayer were to inherit his wealth and reputation, but Willems, enveloped in his own egotistic world, is doomed, and Almayer is an incompetent, embittered fool. The romance of Brooke's career and the imperial successes of the fiction of romance and adventure are both suggested and subverted in Lingard's history. Such fame and glory as Brooke acquired were only possible in the early nineteenth century or in the romances of Empire; at the close of the century Conrad casts a more cynical eye over the whole imperial venture.

The serpent in 'paradise'

Immediately after Lingard pompously outlines his prestige to Willems we hear the voice of Babalatchi preaching intrigue and revolution to the indolent Lakamba. Babalatchi and Willems were originally to form the duo of vagabonds after whom Conrad was to name his book, before that is Mrs Wood published *The Vagabonds* in 1894 and caused him to rethink.[11] In the final version Babalatchi is the motivating force behind the take-over of Lingard's 'paradise'. Squatting by a fire fomenting unrest, our first view of Babalatchi in *An Outcast* emphazises his savagery:

> The burst of clear flame lit up his broad, dark, and pock-marked face, where the big lips, stained with betel-juice, looked like a deep

and bleeding gash of a fresh wound. The reflection of the firelight gleamed brightly in his solitary eye, lending it for the moment a fierce animation that died out together with the short-lived flame. (*OI*, 47)

The seediness, uncleanness, and suggestion of danger about this description recall another, much earlier embittered 'native', Magua' in *The Last of the Mohicans*:

[T]here was an air of neglect about his person, like that which might have proceeded from great and recent exertion which he had not yet found leisure to repair. The colours of the war-paint had blended in dark confusion about his fierce countenance, and rendered his swarthy lineaments still more savage and repulsive than if art had attempted an effect which had been thus produced by chance. His eye alone, which glistened like a fiery star amid lowering clouds, was to be seen in its state of native wildness. (*LM*, 11–12)

We are reminded also of the shrunken figure of Gagool with her 'sunken slit, that represented the mouth' and her eyes 'still full of fire and intelligence' (*KSM*, 157–8). Babalatchi clearly follows a tradition of deformed, malevolent 'native' villains.

Pock-marked faces or physical deformities indicate some degree of depravity or unhealthy living, as in Dr Jekyll's alter-ego, Mr Hyde: 'There is something wrong with his appearance; something displeasing, something downright detestable. I never saw a man I so disliked, and yet I scarce know why. He must be deformed somewhere; he gives a strong feeling of deformity, although I couldn't specify the point' (*Jekyll and Hyde*, 22). Dr Lanyon describes Hyde as 'hardly human' and 'troglodytic' (*Jekyll and Hyde*, 37). Later Hyde brutally murders Sir Danvers Carew by trampling him under foot 'with ape-like fury' (*Jekyll and Hyde*, 49). Hyde is the primitive other self of Jekyll, the 'savage' part of his nature normally kept under control by his civilized self. Quatermain argues for a fundamental kinship between the 'savage' and the 'civilized' races: 'It is a depressing conclusion, but in all essentials the savage and the child of civilisation are identical' (*AQ*, 4). It is Quatermain's contention that human nature is nineteen parts savage and one part civilized: the one part civilized distinguishes the white man from the 'savage' (*AQ*, 6).[12] Despite his oratory skills, we are in no doubt as to Babalatchi's place in this evolutionary order: he is a 'savage statesman', and a 'barbarous politician' (*OI*, 214). Conrad, however, adds a new dimension to

Haggard's simplistic view of human nature: even a 'savage' is allowed a moment of emotional intensity. Thus upon the death of Omar:

> For the space of about thirty seconds, a half-naked, betel-chewing pessimist stood upon the bank of the tropical river, on the edge of the still and immense forests; a man angry, powerless, empty-handed, with a cry of bitter discontent ready on his lips; a cry that, had it come out, would have rung through the virgin solitudes of the woods, as true, as great, as profound, as any philosophical shriek that ever came from the depths of an easy-chair to disturb the impure wilderness of chimneys and roofs. (*OI*, 215)

In the urban jungle of Europe agonized grief has no more profound expression than that to be found in the Malay backwaters. Conrad stresses a common humanity; but the 'savage' mind can only maintain this level of 'human' feeling for thirty seconds. It is his nature to scheme, and duly Babalatchi abandons his grief and immerses himself in his plans, 'a victim to the tormenting superstitions of his race' (*OI*, 215).

Babalatchi's schemes, like those of Magua or Gagool, are designed to oust the invading imperialists. He is a savage threat like the half-clothed Malay pirate of plate 13, viciously handling the white-suited adventurer who, incidentally, bears a strong resemblance to Willems. But Conrad sets his narrative in opposition to the conventions of the imperial romance. Rather than being defeated, Babalatchi's schemes expose the delusions of both Lingard and Willems. In a deliberate inversion of the popular formula Malays defeat Europeans and install 'native' power. In Conrad's fiction the stability of European imperialism at the end of the nineteenth century, and claims for white superiority are in doubt. Lingard's dreams of Arcadian happiness for Sambir are shattered when, through the agency of Willems, Babalatchi brings Abdulla up the river. Willems's self-righteousness and protestations of white superiority are revealed as hollow rhetoric when Babalatchi, serpent-like, manipulates his obsession for Aïssa and thus persuades him to betray his 'father' and his race. The assumptions of racial purity and heroism, of 'good' defeating 'evil' that are the hallmarks of the romance are undercut by the reversals of Conrad's narrative where heroic action is a thing of the past. Babalatchi's history is one of heroic deeds, piracy and fierce battles against an invading race. As White comments, Babalatchi's story is 'more truly the stuff of adventure' than that of Willems (White, 148).

Furthermore, within the multi-voiced narrative of *An Outcast* Babalatchi's voice is as potent as any of the white voices we hear.

When Lingard protests to him of the benevolence of his enterprise Babalatchi has an equally persuasive argument:

> 'This is a white man's talk,' exclaimed Babalatchi, with bitter exultation. 'I know you. That is how you all talk while you load your guns and sharpen your swords; and when you are ready, then to those who are weak you say: "Obey me and be happy, or die!" You are strange, you white men. You think it is only your wisdom and your virtue and your happiness that are true.' (*OI*, 226)

This is a perspective that Babalatchi shares with Magua, but in Conrad's fiction it has a power never available in the imperial romance. The Malay subjects of Conrad's fiction, unlike Henty's or Haggard's grateful 'natives', perceive the imperial venture as one of exploitation and cultural blindness:

> What Babalatchi points out is the tremendous gap that separates culture from culture and that makes a mockery of European pretensions to enlightened rule. ... Thus even the most benign imperialist can never truly perform the function (advocated by Kipling and others) of protecting the colonized peoples from change. Whether such a program is advocated naively or with the ulterior purpose of protecting monopolies on psychological and economical exploitation, it is doomed to failure. (McClure, 112–13)

At the end of the novel Almayer bitterly outlines Lingard's failure to the Roumanian orchid-hunter. Babalatchi is the 'Shahbandar of the State', Lakamba 'calls himself a Sultan', and Abdulla has well and truly replaced Lingard:

> He lives here because—he says—here he is away from white men. But he has hundreds of thousands. Has a house in Penang. Ships. What did he not have when he stole my trade from me! He knocked everything into a cocked hat; drove father to gold-hunting—then to Europe, where he disappeared. (*OI*, 364)

'Natives' of imperial romance, like Magua, may dream of such an overthrow, but it is an impossibility because the European is always superior, intellectually, morally, and politically. Conrad, subverts these assumptions, undercuts the simple 'truths' of imperial romance, and presents alternative voices and alternative resolutions to racial conflicts. Babalatchi challenges the destiny of dissenting 'native' stereotypes by actually ousting white rule. He is the serpent in Lingard's paradise who, with cunning and eloquence, effects Lingard's loss of control of his Eden.

An oriental *femme fatale*

In a letter to Marguerite Poradowska, while he was still in the early stages of planning *An Outcast* Conrad mused half-humorously, half-seriously: 'Do you think one can make something interesting without any women?!'[13] Obviously he decided he couldn't. Aïssa is central to the novel as the temptation that leads Willems to abandon his 'father' and his racial identity. Like Babalatchi, Aïssa in many ways conforms to the stereotypes of nineteenth-century romance literature. She is a *femme fatale*, even more threatening to the male than Nina Almayer, perhaps because she is half-Arab. Aïssa is dangerous, like Hawthorne's Zenobia, in *The Blithedale Romance* (1852)[14] whose beauty 'sometimes compelled' the hero Coverdale to shut his eyes 'as if it were not quite the privilege of modesty to gaze at her' (*BR*, 44). Zenobia is an 'enchantress': the exotic flowers she wears seemed to have 'sprung passionately out of a soil, the very weeds of which would be fervid and spicy' (*BR*, 45). She is associated with magic, spells, and illusions as if there were something unearthly about her, or rather too earthy, in that this is profane rather than sacred magic: black not white.

The implicit danger of the *femme fatale* is more pronounced when she is Oriental like Ayesha in *She*; even the name Aïssa recalls that of Haggard's earlier creation. Stunningly beautiful temptresses, with masses of long black hair signifying their sensuality (see Ayesha in plate 7), they represent nineteenth-century popular notions of Eastern femininity: mysterious, half-perceived, never to be understood, but above all exotic, exciting sexual passion, and capable of destroying the male. While he was writing *Almayer's Folly*, Conrad drew the sketch of an exotic woman (plate 8). Flimsily dressed in a transparent top with a sarong wrapped loosely around the waist, and toying with a large snake, she is, as Kenneth Inniss notes, 'in accord with every Westerner's image of the desirable girl from *The Arabian Nights*' (Inniss, 39). The drawing depicts the same stereotype of Eastern female sensuality and danger that Conrad used in creating his Eastern heroines. Aïssa is even more in that mould than Nina. Willems's first glimpse of her is exciting and suggestive:

> As he approached her the woman tossed her head slightly back, and with a free gesture of her strong, round arm, caught up the mass of loose black hair and brought it over her shoulder and across the

lower part of her face. The next moment he was passing her close, walking rigidly, like a man in a trance. (*OI*, 68)

Covering her face is a sign of Islamic modesty, but apart from that Aïssa has the same effect on Willems as Ayesha does on Leo and Holly; Aïssa could almost be the Ayesha of plate 7. Said pinpoints three features of Western perceptions of Oriental women to which both Aïssa and Ayesha conform: 'They express unlimited sensuality, they are more or less stupid, and above all they are willing' (*Orientalism*, 207). Their 'stupidity' is, in Aïssa's case, her 'savagery'; in Ayesha's, her naivety; their willing sensuality is expressed in the flowing hair and gauzy, revealing wrappings that invite the male gaze. The Eastern woman is visually sensual in her apparent physical abandon. Few English heroines would be seen in the position of Aïssa when Willems eventually finds her in Lakamba's campong: 'He rushed up the enclosure like a tornado, pressing the girl to his breast, her arms round his neck, her head hanging back over his arm, her eyes closed and her long hair nearly touching the ground' (*OI*, 108). This is the melodrama of imperial romance with overt suggestions of Oriental female sexual abandon. The typical English woman, chaste, tightly corseted, immaculately coiffured, is far from inviting sexuality; she must be chivalrously protected from any sexual threat. When young Ethel in *Out on the Pampas* is taken by the 'Indians' Mr Hardy is horrified: 'Carried off!…It is worse than death' (*OP*, 225). The English woman is emblematic of a known middle-class order, safe and inviolable.

Joanna de Groot indicates how, particularly in nineteenth century travel writing, 'women were presented as the *means* for imagining or finding out about the Orient' (de Groot, 105). The mystery of woman and the male desire to explore that mystery constitutes the romantic danger of the Oriental *femme fatale*. Thus Stott writes of Haggard's males: 'Desire, the natural impulse that begets curiosity to lift the veil on the mysteries of Woman and the mysteries of Africa or the Unknown, is the compulsion behind the quest and a compulsion which leads dangerously towards fatality' (Stott, 92). The mystery of the Eastern woman can even be evil, as when Holly beholds Ayesha's face: 'I have heard of the beauty of celestial beings, now I saw it; only this beauty, with all its awful loveliness and purity, was *evil*—or rather, at the time, it impressed me as evil' (*S*, 153). Once Ayesha lifts her veil to reveal her unearthly beauty Leo is enslaved:

I saw him struggle—I saw him even turn to fly; but her eyes drew him more strongly than iron bonds, and the magic of her beauty and concentrated will and passion entered into him and overpowered him ... It sounds horrible and wicked indeed, but he should not be too greatly blamed, and to be sure his sin has found him out. The temptress who drew him into evil was more than human, and her beauty was greater than the loveliness of the daughters of men. (S, 223–4)

Aïssa has the same effect: as if she has cast a spell, her gaze compels Willems:

He heard her rapid breathing and he felt the touch of a look darted at him from half-open eyes. It touched his brain and his heart together. It seemed to him to be something loud and stirring like a shout, silent and penetrating like an inspiration. The momentum of his motion carried him past her, but an invisible force made up of surprise and curiosity and desire spun him round as soon as he had passed. (OI, 68–9)

This recalls the fascination of another mysterious beauty: the Veiled Lady in *The Blithedale Romance* tempts Theodore, but warns of the consequences of her beauty:

'Dost thou hesitate,' said the Veiled Lady, 'to pledge thyself to me, by meeting these lips of mine, while the veil yet hides my face? Has not thy heart recognised me? ... Still, thou mayst lift the veil! But from that instant, Theodore, I am doomed to be thy evil fate; nor will thou ever taste another breath of happiness!' (BR, 113)

The veil, the danger, and the irresistible beauty that enslaves also characterize Aïssa:

He had been frightened by the vague perception of danger before, but now, as he looked at that life again, his eyes seemed able to pierce the fantastic veil of creepers and leaves, to look past the solid trunks, to see through the forbidding gloom—and the mystery was disclosed—enchanting, subduing, beautiful. He looked at the woman. Through the checkered light between them she appeared to him with the impalpable distinctness of a dream. The very spirit of that land of mysterious forests, standing before him like an apparition behind a transparent veil—a veil woven of sunbeams and shadows. (OI, 70)

Having Willems associate the woman with nature and the jungle, Conrad insists upon her 'otherness', her strangeness and mystery, and the threat she poses to racial and masculine identity. The appeal of the woman is thus equated with the romantic appeal of the East, dark, alluring, and unfathomable, threatening a loss of the masculine self into the chaos of the jungle and the 'irrational' female temperament. The mid-to-late nineteenth-century view of the balance of male and female characteristics, that is, male rationality complemented by female sensitivity to produce a harmonious union, is threatened by the overly sensual nature of the Oriental female. Stott outlines the perception of Aïssa as part of the deadly anarchy of the natural world:

> Willems, in his attempt to comprehend the incomprehensible Oriental landscape of the Malay jungle, characterises its mystery as erotically feminine but also poisonous and deadly. In Conrad's early Malayan tale and in *Heart of Darkness*, the native women are framed and held by the jungle but are also inseparable from it; they are like carnivorous jungle plants—*fleurs du mal*—alluring and deadly. The contours of these women, pictured or framed against a 'riot of foliage', in twilight or in checkered green sunlight, dissolve into the erotic confusion around them. (Stott, 128)

The association of Aïssa with the untamed wilderness emphasizes her position on the evolutionary ladder: she is a 'savage', frequently characterized as a wild animal. She casts 'sidelong' glances, and has 'the expression of a wild and resentful defiance' (*OI*, 71). More than once Conrad mentions her 'distended nostrils', and Willems watches 'the gradual taming of that woman' (*OI*, 76). Like a timid animal she must be coaxed nearer, for Willems 'knew from experience how a slight movement of his could frighten her away' (*OI*, 76). Babalatchi holds her back from Willems like a dog on a leash: 'Fool!' muttered Babalatchi, looking up at Aïssa, who stood with set teeth, with gleaming eyes and distended nostrils, yet obedient to the touch of his restraining hand'. He releases her with the authority of masterly control, and like an arrow 'she flew down the enclosure, and disappeared through the gate of the courtyard' (*OI*, 107). Just as Ayesha inhabits her womb-like caves of Kôr luring Holly and Leo spider-like into her web of sensuality, Aïssa is the 'very spirit of that land of mysterious forests', manifesting its romance, its fecundity, and its threat to male self-control (*OI*, 70).

Deep in the caves of Kôr Holly watches Ayesha capturing the very essence of Leo: 'I saw his wonder and astonishment grow into admiration, then into longing, and the more he struggled the more I saw the power of her dread beauty fasten on him and take hold of his senses, drugging them, and drawing the heart out of him' (*S*, 222–3). There is a sense of horror, powerlessness, and deadly danger in Leo's fascination. Willems's surrender to his passion for Aïssa has the same effect. Losing his sense of reality in her embrace, Willems is vulnerable to Omar's murderous attack:

> Glancing upwards he saw the motionless head of the woman look-ing down at him in a tender gleam of liquid white between the long eyelashes, whose shadow rested on the soft curve of her cheek; and under the caress of that look, the uneasy wonder and the obscure fear of that apparition, crouching and creeping in turns towards the fire that was its guide, were lost—were drowned in the quietude of all his senses, as pain is drowned in the flood of drowsy serenity that follows upon a dose of opium. (*OI*, 147)

Aïssa acts to save him while Willems, like Leo, is left with a sense of complete loss of control, as if drugged: 'It was not death that frightened him: it was the horror of bewildered life where he could understand nothing and nobody round him; where he could guide, control, com-prehend nothing and no one—not even himself' (*OI*, 149). Watts notes how frequently in Conrad's fiction 'a passionate sexual encounter seems, paradoxically, to emasculate the man, to be subversive, making him bewildered and self-doubting, and it sometimes results in his destruction' (Watts, 98–101). In the embrace of the woman and the Malay forest Willems's fantasy of himself as the imperial hero, master of himself and the conquered people, dissolves into the 'horror of bewil-dered life'. Willems comes face to face with the unfathomable nature of existence itself. Thus Conrad endorses the white male stereotype of imperial romance where women are treacherous: they are all Delilahs. The 'native' woman is especially dangerous: she may even carry dis-ease, 'the pox'. On one level, Conrad subverts conventional assump-tions of heroism in the imperial romance: at another he sanctions the fear of Oriental female sexuality as expressed in such literature.

A doubled-up crone

Another side to the characterization of Aïssa indicates Conrad's further endorsement of the conventional romance representation of Oriental women. Implying the transience of passion and the illusion of the ideal, Conrad juxtaposes Aïssa with the unnamed old woman who constantly hovers in the background. This woman recalls the familiar hag-like creature of imperial romance, in particular of Gagool in *King Solomon's Mines*. She carries intimations of witches, of the strange and uncanny, vaguely recalling the weird sisters in *Macbeth*: 'The water in the iron pan on the cooking fire boiled furiously, belching out volumes of white steam that mixed with the thin black thread of smoke. The old woman appeared to him through this as if in a fog, squatting on her heels, impassive and weird' (*OI*, 348). While 'squatting over the fire', 'lifting up her bleared eyes to gaze', or stretching 'a tremulous and emaciated arm towards the hut', she embodies the decay and ugliness that is the underside of life in Sambir (*OI*, 99). She is a reminder that the glamour of Aïssa's loveliness and sensuality must inevitably fade. Willems notices her in the hut after Lingard's departure: 'A low moan ending a broken and plaintive mutter arrested Willems on the threshold. He peered round in the half-light under the roof and saw the old woman crouching close to the wall in a shapeless heap, and while he looked he felt a touch of two arms on his shoulders. Aïssa!' (*OI*, 285). The vision of the 'shapeless heap' and Aïssa's touch happen simultaneously, thus conflating the younger woman with the older one, for the reader and probably for Willems too.

Aïssa's fate mirrors that of the old woman: at the end of the novel she is 'tamed' by the indomitable Nina, who will herself become the Oriental beauty that Aïssa was. Her life becomes meaningless, and her once statuesque beauty gives way to the hag-like appearance of the old woman. Almayer has the final word on Aïssa:

> 'Now of course she lives with my serving girls, but does what she likes. As long as I have a handful of rice or a piece of cotton in the store she shan't want for anything. You have seen her. She brought in the dinner with Ali.'
> 'What! That doubled-up crone?'
> 'Ah!' said Almayer. 'They age quickly here.' (*OI*, 366)

Such is the destiny of women in Conrad's Sambir once they have lost their sexual attractiveness. Aïssa's life has little more value than that of a faithful old dog to whom Almayer is grateful for having once saved Nina's life. She has shrivelled up just as Ayesha did when she stepped into the flame of Life: 'She raised herself upon her bony hands, and blindly gazed around her, swaying her head slowly from side to side as does a tortoise. She could not see, for her whitish eyes were covered with a horny film. Oh the horrible pathos of the sight!' (*S*, 287).

In nineteenth-century fiction female sexual precocity brings dire consequences. The fate of Caroline Brithwood in *John Halifax, Gentleman* is a warning to young women not to allow their passions to overcome their sense of propriety. Encountering Caroline years after she left her husband the Halifax family see, not a vibrant and elegant young noblewoman, but a degraded and queer parody of her former self. Phineas Fletcher views her with horror: 'And surely when, as she turned from side to side, I caught her full face—what a face it was!—withered, thin, sallow almost to deathliness, with a bright rouge spot on each cheek, a broad smile on the ghastly mouth' (*JH*, 500). The innocent young Maud is advised not to look at her for Phineas 'was sure this must be the wreck of such a life as womanhood does sometimes sink to' (*JH*, 500). Just as Aïssa is taken in by the Almayer household, so Caroline is cared for by the Halifaxes, but of course with more 'Christian charity' than is evident in Almayer's 'care'. Such is the destiny of nineteenth-century women who give in to their sexuality: beauty is defaced, promiscuity results in premature ageing, and the self-righteous of the community watch over the final days of the 'fallen woman'. Zola's Nana is the final word on the consequences of such female 'debauchery'.

Race and marriage

The woman 'with the steadfast heart' becomes the 'doubled-up crone' of the novel's end accepting scraps from Almayer's table. Almayer's comment, 'They age quickly out here', indicates the European man's sense of racial difference, and the male sense of woman's 'otherness'. The racial gulf that Willems perceives between himself and the 'native' woman Aïssa is central to the racial prejudices of imperial romance: miscegenation is taboo and brings with it only disaster. Conrad exploits this sense of racial and sexual 'otherness' in his exploration of the effects of Willems's decision to step from 'the straight and narrow path of his peculiar honesty', and in doing so endorses the assumptions of imperial fiction about 'native' women.

Retreating into the forests with Aïssa, Willems enters a moral wilderness that he comes to closely associate with the woman. It is crucial to remember, however, that Willems was a moral degenerate before he ever saw Aïssa. His 'peculiar honesty' had never involved a sense of loyalty to anyone but himself, as proven by his callous rejection of Aïssa once his passion is spent. His passion is the final chapter in the story of his self-destructive surrender to the demands of his own ego. His pursuit of her through the seductive veil of the Malay forest leads to Aïssa's recognition that Willems was 'a man ready to be enslaved' (*OI*, 75). His boastful representation of himself, provides Aïssa with the material with which to fabricate her own fantasy: 'She could not understand all he told her of his life, but the fragments she understood she made up for herself into a story of a man great amongst his own people, valorous and unfortunate; an undaunted fugitive dreaming of vengeance against his enemies' (*OI*, 75). Neither her version of Willems nor his version of himself is the true one. The point is that through his romantic fictions of his own 'greatness' Willems has in fact enslaved Aïssa. Both are victims of romantic dreams of wronged manhood vindicating itself through heroic action.

Willems ignores Almayer's cynical warnings: 'But that girl. Hey! You stole her. You did not pay the old fellow. She is no good to him now, is she?' (*OI*, 89). In a rare moment of insight, Almayer recognizes that there is a racial and cultural gulf between Willems and Aïssa that neither race will tolerate. Almayer understands the conditions under which white men acquire 'native' mistresses. Willems doesn't play by the rules: like the Dutchman in 'Karain' who 'steals' Matara's sister, Willems invites Omar's murderous attack when he 'steals' Aïssa. In imperial romance such situations are avoided: either the 'dusky native' woman is fortuitously killed off, like Haggard's Foulata and Ustane, or she is resisted as when Kim resists the Woman of Shamlegh (*K*, 302–6). Miscegenation brings destruction, as Kipling's heroes Dravot and Carnehan discover in 'The Man Who Would Be King' (1888). Carnehan quaintly warns Dravot of the dangers of becoming involved with women: '"For the last time o' asking, Dan, do *not*," I says. "It'll only bring us harm. The Bible says that Kings ain't to waste their strength on women, specially when they've got some new raw kingdom to work over."' (in *Twenty-One Tales*, 69). Kipling is making a point here about the stability of the Empire. Martin Seymour-Smith claims that Kipling 'knew that an empire might fail if one of its founders has a defect of character' (Seymour-Smith, 196), a point Conrad endorses in *Lord Jim*.

The Indian girl whom Dravot tries to marry effectively brings about his death. Kipling's heroes resemble Willems in as much as they believe the 'natives' regard them as gods. But they at least have power and a fleeting 'greatness'; Willems's pretensions to power and greatness have substance only within his own imagination. Kipling's point was that the white race could maintain its hold over the Empire only whilst it remained detached from personal involvement with the Indian population; once Dravot 'sinks' to the level of contemplating a 'native' wife he is vulnerable and no better than the Indians themselves. Where

Conrad differs from Kipling is in his scepticism. Kipling's heroes are always superior even if at times it is only by virtue of being representatives of the imperial power. And Kipling's 'shady men', as Martin Green calls them are 'after all romantically large' (Green, 307). In Willems's case, however, whiteness and European identity are no proof against moral degeneracy. Effectively 'going native', Willems loses all claim on so-called civilized society.

Racial identity: dressing up for Empire

The hero of imperial romance consciously chooses to adopt the attire of the locals for the good of the Empire; it is only a pretence of 'going native'. So Dick Holland in plate 16 spends weeks practising to be an Indian in order to find his father and help defeat the 'wicked' Tippoo. He is even advised by his Indian uncle: 'After a week or two you must stain your face, arms and legs, and go out with Rajbullub in the evening. You must keep your eyes open and watch everything that passes, and do as you see others do' (*TM*, 176). Kim is similarly 'stained' to pass as an Indian. As Mahbub explains, the purpose is protection: 'Tonight we change thy colour. This sleeping under roofs has blanched thee like an almond' (*K*, 226). Kim and Dick disguise themselves as Indians for purposes of imperial espionage. There is never any doubt as to their allegiance, or to the fact that they can resume their white identity at will. It is as Brantlinger observes, the 'wish-fulfilment pattern' of the imperial romance where 'the civilized hero acquires a savage identity and yet remains civilized' (*Rule of Darkness*, 66). Even Fenimore Cooper's hero, Natty Bumppo, who chooses to live as a North American Indian, is rarely compromised when it comes to choices of loyalty. Indeed, as Green notes, Bumppo 'is a savage, except that he has the highest principles of civilization, in simple form' (Green, 133).

Willems has no such control either over his identity or his loyalties, if he ever had any. Returning to Almayer's campong, desperate to retrieve Aïssa from Babalatchi, he is a 'masquerading spectre of the once so very confidential clerk of the richest merchant in the islands':

His jacket was soiled and torn; below the waist he was clothed in a worn-out and faded sarong. He flung off his hat, uncovering his long, tangled hair that stuck in wisps on his perspiring forehead and straggled over his eyes, which glittered deep down in the sockets like the last sparks amongst the black embers of a burnt-out fire. An unclean beard grew out of the caverns of his sunburnt cheeks. The hand he put out towards Almayer was very unsteady. The once firm mouth had the tell-tale droop of mental suffering and physical exhaustion. He was barefooted. (*OI*, 87–8)

Romantic 'dressing-up' in the imperial romance as portrayed in plate 16 carries overtones of patriotic heroism and good clean fun for plucky young English boys. Not so for Willems: the glamour of his liaison with Aïssa gives way to a sordid physical decline that emphasizes his moral bankruptcy. He is a slave to his physical passion, and even that is all but spent, as indicated by the dying sparks of his eyes and his cavernous cheeks. Willems's physical disintegration is thus connected to his moral breakdown. He does not even have the dubious redeeming features of Kurtz's eloquence and reputation. Willems is not in disguise: he appears as what he is, a degenerate remnant of 'civilization'. In his impeccable white suit the imperial adventurer of the romance maintains his racial identity. Half of Willems's symbolic costume has been discarded; what remains is soiled and torn. From the waist down his identity is Malay, given to unrestrained physical passion. Willems's blatant parading of his 'depravity' disgusts that other would-be imperial hero, Almayer. Indeed Almayer articulates European censure of Willems's racial betrayal in 'going native'.[15]

Lingard's shame

Abandoned in the depths of the forest by Lingard, Willems fantasizes about escape to the land to which Henty's boys return, to the elegant lifestyle suggested by the dining room of Haggard's gentlemen in plate 3:

> The superior land of refined delights where he could sit on a chair, eat his tiffin off a white tablecloth, nod to fellows—good fellows; he would be popular; always was—where he could be virtuous, correct, do business, draw a salary, smoke cigars, buy things in shops—have boots … be happy, free, become rich. (*OI*, 329–30)

The trouble is, the hero of an adventure story would never betray his race and would certainly never take a Malay/Arab lover. Much of Willems's dream is a sanitized version of his circumstances before he 'stepped off the straight and narrow path of his peculiar honesty'. Escape relies upon action: Willems is even incapable of building a raft because all he has is a pocket-knife. The only two acts he effects within the novel are in themselves subversive: the stealing of Hudig's money and the betrayal of Lingard to Abdulla. For the rest, Willems drifts into dissipation just as he drifts deeper into the recesses of the Malay forest.

The strong bonds of loyalty between white heroes are tested and often strained in the imperial adventure story. The fact that they survive the test and are thus fit to return home is evidence of racial superiority. So Ignosi tempts Quatermain, Curtis, and Good with all the benefits his race and country can provide:

> 'Ye who stood by me in rebellion and battle, will ye leave me in the day of peace and victory? What will ye—wives? Choose from among the maidens! A place to live in? Behold, the land is yours as far as ye can see ... If there is anything more which I can give, that will I give you.' (*KSM*, 338)

On behalf all three Quatermain declines, proving his racial loyalty: 'Nay, Ignosi, we want none of these things ... we would seek our own place' (*KSM*, 338). Haggard's heroes return to England as 'good fellows', racially and physically untainted having resisted the temptations of the 'dark continent'. It is this 'civilized' life for which Willems yearns. But Conrad reaches beyond the simple messages of the romance: the temptations that Haggard's heroes reject are the very ones to which Willems succumbs. Near the climax of the novel, in Lingard's eyes, he is 'not a human being that may be destroyed or forgiven', rather he is 'a something without a body and that must be hidden' (*OI*, 275). Echoing Leonard, Lingard denies him racial distinction: 'You are neither white nor brown. You have no colour as you have no heart' (*OI*, 276). 'Whiteness' does not automatically imply moral purity as Willems assumes.

Having no allegiances Willems is a renegade undermining Lingard's imperial scheme; in assisting Abdulla he forfeits the status of 'civilised white man'; by attacking Almayer's campong and usurping Lingard's 'Empire' Willems behaves like the Sulu pirates of old, so prominent in Babalatchi's fireside narratives. Unable to grasp that for his fellow Europeans he is now more 'Malay' than 'white', Willems appeals to Almayer's racial loyalty in words that echo the imperial romance: 'We are both white men, and should back each other up'. Almayer, however, identifies Willems with the Malays calling Willems a thief: 'but he never looked, and went away, one hand round that woman's waist, the other on Babalatchi's shoulder' (*OI*, 186). Willems has done what Quatermain could never do: he has turned his back on his own race and embraced the 'enemy'.[16] As Alan Sandison remarks, Willems 'is the reminder that a good man in this sense—a good chap, a fine fellow—doesn't really exist; that he is nothing but a myth made corporate, raised in the interest of brotherhood and integrity'. He is 'the Judas of the Conrad system' (Sandison, 124).[17]

Henty's boys are physically more agile than his 'indolent' Indians; Ballantyne's young adventurers in *The Coral Island* are intellectually sharp in contrast to the sluggish intelligence of his Polynesians. The public school fraternal bonds, chivalry, and Christian ethics of the hero of adventure are the English characteristics that allow them to triumph over the 'inferior native'. Conrad too, makes racial distinctions: his Malays are indeed often 'savages' like the scheming Babalatchi or the indolent Lakamba but such distinctions are not straightforward. Willems's European blood is no assurance of 'superiority'. He tries despairingly to distance himself from Aïssa, citing her eyes as evidence of her 'otherness':

> 'Look at them! You can see nothing in them. They are big, menacing—and empty. The eyes of a savage; of a damned mongrel, half-Arab, half-Malay. They hurt me! I am white! I swear to you I can't stand this! Take me away. I am white! All white!'
>
> He shouted towards the sombre heaven, proclaiming desperately under the frown of thickening clouds the fact of his pure and superior descent. (*OI*, 271)

Willems has broken every rule in the book of imperial adventure. Lingard declares that Willems is 'not fit to go amongst people' (*OI*, 275). He might well have added 'people of any colour'. In a counterpoint to the conventional imperial hero, Willems is a 'tall madman making a great disturbance about something invisible; a being absurd, repulsive, pathetic, and droll' (*OI*, 271): he is Lingard's 'shame', a moral weakness, that must be hidden to sustain the illusion of white superiority.

Subverting the myth of heroism

Citing, among others, Haggard, Kipling, and Jules Verne, Said points to the 'exhilaration and interest of adventure in the colonial world' that informed the fictions of 'frank exoticism and confident empire' which, 'far from casting doubt upon the imperial undertaking, serve to confirm and celebrate its success':

> Against this optimism, affirmation, and serene confidence, Conrad's narratives … radiate an extreme, unsettling anxiety … Conrad's tales and novels in one sense reproduce the aggressive contours of the

high imperialist undertaking, but in another sense they are infected with the easily recognizable, ironic awareness of the post-realist modernist sensibility. (*Culture and Imperialism*, 227)

Some early reviewers of *An Outcast* seem to have recognized the 'aggressive contours of the high imperialist undertaking', but failed to see the ironic treatment of such material; perhaps they didn't want to. Conrad was doing something radically new with the motifs of imperial romance: he employed some of its strategies and endorsed some of its assumptions, but Conrad was not a writer of romantic adventure. Green points to the 'highly operatic' nature of the narrative in *An Outcast*. He cites the 'striking postures and gestures that are held unchanging over several pages', but concludes that 'the action is static': 'One feels that the central characters, who embody the story, are paralysed; they ought to move, but they can't and one feels that about Conrad often' (Green, 308–9).

That sense of paralysis is precisely the frustration felt by the reviewer in the *National Observer*. Used to a diet of imperial fiction that lionized its heroes, celebrated the Empire, and relied on action for narrative impetus, it is perhaps not surprising that some of Conrad's early readers were puzzled. Heroic action and paralysis did not belong in the imperial narrative. It is, however, very much part of Conrad's strategy that these two notions should coincide in his novel. The heroic, romantic action of the past is made to comment on the sordid reality of the present. Babalatchi, Aïssa, Omar, and, to some degree, Lingard, have a history of deeds of courage, endurance, fidelity, and romance which ironizes Willems's naive dreams of success, wealth, and reputation. The past is where heroic action is possible, in deed, or in imagination; the present is replete with inaction, treachery, and moral cowardice.[18]

The impossibility of positive action is made strikingly, and ironically, apparent as Lingard and Almayer ineffectually try to swat a bluebottle on Almayer's verandah. Lingard tries to strike it with his hat while Almayer dodges his head out of the way. The two are portrayed comically 'with heads thrown back and arms gyrating on high, or again bending low with infuriated lunges':

But suddenly the buzz died out in a thin thrill away in the open space of the courtyard, leaving Lingard and Almayer standing face to face in the fresh silence of the young day, looking very puzzled and idle, their arms hanging uselessly by their sides—like men disheartened by some portentous failure. (*OI*, 169).

No adventure hero would have been defeated by a fly, let alone made to look so foolish and inept; they had just been discussing Willems.

Romance, adventure, and positive action: these are things of the past, for which Conrad's characters yearn but can never achieve. Babalatchi's past is full of romance:

> He was a vagabond of the seas, a true Orang Laut, living by rapine and plunder of coasts and ships in his prosperous days; earning his living by honest and irksome toil when the days of adversity were upon him. So, although at times leading the Sulu rovers, he had also served as Serang of country ships, and in that wise had visited the distant seas, beheld the glories of Bombay, the might of the Mascati Sultan; had even struggled in the pious throng for the privilege of touching with his lips the Sacred Stone of the Holy City. (*OI*, 51–2)

This is the romance of the Orient, like *The Arabian Nights Entertainment*.[19] It occurred in the distant past, and even before the narrative present of the novel commences romance has died: The Sultan of Sulu rejects violence and insurrection, and Babalatchi accepts that 'There was nothing to be done. Times were changed' (*OI*, 54). The glorious adventures of Babalatchi, Omar, and Aïssa, end in exile in the backwater of Sambir. The prau that carried them there languishes on a mud-bank: it 'rotted in the rain, warped in the sun, fell to pieces and gradually vanished into the smoke of household fires of the settlement' (*OI*, 56). His once illustrious leader, Lakamba, is now a lazy, slow-witted figurehead, spending his days dozing on mats, or staring vacantly into the embers of the fire. Omar is a blind cripple. Aïssa betrays him in her liaison with Willems and becomes the 'doubled-up crone' of the novel's end. The heroic past is reduced to petty intrigue as Babalatchi plots, schemes, and betrays instead of indulging in the 'manly pursuits of throat-cutting, kidnapping, slave-dealing, and fire-raising' (*OI*, 52) like the Dyaks of plate 14.

Towards the end of his article, 'Well Done', Conrad gives his impression of the adventurer: 'A successful highwayman showed courage of a sort, and pirate crews have been known to fight with courage or perhaps only with reckless desperation in the manner of cornered rats' (*NLL*, 189–90). There is clearly no admiration for piracy. Writing this twelve years after the publication of *An Outcast*, it is possible that Conrad's opinions may have altered. Certainly he invokes the spirit of romance and adventure in Babalatchi's tales, but the underlying irony of 'manly pursuits' is unmistakable. About adventurers in general Conrad has this to say:

> I have noticed that the majority of mere lovers of adventure are mightily careful of their skins; and the proof of it is that so many of them manage to keep it whole to an advanced age. You find them in mysterious nooks of islands and continents, mostly red-nosed and watery-eyed, and not even amusingly boastful. (*NLL*, 190)

There is more than a hint of Lingard here. Ultimately for Conrad, adventure and the adventurer are hollow concepts with no human value: 'There is nothing more futile under the sun than a mere adventurer…Adventure by itself is but a phantom, a dubious shape without a heart' (*NLL*, 190). Time and again Conrad's characters discover the truth of these statements. Willems is one of a series of Conrad's heroes whose illusions are systematically shattered. Hampson says that 'Willems is the prototype of those Conradian heroes who betray an ideal conception of the self and "spoil" their lives' (*Betrayal*, 32): one thinks in particular of Jim and Nostromo.

One Conradian character does gain a kind of heroic status: the Captain of the *Nan-Shan* in *Typhoon*, MacWhirr. This dogged, uninspired nonentity of a man is a qualified hero because of his tenacity to one simple idea. He is no romantic hero: he neither possesses nor dreams of acquiring the characteristics that would make him so. As Conrad says: 'The mere love of adventure is no saving grace. It is no grace at all. It lays a man under no obligation of faithfulness to an idea and even to his own self' (*NLL*, 189). Faithfulness is what Willems singularly lacks and MacWhirr singularly possesses. Sticking doggedly to one idea, MacWhirr saves himself and his ship; Willems vacillates, deviates, betrays, and, ultimately destroys the lives of those who trusted him. Surrendering himself to the 'adventure' of his love affair with Aïssa, Willems loses his 'civilized' identity. This is emphasized when Willems witnesses, in a kind of dream, the retreat of part of himself: 'It was like an evasion, like a prisoner breaking his parole—that thing slinking off stealthily while he slept' (*OI*, 145). This returns us to the inaction, the paralysis that bothered the *National Observer*'s reviewer. The writer of adventure stories would not allow a fragmentation of the hero's self. At the first sign of moral dissolution the true adventure hero leaps to action and reaffirms his imperial purpose; Willems passively watches his own disintegration. Conrad's point is that 'There is nothing in the world to prevent a mere lover or pursuer of adventure from running at any moment' (*NLL*, 190). Running is exactly what Willems does, from his wife, his 'father', his race, his lover, and ultimately from himself. It is the opposite of the heroic action of the romance.

As we read *An Outcast of the Islands* it is obvious that for all the invocation of the motifs of romance and adventure, the story is consciously anti-heroic. It subverts the heroic code, pointing instead to the futility of a life based on dreams. Real life for Conrad, and his protagonists, is punctuated by disillusion, not romance. In 1890, in despondent mood, Conrad wrote to Marguerite Poradowska:

> One doubts the future. For indeed—I ask myself—why should anyone believe in it? And, consequently, why be sad about it? A little illusion, many dreams, a rare flash of happiness followed by disillusionment, a little anger and much suffering, and then the end. Peace! That is the programme, and we must see this tragi-comedy to the end. One must play one's part in it. (*Letters 1*, 51)

It is a gloomy enough programme too, but it hints at Conrad's emerging 'ironic awareness of the post-realist modernist sensibility'. This is a vision that in Conrad's fiction confronts the complacency of the nineteenth-century literature of romance, adventure, and empire with the need for something more than simply appearing to be 'one of us'.

5

'Karain':
Constructing the Romantic Subject

'Something magazine'ish'

In April 1898 Conrad wrote to Cunninghame Graham: 'I am glad you like *Karain*. I was afraid you would despise it. There's something magazine'ish about it. Eh? It was written for Blackwood' (*Letters 2*, 57). Those 'magazine'ish' elements include a ghost, an exotic Malay chieftain, charms and talismans, love, betrayal, and questions of honour, and it is likely that it was precisely these 'magazine'ish' qualities that Conrad was looking for to ensure publication for this short story. In 1896 Edward Garnett had advised Conrad not to continue with *The Sisters*. Watt suggests that Garnett was effectively warning Conrad 'against trying to be a more ambitious and highbrow kind of novelist'. 'Karain' is evidence, Watt asserts, that Conrad had 'more or less accepted Garnett's typecasting' (Watt, 27). Significantly Conrad is aware of similar qualities in an earlier tale, 'The Lagoon' (1897). Writing to Garnett in August 1896, he calls this tale 'a tricky thing' and identifies exotic elements that would appeal to a magazine readership: 'the usual forests river—stars—wind sunrise, and so on—and lots of secondhand Conradese in it. There is only 6000 words in it so it can't bring in many shekels...Don't you think I am a lost soul?' He concludes: 'I would bet a penny they will take it' (*Letters 1*, 301). *Cornhill Magazine* duly accepted it.

Obviously Conrad was preoccupied with earning money. He was writing stories with a specific audience in mind, and with a view to specific publications. However, it is unlikely that he wrote 'Karain' just for *Blackwood's*, as he claims in his letter to Cunninghame Graham. There is a good deal of evidence to indicate that it was Garnett's idea to approach William Blackwood. Garnett recounts how, standing on the pavement opposite Newgate Prison, he 'declared positively [to Conrad] that *Karain* was destined by Providence for *Blackwood's Magazine'*. Conrad thanked him fourteen years later saying 'it was you who turned *Karain* on to Maga, with inspired judgment'(Garnett, xxviii–xxix). And we do not just have Garnett's word for it: on 7 February 1897 Conrad wrote to T. Fisher Unwin asking him to 'place' 'Karain' and suggesting *Cornhill Magazine* as he had 'some kind of intimation to the effect that they would take [his] stories there' (*Letters 1*, 338). On the same day he wrote to Garnett calling 'Karain' a 'Malay thing' and signalling his intention to send the story to Unwin: 'It will be easy and may bring a few pence' (*Letters 1*, 338). Thus it would seem that Conrad was consciously courting an audience of imperial romance enthusiasts in order to supplement his income: he wanted to be published in a widely circulated magazine, which would usually mean one that sympathized with imperialism. He had written a framed story with a colonial/imperial background and which observed some conventions and attributes of traveller's tales. In short, he had written the perfect story for *Blackwood's*.[1]

If that is the case Conrad's comment to Cunninghame Graham about 'Karain' and *Blackwood's* needs to be treated cautiously. Graham was, after all, by no means an advocate of imperialism. As Laurence Davies has commented: 'Conrad usually shapes his letters to reflect the interests, passions, and quirks of his correspondents'.[2] Davies says that 'Graham, being neither an imperialist nor a Tory, would never want to publish in *Blackwood's*, even if they would have him'. Moreover, he was 'a writer who did not hide or dissemble his anti-colonialist views'. Conrad would have been keenly aware of *Blackwood's* reputation as a conservative magazine that published stories of imperial adventure. As such he was no doubt worried that Graham would disapprove of his publishing a story there and therefore his tone could be construed as apologetic. Claiming that he wrote the story for *Blackwood's* is probably Conrad's excuse for the imperial romance overtones of 'Karain'.

'Karain' appeared in *Blackwood's Magazine* in November 1897, marking the beginning of Conrad's relationship with the house of Blackwood.[3] Their literary adviser, David Meldrum, was so impressed with the story that he wrote to William Blackwood: 'Conrad is a capital man, and this is a capital story—extremely strong and good on the literary side' (in Blackburn, 3). Sherry notes how *Blackwood's* was highly regarded: '"It was…the ambition of all young writers in my day to find themselves in *Blackwood*," wrote Sir Hugh Clifford, and William Blackwood was sympathetic and helpful and patient with young talent'

(*CH*, 3). Furthermore, *Blackwood's* was staple reading for the British audience out in the colonies, and Conrad would thus benefit from the association by gaining a wider readership. The 'magazine'ish' qualities of 'Karain' thus secured for Conrad a profitable liaison with one of the foremost magazines of his day and brought him those 'few pence' he needed to ease his financial circumstances.

Indeed Conrad was very successful in his attempt to capitalize on unalloyed romance. In January 1899 the *Academy* awarded Conrad a prize of fifty guineas for his literary achievement, an accolade he shared with Sidney Lee and Maurice Hewlett. *Academy* singled out *Tales of Unrest* and *Youth* as the volumes they wished to 'crown', and special mention was given to 'Karain'. Conrad, says the *Academy's* reviewer, brings 'the East to our very doors, not only its people ... but its feeling, its glamour, its beauty and wonder' (*CH*, 110). While many reviewers complained that the stories in *Tales of Unrest* were gloomy and morbid,[4] the *Academy* was particularly impressed with Conrad's evocation of an exotic East, leaving little doubt that 'Karain' was a strong contributory factor in the decision to honour him. Of course Conrad was understandably pleased: not only did the award bring a much-needed injection of cash, but it boosted his confidence at a time when he was in one of his recurring periods of self-doubt, and still considering returning to sea (see *CH*, 13–14).

Creating the romantic distance

Karain's tale is one of betrayal of a friend because of a woman. Some similarities with *An Outcast* are thus evident, but the short story receives different treatment. To Willems's story of betrayal is added one of moral degeneracy. Furthermore, Willems condemns himself through his own words and thoughts: no narrator is necessary to enable our censure. Karain, however, is held at a romantic distance from the reader through the device of his English interlocutors. His tale is told without the self-reflection of Marlow, who questions and often obscures meaning. Rather it is told in the simple language of fireside tales that acquire the quality of myths or legends. As Mark Conroy observes, Conrad's storytellers are often 'attempts to recuperate some of the interpersonal warmth and commonality of the folk-tale' (Conroy, 10). With 'Karain' Conrad moves away from preoccupations with Western bourgeois values and focuses instead upon what he presents as a simple Eastern culture. This allows for a more overtly romantic narrative, one that will satisfy magazine readers looking for a taste of the exoticism and romance of the Orient, far removed from the vexed problems of late nineteenth-century city life.

'Karain' concerns three Englishmen, Hollis, Jackson and an unnamed narrator, who sell guns to a Malay leader, Karain.[5] On their last visit Karain comes to the cabin of their schooner with a tormenting secret. Years earlier, the sister of Karain's friend, Pata Matara, ran away with a Dutchman. The friends embark on a quest to seek out the lovers and kill them. But Karain becomes obsessed with the image of Matara's sister and when the lovers are eventually found he kills Matara rather than the sister. Karain becomes a wanderer, haunted by the ghost of his dead friend, until a shaman charms away the ghost. When the old man dies Hollis provides Karain with a 'charm', a Jubilee sixpence, to ward off the ghost. Convinced by the power of this token, Karain returns to his people. The story ends with the narrator meeting Jackson years later in the streets of London.

This is a narrative in the romance tradition which, as Gillian Beer says, 'invokes the past or the socially remote' (Beer, 2). 'Karain' begins: 'We knew him in those unprotected days when we were content to hold in our hands our lives and our property' (*TU*, 3). Here is a sense of the remote past of youth, free and unfettered, adventuring heroically in the distant East. Conrad presses that point home by referring to the memories of the romantic past that are revived by reports of 'uprisings in the Eastern Archipelago' (*TU*, 3). Out of the 'befogged respectability' of the newspaper the land of romance and adventure emerges, distinct and gleaming. As in *The Scarlet Letter*, the present becomes hazy and indistinct as the romance rises dream-like from the imagination and takes on a palpable air of reality. For Hawthorne it is the atmosphere of moonshine that invokes the romantic:

> It would be too much in keeping with the scene to excite surprise, were we to look about us and discover a form, beloved, but gone hence, now sitting quietly in a streak of this magic moonshine, with an aspect that would make us doubt whether it had returned from afar, or had never once stirred from our fireside. (*Scarlet Letter*, 42)

Conrad's method is strikingly similar. A cluster of images that transport us back in time and over distance to the exotic land of Karain evokes the romance:

> A strange name wakes up memories; the printed words scent the smoky atmosphere of to-day faintly, with the subtle and penetrating

perfume as of land breezes breathing through the starlight of
bygone nights; a signal fire gleams like a jewel on the high brow of a
sombre cliff; great trees, the advanced sentries of immense forests,
stand watchful and still over sleeping stretches of open water; a line
of white surf thunders on an empty beach, the shallow water foams
on the reefs; and green islets scattered through the calm of noonday
lie upon the level of a polished sea, like a handful of emeralds on a
buckler of steel. (*TU*, 3)

Karain's kingdom is remote, a 'conquered foothold that, shaped like a
young moon, lay ignored between the hills and the sea' (*TU*, 4). As
Hampson has pointed out in an article for *Tenggara*,[6] the narrative perspective 'denies subjectivity and historical specificity' (*Tenggara*, 111).
For the narrator and his companions it is a magic kingdom: 'It
appeared to us a land without memories, regrets, and hopes; a land
where nothing could survive the coming of the night, and where each
sunrise, like a dazzling act of special creation, was disconnected from
the eve and the morrow' (*TU*, 5). Such is the mytho-magical quality of
the unexplored East: no gas lamps or electric lights, no broughams and
busy streets to perpetuate the hum of life in the cities once night falls.
The glittering world of romance appears and disappears mysteriously
with the setting of the sun. Like the 'privileged man' in *Lord Jim* sitting
in his London flat on a grey evening, the reader of 'Karain' is far
removed from the fog and bustle of the European city.

The narrative is replete with strange and exotic images. The colourful
'natives', are an 'ornamented and barbarous crowd, with the variegated
colours of checkered sarongs, red turbans, white jackets, embroideries;
with the gleam of scabbards, gold rings, charms, armlets, lance blades,
and jewelled handles of their weapons' (*TU*, 4).[7] The Malays are vividly
characterized by their 'independent bearing, resolute eyes', and their
'restrained manner'. They speak softly of 'battles, travels, and escapes;
boasting with composure, joking quietly; sometimes in well-bred mur-
murs extolling their own valour, our generosity; or celebrating with
loyal enthusiasm the virtues of their ruler' (*TU*, 4). Image upon image
of romantic exoticism creates a feast of visual stimulation, making the
Eastern setting and atmosphere vividly, but romantically present. It is
the East of Henty's fiction. There is no hint of the subtle irony or suggestions of sordid reality beneath the exotic surface, such as we find in
Almayer's Folly and *An Outcast*; it seems, in fact, to have little to do
with Western moral values.

A 'tableau vivant'

Karain too is remote yet intensely, physically, present, infinitely exotic, the epitome of Western impressions of the Oriental. Said famously observes that 'the Orient is *for* the European observer', and he speaks of the Western perception of the East as a 'spectacle, or *tableau vivant*' (*Orientalism,* 158). The Orient is romanticized and distanced by presenting it as a theatre for the entertainment of European visitors. It is never 'real' in the sense that the London of *The Secret Agent* is 'real'. Karain's Eastern village is 'the stage where, dressed splendidly for his part, he strutted' (*TU,* 6). For the European seamen this setting has the 'suspicious immobility of a painted scene' (*TU,* 7), which Karain filled 'with barbarous dignity' (*TU,* 8). He is 'incomparably faithful to the illusions of the stage, and at sunset the night descended upon him quickly, like a falling curtain' (*TU,* 9). The theatrical imagery endows Karain with larger than life heroic qualities: in the limelight, glamorous and romantic, his grandiose gestures demand the audience's attention. Ultimately the imagery of the theatre creates the romantic distance whereby the reader is made a spectator. The action taking place on that Eastern shore is that of a world from which we are barred but which we can observe from the decks of the schooner. The boat is a floating gallery, which, in its compact efficiency, symbolizes the reality, and indeed the reliability, of English cultural and political systems. The 'two ship's chronometers ticking off steadily the seconds of Greenwich Time' and the guns that the schooner is carrying further emphasize this 'reliability': indeed the narrator finds the ticking chronometers a 'protection and a relief' (*TU,* 40).[8]

Karain's physical presence is evidence of the magnificence of the East; his story confirms its otherness, its Oriental strangeness. As Said puts it: 'The Orient is *watched*, since its almost (but never quite) offensive behaviour issues out of a reservoir of infinite peculiarity; the European, whose sensibility tours the Orient, is a watcher, never involved, always detached' (*Orientalism,* 103). The sense of the European as 'watcher' is strongly present in Conrad's narrative. Karain's Eastern community is described in broad splashes of colour and details of unusual, distinctly non-European dress. The festival atmosphere of a pageant is evoked:

> Before sunset he would take leave with ceremony, and go off sitting under a red umbrella, and escorted by a score of boats. All the paddles flashed and struck together with a mighty splash that reverberated

loudly in the monumental amphitheatre of hills. A broad stream of dazzling foam trailed behind the flotilla. The canoes appeared very black on the white hiss of water; turbaned heads swayed back and forth; a multitude of arms in crimson and yellow rose and fell with one movement; the spearmen upright in the bows of canoes had variegated sarongs and gleaming shoulders like bronze statues; the muttered strophes of the paddler's song ended periodically in a plaintive shout. (*TU*, 10)

This is indeed the *tableau vivant* of which Said speaks. The crowds of the East, with their strange costumes and habits dominate the land-scape. As Douglas Kerr comments, the crowds of the East are an 'essen-tial part of the first impressions of all travellers who have set out to see the east and find their gaze returned':

The oriental crowd was the focus of the most urgent anxiety of colo-nialism, an anxiety present in extreme form in De Quincey, but visi-ble everywhere in colonialist writing, and not least in those adventure stories for boys that so frequently have a scene in which some plucky hero faces down, outwits or in some cases converts a hostile—often fanatical—crowd.[9] (Kerr, 51)

The multitudes of 'natives' in 'Karain' thus recall Henty's 'hordes' and 'black masses': Conrad's Malays 'swarmed on the beach' much as Henty's South Americans rush from their huts 'like swarms of bees' (*OP*, 285).

Eastern splendour is apparent in the richly embroidered garments, the 'shimmer of silks', colourful sarongs and turbans. This is the language of popular romance: numerous references to the rich silks and damasks of Indian dress in *The Tiger of Mysore* create the magnificence of India. Dick Holland's disguise, as seen in plate 15, is typically gorgeous: 'Dick's dress consisted of a steel cap with a drooping plume of red horsehair, and a red tunic with a blue sash. Over it was worn a skirt of linked mail, which, with leggings fitting tightly, completed the costume' (*TM*, 197). He com-ments to his companion that they are a 'rum-looking couple', but asserts that he had seen 'plenty of men just as gaudy in the train of some of the rajahs' (*TM*, 197). The East is thus summed up as a mass of shimmering colour, populous, inscrutable, and suggestive of danger and mystery.

A savage gentleman

Karain forges a close bond with the narrator of his story: 'He was an adventurer of the sea, an outcast, a ruler—and my very good friend'

(*TU*, 8). But as 'one of them', a native, Karain anticipates Dain Maroola and Dain Waris. He is the 'noble savage' of romance and adventure novels, in the tradition of the fearsome Umslopogaas of *Allan Quatermain* (plate 9) or Ignosi in *King Solomon's Mines* rather than the bloodthirsty Dyaks of plate 14. Quatermain knows Umslopogaas for 'a great warrior of the royal blood, faithful to the death'; in Zululand 'where all men are brave' they tell fireside stories of his 'strength and deeds' (*AQ*, 17). Karain is trusted and admired by his friends for his 'European' qualities: 'He was plotting and preparing a war with patience, with foresight—with a fidelity to his purpose and with a steadfastness of which I would have thought him racially incapable' (*TU*, 18).

The typical native of romance is intrinsically treacherous and hostile to 'whites'. Umslopogaas and Ignosi are exceptions and thus worthy companions for white heroes. Karain, too, possesses traits that qualify him for special attention: he talks of himself as 'a private gentleman coming to see other gentlemen whom he supposed as well born as himself'; he smiles with 'discreet politeness' (*TU*, 12), and speaks with 'wonder and chivalrous respect' of the Queen; the 'quiet dignity of his bearing' transforms the 'dimly-lit cuddy of the schooner into an audience-hall'; his 'splendour' is 'spotlessly neat' (*TU*, 13). Dignity, chivalry, discreet politeness, and cleanliness are the characteristics of the English gentleman to which Karain's friends respond. They marvel at his Oriental otherness, but embrace him as a friend, superior to his 'kind' because he demonstrates traits respected by the English as evidence of breeding.

Yet it is made clear that Karain is still a 'primitive'. His sagacity is 'limited by his profound ignorance of the rest of the world'. He cannot be dissuaded from war because of his 'eagerness to strike a blow for his own primitive ideas':

> He did not understand us, and replied by arguments that almost drove one to desperation by their childish shrewdness. He was absurd and unanswerable. Sometimes we caught glimpses of a sombre, glowing fury within him—a brooding and vague sense of wrong, and a concentrated lust of violence which is dangerous in a native. (*TU*, 18)

For a fleeting moment we glimpse the 'savage' beneath Karain's civilized surface, the Hyde lurking in the shadows. The danger inherent in the 'native' hinted at here is more actively present in John Laputa (see plate 16), the African hero of Buchan's *Prester John* (1910), of whom Street remarks: 'Laputa is black, so, however 'civilized' he becomes, there will always be the danger that his inherent 'savagery' will come to the surface in times of stress' (Street, 145). For all the elements in his character that render Karain attractive, he is ultimately 'a native', and as such dangerous and unpredictable. Conrad's worldly English gunrunners trust Karain, but it is with the arrogance of a self-conscious superiority. His 'childish shrewdness' echoes the literature of empire where the 'native' is a child to be guided and indulged by superior European imperialists. Joanna de Groot argues that women and 'natives' are 'portrayed and treated as children in need of the protection and care of male/imperial authority by virtue of their weakness, innocence, and inadequacy' (de Groot, 98); they are inferior to the European male.

An Eastern secret

Karain presents an enigmatic mystery. Here we should note that in accordance with the theatricality of Eastern romance the suggestion is that Karain is acting:

> He was ornate and disturbing, for one could not imagine what depth of horrible void such an elaborate front could be worthy to hide. He was not masked—there was too much life in him, and a mask is only a lifeless thing; but he presented himself essentially as an actor, as a human being aggressively disguised. His smallest acts were prepared and unexpected, his speeches grave, his sentences ominous like hints and complicated like arabesques. (*TU*, 6)

An ominous note is struck too, when we are told that Karain 'summed up his race, his country, the elemental force of ardent life, of tropical nature. He had its luxuriant strength, its fascination; and, like it, he carried the seed of peril within' (*TU*, 7). The narrator draws upon the notion of danger inherent in the supposed inscrutability of the East and Karain's 'secret' thus becomes emblematic of Eastern mystery.[10]

The secret is hinted at through the taciturn presence of Karain's faithful retainer, the 'silent old fellow in a richly embroidered black jacket' (*TU*, 5). The shaman is variously described as the 'old sword-bearer' (*TU*, 11), a 'wizard, the man who could command ghosts and send evil spirits against enemies' (*TU*, 16), and an 'old sorcerer' (*TU*, 17). He is 'impenetrable and weary' but 'always there' (*TU*, 12), like some magician in an old romance of the Orient. Robert F. Lee says he is 'symbolic of that great detachment, that overpowering objectivity which is, and was, for the Rajah (the East) the only power of the Orient able to protect him from the avenging spirits of his broken taboos' (Lee, 31). But Lee, like Conrad, responds to popular notions of Eastern inscrutability, the East as a construct of the Western imagination. This is what Said calls 'a distillation of essential ideas about the Orient'; the very use of the word 'Oriental' is 'a reference for the reader sufficient to identify a specific body of information about the Orient' (*Orientalism*, 205). The tale's setting allows Conrad to tap his readers' preconceptions about the East in order to create a 'magazine'ish' quality. 'Karain' thus differs from Conrad's Malay novels in that it uses romance and exoticism solely for the purpose of attracting an audience; it is self-consciously romantic with no intention to subvert the genre as in *Almayer's Folly* and *An Outcast*. The characterized narrator also helps Conrad to create a narrative style that is distinct from the ironic tones of those novels.

This Eastern world of romance, Karain's world, is trapped in time, vivid and vibrant. While it interacts with the commercial world of the crew, this Eastern kingdom is never part of that commercial world. The schooner's crew moves to and fro across the Eastern seascape pursuing their vaguely illegal activities with the assurance of white imperial entrepreneurs, selling outdated rifles to 'native' chiefs. Those 'very respectable people sitting safely in counting-houses' (*TU*, 19), who allow the gunrunners one more trip, are a reminder of the commercial, imperial world of which Karain is romantically ignorant. There is a stark contrast between Karain's colourful, exotic and warlike kingdom, a mythic world, and the measured, controlled world of politics and business that his English friends regard as 'real'.

After three days of transactions and no sign of Karain, his secret is finally revealed. The silence becomes oppressive, as the immobility on shore and the impending storm warn of a crisis:

> Ragged edges of black clouds peeped over the hills, and invisible thunderstorms circled outside, growling like wild beasts. We got the schooner ready for sea, intending to leave next morning at daylight. All day a merciless sun blazed down into the bay, fierce and pale, as if at white heat. Nothing moved on the land. The beach was empty, the villages seemed deserted; the trees far off stood in unstirring clumps, as if painted; the white smoke of some invisible bush-fire spread itself low over the shores of the bay like a settling fog. (*TU*, 20)

The paralysis of the scene, the subsequent 'whirling vapours' and 'single clap of thunder' giving way to an airless and debilitating heat, suggest a straining tension about to snap: the mysterious East is poised to reveal one of its secrets, and Karain appears in the cabin with the dramatic impact of an apparition. Much like Willems's appearance in front of Almayer, Karain's dishevelled state speaks of an inner turmoil:

> Then we heard startled voices on deck crying in the rain, hurried footsteps overhead, and suddenly Karain appeared in the doorway of the cabin. His bare breast and his face glistened in the light; his sarong, soaked, clung about his legs; he had his sheathed kriss in his left hand; and wisps of wet hair, escaping from under his red kerchief, stuck over his eyes and down his cheeks. He stepped in with a headlong stride and looking over his shoulder like a man pursued. (*TU*, 21)

In the small ship's cabin, romance, in the form of Karain, confronts the 'real' world and seeks refuge in its 'rationality'. The crew of the schooner are transfixed by the sight: Karain is 'enigmatical and touching, in virtue of that mysterious cause that had driven him through the night and through the thunderstorm to the shelter of the schooner's cuddy' (*TU*, 23).

The language of romance

The mythic mode of this tale acquires concrete form in the figure of Karain: 'His dark head and bronze torso appeared above the tarnished slab of wood, gleaming and still as if cast in metal' (*TU*, 27). The statue-like pose echoes the immobility on the shore: it is again as if time is frozen. The present fades as Karain's tale shifts the narrative focus from the airless cuddy of the schooner onto the timeless domain of romance where customs, beliefs, and experience challenge Western cultural and ethical assumptions. The frame narrator can only provide the visual spectacle of the East by peering in from outside; Karain, the authentic 'Oriental', speaks for the East as part of it. As he confides his tale, we are no longer spectators but the recipients of 'the futile tale of the burden of life' (*TU*, 26) coming from the heart of this region of romance.

Karain's story is recounted in the strangely archaic language that characterizes the 'native' of romance. One thinks for instance of Haggard's Mopo telling the story of Umslopogaas and Nada. The story is placed historically, citing unknown tribes from a distant past: 'Before the Zulus were a people—for I will begin at the beginning—I was born of the Langeni tribe. We were not a large tribe...' (*NL*, 30). In similar epic mode in a much earlier romance well-known to Conrad, Chingachgook tells Hawkeye the history of his people: 'The first palefaces who came among us spoke no English. They came in a large canoe, when my fathers had buried the tomahawk with the red men around them. Then ... we were one people and we were happy' (LM, 32). Karain's narrative creates the same distance: 'It was after the great trouble that broke the alliance of the four states of Wajo. We fought amongst ourselves, and the Dutch watched from afar till we were weary' (TU, 28). Karain's 'simple' language is in contrast to the frame narrator's ponderous style. He speaks in metaphor and simile without the technical definitions available to the initiated Westerner: the Dutch warships are 'fire-ships'; Karain's friendship with Matara is figured in terms of action: 'We had shared hunger, danger, fatigue, and victory. His eyes saw my danger quickly, and twice my arm had preserved his life' (TU, 28). Sentences are frequently short and suggestive: 'It was his destiny. He was my friend. And he was great amongst us—one of those who were near my brother, the Ruler' (TU, 28). The Dutchman who 'steals' Matara's sister is drawn with similar broad strokes:

> He despised our joys, our thoughts, and our sorrows. His face was red, his hair like flame, and his eyes pale, like a river mist; he moved heavily, and spoke with a deep voice; he laughed aloud like a fool, and knew no courtesy in his speech. He was a big, scornful man, who looked into women's faces and put his hand on the shoulders of free men as though he had been a noble-born chief. We bore with him. Time passed. (TU, 29)

This is a man at odds with his cultural surroundings. Putting his hand on the shoulders of Malays is an affront, as the narrator knows: when the schooner's crew entertain Karain at night it is 'in a free and easy manner, which just stopped short of slapping him on the back, for there are liberties one must not take with a Malay' (TU, 12). The Dutch trader offends through arrogant dismissal of the culture he has invaded: he is a man like Willems, and significantly he is Dutch.

The romance mode of the tale is emphasized by the device of telling a tale within a tale. In the close atmosphere of a ship's cabin, with a violent storm raging outside, an earlier haunted soul, Frankenstein, had confessed his mournful story to another astonished listener. Here there are three astonished recipients of an anguished tale while nature storms outside. The cuddy harbouring the white men is the world of Western 'rationality': the schooner and its officers penetrate the land of romance but remain representative of the Western world of commerce and 'real' lives toiling in the cities of Europe. Into this familiar world comes Karain with a story of romance that assumes epic proportions. The cabin is real, a place where white men play guitars and languish in the heat awaiting the conclusion of transactions with the Malays. It is familiar to them, but strange to Karain:

> He looked round the little cabin, at the painted beams, at the tarnished varnish of the bulkheads; he looked round as if appealing to all its shabby strangeness, to the disorderly jumble of unfamiliar things that belong to an inconceivable life of stress, of power, of endeavour, of unbelief—to the strong life of white men, which rolls on irresistible and hard on the edge of outer darkness. (*TU*, 25–6)

Karain's world is, by contrast, vague and unspecified. Only Pata Matara is named; the rest of the characters are types: Karain's brother is the 'Ruler'; Matara's sister is 'the woman who had broken faith and therefore must die' (*TU*, 33); the Dutchman is the representative of a ruthless imperialism invading the East to steal its riches (a woman with a 'ravishing face'). Even the land and its people remain unnamed. Andrzej Braun identifies it as the kingdom of Wadjo for which Conrad has a 'special predilection'.[11] Braun states that Wadjo is a 'mysterious and romantically exotic state' that 'overwhelms one's imagination with its history and isolation' (Braun, 3). Within the tale it is a vaguely suggested Malay state where time is measured in terms of moons that have 'grown full and withered' (*TU*, 31).

The whole of Karain's sorrowful story is related in the same manner, with vague suggestiveness and epic allusions. His many adventures become an 'obscure Odyssey of revenge' (*TU*, 40), the wanderings in the wilderness of warriors far from home:

> We lost ourselves in the fields, in the jungle; and one night, in a tangled forest, we came upon a place where crumbling old walls had fallen amongst the trees, and where strange stone idols—carved images of devils with many arms and legs, with snakes twined round their bodies, with twenty heads and holding a hundred swords—seemed to live and threaten in the light of our camp fire. (*TU*, 32)

The range of work they undertake on their wanderings is so large as to be almost unbelievable. Lee claims that any one acquainted with the East would know that the two friends could not realistically have done all that Karain claims, for in 'one job alone, that of pearl diving, it is almost essential to be born and reared'. Perhaps, but Lee is more to the point when he concludes that for anyone who knows 'Conrad's Eastern background he has openly declared himself' (Lee, 26): Karain's story is deliberate romance.

Breaking the bonds of male friendship

Matara's sister breaks taboo in abandoning her race for a sexual liaison with a white man; for this she must die, in order to restore honour to Matara and his people. Matara and Karain embrace exile by seeking out the lovers. This is a familiar nineteenth-century romance structure: the woman is, like Eve, responsible for the fall or the exile of the man; Bertie Cecil in *Under Two Flags* becomes a wanderer to save a woman's reputation; George Talboys in Miss Braddon's *Lady Audley's Secret* (1861) disappears and is presumed murdered by his bigamous wife.

The reason for this negative representation of women perplexes Rebecca Stott: 'Why is it that male authors of this period need to create a "type" of fictional female who is sexually assertive, a figure who stimulates male sexual anxieties and who brings moral atrophy, degeneration, or even death to the male protagonists?' (Stott, ix). Part of the answer can be found in 'Karain'. Matara's sister is unnamed because she is presented as a 'type' of Oriental female seductiveness. Karain may have already been obsessed with her before her flight with the Dutchman: he mentions having seen her carried on the shoulders of slaves 'with uncovered face' (*TU*, 29). As Berthoud observes, in traditional Muslim society to go unveiled 'would be a sign of shamelessness in that it would indicate a desire to provoke sexual response' (*AF* [World's Classics edn], 228). It may be that Karain accompanies Matara not simply out of duty and friendship, but also through a sublimated passion for the sister. Be that as it may, by the time they find the lovers Karain has vowed secretly to protect her. She is responsible for Karain's loss of masculine reason: 'The fire of anguish burned in my breast, and she whispered to me with compassion, with pity, softly—as women will; she soothed the pain of my mind; she bent her face over me—the face of a woman who ravishes the hearts and silences the reason of men' (*TU*, 36). For a second time this power is ascribed to her.[12] Furthermore, she is, apparently, treacherous in denying ever having seen Karain, and his sense of rejection is overpowering:

What! Never before? Had she forgotten already? Was it possible? Forgotten already—after so many years—so many years of wandering, of companionship, of trouble, of tender words! Forgotten already!...I tore myself out from the hands that held me and went away without a word...They let me go. (*TU*, 39)

This is a tale of what Brantlinger calls the 'imperial Gothic', one of ghosts and hauntings in the dark forests and jungles of the exotic East.[13] If the 'ghost' of Matara is a subconscious expression of Karain's guilt, then we must also recognize the symbolic force of his vision of the sister. The actual woman never spoke to him and was, possibly, oblivious to his existence, yet she is still blamed for his loss of reason. She is perceived as unfaithful, true to the 'type' of *femme fatale*, when she denies him; yet this denial probably saves his life, and as such may have been calculated to do so. But, as a lovely and sexually assertive woman, Matara's sister is perceived as a living temptation to betray male friendships. The very existence of such a woman is a threat whether she wills it or not: parading with 'uncovered face' announces her 'shamelessness'; running away with the Dutchman she wilfully exposes the strength of her sexuality. She thus becomes the object of Karain's fantasies.

Such women can break the powerful ties that bind men to each other. In 'The Lagoon' Arsat's brother believes he sees the division women cause: '"There is half a man in you now—the other half is in that woman. I can wait. When you are a whole man again, you will come back with me here to shout defiance. We are sons of the same mother"' (*TU*, 198). Arsat is separated from his brother, just as the desire for the sexually aggressive and provocative Ayesha (plate 7) causes Holly to resent Leo. Similarly the vision of Matara's sister insinuates itself between Karain and Matara. The trouble is that Matara's sister, the flesh and blood woman, is unaware of the effect of her 'spectre' upon Karain and certainly never wills the catastrophe. Karain's vision of the woman is an illusion based on the assumptions of the romance stereotype of the *femme fatale*.

To return to Stott's question: why did male writers create these 'types' of women? Why did Conrad employ this 'type'? One thing is clear: the moral crises in the lives of both Karain and Arsat are generated by their obsessions with irresistibly beautiful and sexually powerful women. The rigid moral codes that had previously been the guiding principles of their lives disintegrate when confronted by the sensual power of woman. Submissive, obedient wives pose no threat to the nineteenth-century male, but the intrusion of a sexually confident female into the world of masculine domination fractures the system that helps men make sense of their lives. Sexually emancipated women threaten the 'male world' with anarchy. The *femme fatale* of nineteenth-century romance is a reminder of the dangers inherent in female emancipation; it indicates a yearning for the female stereotype of Coventry Patmore's 'angel in the house', and underlines the misogynist nature of Conrad's drawing in plate 8. The fear of a *fin de siècle* moral and social crisis, generated by female emancipation, is thus revealed between the lines of an ostensibly romantic tale about exotic 'natives'.

Conroy notes that, when Matara's sister denies that she knows Karain, 'her words kill off her own phantom': 'But she makes room for another phantom, because in place of the vision of her is the guilt-inducing ghost of the man Karain has just killed for her sake' (Conroy, 6). Matara is the 'true' friend, murdered in pursuit of an ideal woman. Arsat abandons his brother to certain death at the hands of the Rajah's men in order to save Diamelen, the servant woman he has 'stolen' from the Rajah's wife. But the ecstasy of Arsat's union with her is also short-lived: as she dies of tropical fever the ephemeral nature of happiness acquired through betrayal is made clear. It is a lesson later to be learned by another of Conrad's heroes, the Capataz, Nostromo.

The sacred male bond

The spectre of Matara that haunts Karain is the nagging voice of male comradeship and loyalty. Karain endures a living death. 'My heart was torn with a strange fear, but could not die', he says mournfully as if seeking the release of death (*TU*, 42). A new fidelity and a new male comradeship with the old 'sorcerer' exorcizes the ghost of Matara and positive action ensues:

> We were welcomed by the great; his wisdom and my courage are remembered where your strength, O white men, is forgotten! We served the Sultan of Sula. We fought the Spaniards. There were victories, hopes, defeats, sorrow, blood, women's tears…What for?… We fled. We collected wanderers of a warlike race and came here to fight again. The rest you know. I am the ruler of a conquered land, a lover of war and danger, a fighter and a plotter. (*TU*, 42–3)

Power and glory are now possible through the union of two men in one cause.

The romantic hero is rarely a loner: male friendships form the cornerstone of the romance of adventure; working together men are powerful and invincible, pooling their resources and qualities to form a formidable force. Hawkeye and Chingachgook; Jack, Ralph and Peterkin; Jack Easy and Mesty; David Balfour and Alan Breck; Holly and Leo; Quatermain, Curtis and Good; Kim and the lama: they are all potent male partnerships of the romance, and in each case the hero is dependent for his safety and the successful conclusion of his adventure upon his friend's loyal devotion. So too with Karain: had he remained loyal to Matara their quest would have ended in the death of the lovers and a safe return home, but he broke faith with his companion and the romantic closure is thus denied him. Instead he becomes a lost, haunted soul until a new partnership permits him to embark upon a fresh romantic adventure. The new bond allows for a rebirth and renewed male vigour. Karain moves forward and fulfils his destiny as the exotic romantic hero: he conquers an Eastern people; he rules with the wisdom, confidence, and supreme belief in himself that can only spring from inner serenity, the knowledge that his ghost is kept at bay. With the death of the old man, however, Karain is again vulnerable.

A question of racial identity

Karain reacts to this new disaster by seeking refuge in the 'secure' Western world of the 'unbelievers'. In a reversal of Jim's leap from the Rajah's stockade into the romance world of Patusan, Karain leaps out of his stockade and swims out to the schooner, that haven of Western 'rationality'. Erdinast-Vulcan notes the parallels with Jim's leap and observes that 'Karain wishes to escape into the "civilized" world where facts alone have power, where men "understand all things seen, and despise all else"' (Erdinast-Vulcan, 32–3). But while Jim succeeds in leaping into another identity as a romance hero, Karain's entry into Western society is problematic:

> 'Yes, take him home,' said Hollis, very low, as if debating with himself. 'That would be one way. The ghosts there are in society, and talk affably to ladies and gentlemen, but would scorn a naked human being—like our princely friend. ... Naked ... Flayed! I should say. I am sorry for him. Impossible—of course.' (*TU*, 44)

Hollis is probably quite astute in recognizing that Karain would never be accepted by European society. He does, after all, have Karain's best interests at heart, and decides that Karain must remain with his own people.

It is the convention of romance that few 'natives' accompany their white comrades back to Europe. If they do, they come as servants to their white masters. Hence Mesty in Marryat's *Mr. Midshipman Easy* returns as Jack's cook and butler, holding his 'post with dignity, and prov[ing] himself trustworthy' (*MME*, 315). In Haggard's *The Witch's Head* (1884) the African Mazooku accompanies the blind Ernest Kershaw to England as his faithful guide and servant. When Ernest marries, Mazooka, feeling rejected, returns to Zululand:

> And so my father, it came to pass that Mazooka, thy ox and thy dog, communed with his heart, and said: 'Here is no more any place for thee. Mazimba thy chief has no longer any need of thee, and behold in this land of women thou, too, shalt grow like a woman. So get up and go to thy father and say to him, "O my father, years ago I put my hand between thy hands, and became a loyal man to thee; now I would withdraw it, and return to the land whence we came; for here I am not wanted, and here I cannot breathe."' (*The Witch's Head*, 323)

The aristocratic 'native' is noble and respected only within his own culture. As Hollis acknowledges, taken out of his native environment and placed in white society Karain would stand out, not as superior of his kind, but as a 'savage' representative of his race, a figure of curiosity, and an inferior being. However courteous, clean, and dignified the 'native' prince may be, he is incapable of surviving in European society. Even Nina, a half-Malay, encounters racial antagonism while boarding with Mrs Vinck. By contrast, white men like Jim or Sir Henry Curtis can lead successful romantic lives in the far reaches of the Empire by virtue of their Englishness.

They may be friends with Karain, but in the final analysis the crew of the schooner regard him as 'other'. When he enters the cuddy to seek refuge, their cultural difference is stressed as Hollis, assuming the 'indolent superiority' of the white imperial male, gives Karain his own dry sarong. Lee points to the significance of such items of clothing and concludes:

> Clothes among social equals of different groups in the East are rarely exchanged. Conrad could not have been more specific in indicating that, while standing firm on the main matters of one's background, the individual must, in a realistic approach to life with others, be malleable when the situation warrants it with regard to minor conventions. (Lee, 28)

But Karain's acceptance of the sarong indicates more than a simple rational approach to his situation. The cultural and racial divide between the men in the cabin is being breached: Karain reaches across that divide by accepting the sarong and then stating his intention to enter the world of the white men to escape his 'ghost'. And the narrator seems to be speak for Conrad when he stresses a common human experience:

> There are those who say that a native will not speak to a white man. Error. No man will speak to his master; but to a wanderer and a friend, to him who does not come to teach or to rule, to him who asks for nothing and accepts all things, words are spoken by the camp-fires, in the shared solitude of the sea, in riverside villages, in resting-places surrounded by forests—words are spoken that take no account of race or colour. One heart speaks—another one listens; and the earth, the sea, the sky, the passing wind and the stirring leaf, hear also the futile tale of the burden of life. (*TU*, 26)

In this Conrad seems to reject the romance stereotype of the 'native' as 'other', indicating instead a shared human predicament. And yet, as ever, Conrad's meaning slips away from us: while the story's narrator urges empathy and a fundamental equality, Hollis continues to assert the arrogance of the white man. With the dismissive tone that springs from belief in his own superior intelligence, Hollis calls Karain a 'ceremonious beggar' (*TU*, 22). In the face of Karain's urgency Hollis drawls out his words confirming his view of Karain as 'other' when he says, 'There's no one here but you—and we three' (*TU*, 24). They 'three' are distinct from Karain by virtue of racial difference; and Karain himself sharpens the distinction when he speaks of 'You men with white faces' who have the 'strength of unbelievers' (*TU*, 24–5).

While the narrator cuts through racial barriers, other characters assert racial distinctions and undermine the central narrative voice. Ultimately all three are wary of Karain's 'savage' unpredictability. Their skittish response to his passionate outburst at the end of his tale proves their lack of trust in his mental balance:

> For the first time that night a sudden convulsion of madness and rage passed over his face. His wavering glances darted here and there like scared birds in a thunderstorm. He jumped up, shouting—
> 'By the spirits that drink blood: by the spirits that cry in the night: by all the spirits of fury, misfortune, and death, I swear—some day I will strike into every heart I meet—I … '
> He looked so dangerous that we all three leaped to our feet, and Hollis, with the back of his hand, sent the kriss flying off the table. I believe we shouted together. (*TU*, 43)

While the schooner's chronometer, steadily ticking away Greenwich Time is a reminder of the familiar and 'real' world of England, Karain, the embodiment of romance and Eastern exoticism, presents an unexpected human dilemma. The roles of gunrunner and warlike 'native' chief are comfortable stereotypes allowing for a tacit equality and friendship between men of different races and cultures. But when Karain steps out of his role as picturesque 'native' and exposes his inner anxieties as a human being the white men recoil in confusion, trying to reaffirm his 'native' identity. Hollis decides that Karain will finish by running 'amuck amongst his faithful subjects and send *ad patres* ever so many of them before they make up their minds to the disloyalty of knocking him on the head' (*TU*, 45). The narrator concurs and decides that 'very little more pressing was needed to make him swerve over into the form of madness peculiar to his race' (*TU*, 45). They have 'no idea what to do' and begin to 'resent bitterly the hard necessity of getting rid of him' (*TU*, 46).

Femininity, empire, and racial subjugation

The narrator and Jackson have no desire to get involved with Karain's 'futile tale of the burden of life'. It is the cynical Hollis who with 'the insolent and unerring wisdom of his youth' (*TU*, 46) provides the answer to Karain's predicament. From a crimson quilted box, containing 'charms' 'that have the power to make a young man sigh, an old man smile' (*TU*, 48), Hollis produces a love token, a lady's glove, and a Jubilee sixpence. He defaces the glove by cutting out the palm to make a pouch for the coin and thus creates a new 'charm' for Karain. Hollis exhorts his companions to 'lie a little' for the sake of their friend who is, 'A good fellow—a gentleman in his way. We can't, so to speak, turn our backs on his confidence and belief in us. Those Malays are easily impressed—all nerves, you know—therefore ...' (*TU*, 47). As a gentleman Karain is worthy of their help, but he is also a Malay. When he pleads, 'Take me with you ... Or else give me some of your strength—of your unbelief ... A charm!' (*TU*, 44), Hollis complies. In an ironic twist, the very concept of Empire that maintains that people with a darker skin are inferior and holds them in subjugation is manifest in the icon of Victoria, that releases Karain from the torture of his conscience. As Erdinast-Vulcan puts it, Hollis helps Karain by 'reaffirming the mythical mode of perception' (Erdinast-Vulcan, 33). The 'charm' asserts the power of the West over the superstitious and 'backward' world of the East, confirms Karain's mythic status, and returns him to the world of romance.[14]

The 'charm' functions at various levels: on one level it is 'ostensibly a cheap trick played on a superstitious, "primitive" native' (Erdinast-Vulcan, 32). And we mustn't forget that this sixpence is not even the real thing, a point made with ironic incisiveness: 'It was gilt; it had a hole punched near the rim' (*TU*, 49).[15] At another level it represents 'native' belief in the supremacy of white civilization, and consequently it asserts the ability of the Empire to control the native population. It is also a redemptive gift from white friends to a Malay prince. Yet, still another interpretation of the 'charm' is possible. It is an acknowledgement of a common male experience: anxiety about feminine sexual 'precocity'. When Hollis takes a ribbon out of the box, another love token, smiles at it 'scornfully', then mutilates the palm of the glove, he enacts an exorcism of female sexual power. Destroying a woman's love-token unites the men in the cabin through their fear of female domination: 'Every one of us,' he said, with pauses that somehow were more offensive than his words—'every one of us, you'll admit has been haunted by some woman ...' (*TU*, 47).

In a further ironic twist the face of another woman preserves Karain: the white Empress Victoria – an icon of woman and motherhood as a distant, untouchable ideal, powerfully distinct from the alluring Oriental *femme fatale*. Even the irresistible Ayesha cannot persuade Holly and Leo that she could replace this Queen. Holly 'shudders' at the thought, and when Ayesha declares her intent to overthrow Victoria, the two men break out in dismay, claiming they 'would as soon think of overthrowing [them]selves': 'Again we explained that it was the character of monarchs that had changed, and that the sovereign under whom we lived was venerated and beloved by all right-thinking men in her vast realms' (*S*, 248). The notion of Victoria, placed in opposition to the *femme fatale*, whether she be Ayesha or Matara's sister, is ultimately more powerful. In this way the romance asserts an ideal image of womanhood over those women who seek to seduce men.

Hollis's ability to persuade Karain of the effectiveness of the 'charm' relies upon the 'Victoria myth' having already infected Karain's perceptions of the West:

> Every visit began with that inquiry; he was insatiable of details; he was fascinated by the holder of a sceptre the shadow of which, stretching from the westward over the earth and over the seas, passed far beyond his own hand's-breadth of conquered land. He multiplied questions; he could never know enough of the Monarch

of whom he spoke with wonder and chivalrous respect—with a kind of affectionate awe! (*TU*, 12–13)

This Empress has the power to reach across continents and make subjects of credulous 'natives' who have not yet been colonized. Hollis tells Karain that Victoria is 'the most powerful thing the white men know' (*TU*, 49). Some of his utterances even have the power of rhetoric designed to reflect and strengthen their own belief in the cause of the British Empire:

> 'She commands a spirit, too—the spirit of her nation; a masterful, conscientious, unscrupulous, unconquerable devil…that does a lot of good—incidentally…a lot of good…at times—and wouldn't stand any fuss from the best ghost out for such a little thing as our friend's shot.' (*TU*, 49–50)

And these could almost be the words of Marlow in *Heart of Darkness* asserting that the patches of red on the map of Africa are 'good to see at any time, because one knows that some real work is done in there' (*HD*, 55). This real work is conducted under the maternal eye of the white Empress who is, according to Hollis, 'more powerful than Suleiman the Wise' (*TU*, 49). In Hollis's dismissal of the shooting of Matara lies the sense that the death of the Malay is only 'a little thing' compared with the death of a white man. Marlow's, and probably Conrad's, scepticism about imperialism is inscribed in *Heart of Darkness*: in 'Karain' claims for English superiority in dealing with colonized peoples are made by Hollis and thus, for the purposes of writing saleable romance, Conrad can include such assumptions whilst actually distancing himself from Hollis and his beliefs. Speaking of the 'tale-within-a-tale' narrative technique in *The Arabian Nights Entertainment*,[16] Hampson shows how Conrad uses the same techniques. His comment that Conrad uses the 'interaction' between the 'frame and the framed story' in *Heart of Darkness* 'to produce a radical questioning of values' could be applied in some measure to 'Karain' (in Caracciolo, 220). Karain's story finds its resolution in the frame narrative through the meeting of Eastern and Western cultures, but Conrad's distancing technique allows for a 'radical questioning' of Hollis's assumptions about Victoria.

Karain becomes, symbolically, one of the Queen's colonized subjects, in his own consciousness rather than legally. The Englishmen regard him with affectionate indulgence as they confer the 'charm'. But the comic element to the ritual speaks of a superior intelligence, of white rationality mocking Malay superstition. The mute, statue-like figure of Karain appears as a gullible 'native' while the white men practise their trick upon him. It is like a queer parody of the dignity of John Laputa (plate 16) receiving the Snake of John:

> They looked close into one another's eyes. Those of Karain stared in a lost glance, but Hollis's seemed to grow darker and looked out masterful and compelling. They were in violent contrast together— one motionless and the colour of bronze, the other dazzling white and lifting his arms, where the powerful muscles rolled slightly under a skin that gleamed like satin. Jackson moved near with the air of a man closing up to a chum in a tight place. I said impressively, pointing to Hollis—
> 'He is young, but he is wise. Believe him!'
> Karain bent his head: Hollis threw lightly over it the dark-blue ribbon and stepped back.
> 'Forget, and be at peace!' I cried. (*TU*, 50)

This mock ritual has the air of a confidence trick. While the white men in a serio-comic pantomime adopt the simple idiom of the Malay's English, Karain, the stereotypical superstitious and simple 'native' believes all they say. These men are, indeed, performing a redemptive ritual that will allow Karain to go away and live at peace with himself, but they are, simultaneously, effectively confining him to the ranks of the imperial 'native' subject who is more or less stupid. We are reminded of Kipling's Dravot and Carnehan duping an Indian tribe into believing they are gods, or of Quatermain's trick with the eclipse in *King Solomon's Mines*. Conrad has employed the formulaic romance assumption that the 'native' is an easy victim of white scientific knowledge and trickery; addressed over Karain's head the audience's concurrence with this view of the 'native' is assumed.

The dignified, powerfully romantic, and exotic Karain of the story's opening thus becomes a diminished version of his former self by virtue of the white men's 'gift'. Confirmed in his stereotypical role despite the narrator's assertion of their common humanity, Karain returns to the colourful world of Eastern exoticism where, as a Malay, he belongs. Watching him return to shore, the crew enact the public school ritual of three cheers, and Karain, gravely, points to the 'infallible charm' that allows him to re-enter his romantic kingdom. The comic presentation

of Karain and the mock seriousness of the three white men emphasize the distance between the 'real' world and the romantic 'stage' of
Karain's existence.

The city: an alienating jungle

Romantic distance is re-established as Karain retreats from the prosaic
reality of the schooner's cuddy to the romantic landscape of his
Eastern shore. As the schooner sails towards the 'real' world of Western
commerce the gulf between reality and romance widens. Karain, his
people, and their environment, become again Said's *'tableau vivant'*:

> The bay was waking up. The smokes of morning fires stood in faint
> spirals higher than the heads of palms; people moved between the
> houses; a herd of buffaloes galloped clumsily across a green slope;
> the slender figures of boys brandishing sticks appeared black and
> leaping in the long grass; a coloured line of women, with water bam-
> boos on their heads, moved swaying through a thin grove of fruit
> trees. Karain stopped in the midst of his men and waved his hand;
> then, detaching himself from the splendid group, walked alone to
> the water's edge and waved his hand again. The schooner passed out
> to sea between the steep headlands that shut in the bay, and at the
> same instant Karain passed out of our life forever. (*TU*, 52–3)

'But', says the narrator, 'the memory remains' (*TU*, 53). As the close
of the story returns us to the grimy streets of London the distance created by its opening is again made distinct by the contrast. For the narrator, Karain and his romantic land must stay firmly within the
confines of memory. The 'real' world is the bustling city where 'the
wheels of hansoms turned slowly along the edge of side-walks', where
girls pass by 'talking vivaciously and with shining eyes', and 'a fine old
fellow strutted, red-faced, stroking a white moustache' (*TU*, 55). It has
the colour and detail of Karain's kingdom, but also the comforting
familiarity of Western life.

Jackson, just returned to England, sees another side to this bustling
city life. His 'clear blue eyes' look around contemptuously 'amused and
hard, like the eyes of a boy' and perceive a lurid and grubby reality:

> A clumsy string of red, yellow, and green omnibuses rolled swaying,
> monstrous and gaudy; two shabby children ran across the road;
> a knot of dirty men with red neckerchiefs round their bare throats

lurched along, discussing filthily; a ragged old man with a face of despair yelled horribly in the mud the name of a paper ... (*TU*, 55)

Jackson sees with the eyes of an adventurer, a boy's vision of the grimy city after years of wandering the seas and visiting outposts of the Empire. His comment as he gazes at the busy London streets, 'I'll be hanged if it is yet as real to me as ... as the other thing ... say, Karain's story' (*TU*, 55), is the result of a life of romantic adventuring, a yearning for the lost world of romance and Eastern exoticism from which the traveller must return. For, as Hampson observes:

> In 'Karain', as the *coup de grâce*, all this agglomeration of action and detail seems, to Jackson, less real than Karain's story of 'primitive passion'. As in *The Wasteland* or Ford's *Ladies Whose Bright Eyes*, one 'civilization is superimposed upon another, and modern, western, urban life appears alienated and anæmic in the comparison'. (in Gene M. Moore ed., *Conrad's Cities*, 163)[17]

It would be to miss Conrad's purpose to take the two visions of London as opposing states of mind from which we can extrapolate the author's meaning. For both men see the grimy scene, and both see 'a policeman, helmeted and dark, stretching out a rigid arm at the crossing of the streets' (*TU*, 55). This representative of Western social and political stability is a reminder of the assumption of imperial romance that the East is a place of lawlessness where it is assumed that men who kill their friends encounter no system of institutionalized retribution. This policeman is thus a cryptic reminder of Karain's tale of betrayal, revenge, murder, and retribution.

The narrator concludes that 'decidedly' Jackson had been 'too long away from home' (*TU*, 55). These are the last words of the story, and yet not the last words *on* the story. For, in this final double vision of *fin de siècle* London lies the continued problem of interpreting Conrad's meaning. Anxiety about the alienating effect of city life is threaded through the description of 'the broken confusion of roofs', the streets 'deep as a well and narrow like a corridor', the 'headlong shuffle and beat of rapid footsteps', the 'innumerable eyes', 'blank faces', and the 'ragged strip of smoky sky' that 'extended motionless, like a soiled streamer flying above the rout of a mob' (*TU*, 54–5). While he can confidently affirm that Jackson needs a dose of 'reality' the narrator registers a deep anxiety about the decay and the threat of chaos encoded in this image of London. The city that the narrator sees carries dark hints of Arthur Morrison's Jago and George Gissing's nether world. It is an alienating, disturbing jungle. Cedric Watts observes that the effect of this description of the busy city is to 'undercut ironically the narrator's confidence and to support Jackson's doubts':

> Against the turbulence, overcrowding, noise, ugliness, confusion and squalor associated with the city, Karain's picturesquely tropical world with its archaic values (simple heroism and leadership, passionate actions and betrayals, superstitious credulities) seems 'more real': aesthetically, ontologically and morally better. (in Gene M. Moore ed., *Conrad's Cities*, 22)

Once we recognize these doubts lurking beneath the narrative Jackson's voice becomes more subversive. His doubts counter the apparently positive view of London, and in the end the tale is inconclusive about the value and reality of romance. Indeed Hampson's comment that in *Heart of Darkness* the 'African experience flows back to question London society psychologically, politically and philosophically' (in Caracciolo, 220) is also true of the Malay experience in 'Karain'.

Within the text of the story itself we find unanswered questions. As Karain returns to the 'glorious splendour of his stage' the narrator recoils from a direct authorial judgement and instead offers the interpretation to the reader: 'I wondered what they thought; what he thought; ... what the reader thinks?' (*TU*, 52). As Conroy observes, the slippage is not strictly grammatical, 'but the tense shift is symptomatic, as is the narrator's concern with what, if anything, his reader makes, in emotional significance, of his tale' (Conroy, 9). Jackson intensifies the tale's resistance to simple analysis when, troubled by the reality of Karain's story, he asks the narrator, 'What do you think?' (*TU*, 54). The narrator replies, pointing to the London streets, 'What a question to ask! Only look at all this' (*TU*, 54). 'All this' encompasses the cheery bustle of the city and the grimy underside where the confusion of roofs, chimney-stacks, and houses 'stood resigned and sullen under the falling gloom' (*TU*, 54). It is little wonder that Jackson's response is a meditative, 'Ye-e-e-s' (*TU*, 55). It is clear that Conrad successfully created those 'magazine'ish' qualities he speaks about to Cunninghame Graham. Garnett's warnings 'against trying to be a more ambitious and highbrow kind of novelist' may have been accepted by Conrad, yet 'Karain', despite its overtly romantic subject matter, contains hints of the deep scepticism, and plurality of meaning that are the distinctive features of later works such as *Heart of Darkness*.

'Karain' is a deliberately conceived romantic narrative, but *Lord Jim* offers a more sceptical view of romance. When Jim attempts to create in Patusan the kind of imperial utopia over which Karain rules the ghosts of the past are not so easily laid to rest. The 'charm' that Jim acquires, Doramin's ring, enables his entry into the romantic kingdom of Patusan, but guarantees no immunity from the 'real' world that relentlessly pursues him into the farthest reaches of the exotic East. Karain, the true romance hero, believes in ghosts because they are part of his culture. Thus, even ghosts are dependable: they will disappear when exorcized. The 'real' world offers no such certainties and guarantees. Jim relies on the promises of romance to deliver him from the gnawing knowledge of his human failings. But, unlike the romance stereotype, Karain, Jim is 'one of us', and can never escape his ghost, however deeply he may immerse himself in 'his own world of shades' (*LJ*, 416).

6
Lord Jim:
The Limitations of Romance

Conrad's relationship with *Blackwood's* continued with the publication of *The Nigger of the Narcissus* and *Tales of Unrest*. *Heart of Darkness* began serialization in 1898 in the special 1000th edition of the magazine, which must have brought Conrad great pleasure. *Lord Jim*, originally intended as 'a sketch', grew to such proportions that William Blackwood, frustrated by delays, began its serialization in October 1899 after the completion of just four instalments. In his 1917 Preface Conrad gives Blackwood the credit for prompting him to take up the story after it had been laid aside for some time. Blackburn records how David Meldrum predicted that 'in the annals of Maga … half a century hence it will be one of the honourable things to record of her that she entertained "Jim"' (Blackburn, xiv).[1] As John Batchelor notes, many alterations were made to the original manuscript before it appeared in book form in 1900, and the critical response was generally enthusiastic.[2] For the first time Conrad began to be compared to Henry James, and reviewers tended to be less equivocal and more astute in their judgements of Conrad's work.[3] The *Manchester Guardian* found *Lord Jim* 'touched with romance and profoundly true' (*CH*, 113). Whilst this is a favourable assessment it seems to downplay the overt romance of the second half of the book; and it is curious that reviewers say less about the romance elements in *Lord Jim* than in Conrad's previous works, since it is here that he most self-consciously employs the formula and motifs of that genre.

More recent critics generally agree that the second half of *Lord Jim* is a deliberate imperial romance, that Jim himself perpetuates the romance mode. Yet few have commented on how the novel, from the very beginning, picks up the threads of imperial romance and self-consciously thematizes them. In this chapter I will discuss how the use and subversion of the tropes of the imperial romance in Conrad's earlier Malay fiction are explicit from the outset in *Lord Jim*, and contribute to Conrad's modernist vision in that text.

'One of us'?

Lord Jim is a natural progression from the preoccupations of *An Outcast*. By the time the novel begins its narrative proper, that is, when Marlow takes over the storytelling, the hero, Jim, is, like Willems, an outcast of his kind, taken under the protective wing of a surrogate father figure; like Willems, Jim has romantic illusions about his own future. Both Jim and Willems retreat from the world of commerce and bustling white humanity into a Malay community that has a languid air of timelessness. Jim effects political change in Patusan, just as Willems ousts Lingard from his trading monopoly; he forms a relationship with a 'native' woman, Jewel; finally he meets death in this faraway place at the hands of Doramin. Retribution for betrayal comes for both Jim and Willems in the form of a pistol shot to the breast. Given this brief outline of the parallels in the plots of *An Outcast* and *Lord Jim* it would seem, on the surface, that Conrad was simply reworking old material. But there is a significant shift in perspective between the two novels: the moral tone of the later novel is 'ambivalent and, perhaps, ambiguous' according to John E. Saveson (Saveson, 163), and part of the reason for this disparity lies in Conrad's increased preoccupation with English notions of acceptable behaviour and romantic ideals.

Jim is English, whereas Almayer and Willems are Dutch: Conrad's admiration for English social and political stability is well documented, but he had no such reverence for the Dutch or the Dutch imperial endeavour.[4] In contrast to Willems's squalid, unstable background, Jim is an English country parson's son, like the hero of boys' adventure fiction. Marryat's Jack Easy, for example, is the son of an English gentleman 'who lived down in Hampshire; he was a married man, and in very easy circumstances' (*MME*, 9); the Seagrave family in *Masterman Ready* enjoy similarly genteel circumstances; perhaps the most famous of these adventuring fictional heroes, Ralph Rover, in *The Coral Island* is the son of a sea-captain who retired to a 'small cottage in a fishing village on the west coast of England' (*CI*, 21). Jim's father's living, with its suggestions of a gentlemanly background, could almost have come from the pages of a romance:

> The little church on a hill had the mossy greyness of a rock seen through a ragged screen of leaves. It had stood there for centuries,

but the trees around probably remembered the laying of the first stone. Below, the red front of the rectory gleamed with a warm tint in the midst of grass-plots, flower-beds, and fir-trees, with an orchard at the back, a paved stable-yard to the left, and the sloping glass of green-houses tacked along a wall of bricks. (*LJ*, 5)

There is a sense of permanence and gentility in the description recalling the sentimentality of the opening of *Tom Brown's Schooldays*:

How the whole countryside teems with Saxon names and memories! And the old moated grange at Compton, nestled close under the hillside, where twenty Marianas may have lived, with its bright water-lilies in the moat, and its yew walk, 'the cloister walk,' and its peerless terraced gardens. There they all are, and twenty things beside, for those who care about them, and have eyes. And these are the sort of things you may find, I believe, every one of you, in any common English country neighbourhood. (*TBS*, 14–15)

Tom Brown, as his name suggests, epitomizes English boyhood; Jim is, of course, 'one of us'. Marlow's term, 'one of us', is, however, open to various interpretations. Scott McCracken suggests that the phrase is often a question, '*the* ostensible question of the novel, because although Jim is a professional sailor, an officer, a white European, the ideal of behaviour and superiority which goes with being "one of us" is in doubt' (McCracken, 26). For the moment one meaning will suffice: Jim is an English gentleman; 'he came from the right place' (*LJ*, 43). Some critics assume this to mean that he represented the merchant seaman, that class of men whom Marlow, and Conrad, most admired. Tony Tanner, for example, takes Marlow's phrase to mean that Jim is 'a western seaman', and that he becomes 'by extension one of "us", the readers' (Tanner, 13). But this does not address the full implication of the phrase for Marlow:

He stood there for all the parentage of his kind, for men and women by no means clever or amusing, but whose very existence is based upon honest faith, and upon the instinct of courage. I don't mean military courage, or civil courage, or any special kind of courage. I mean just that inborn ability to look temptations straight in the face—a readiness unintellectual enough, goodness knows, but without pose—a power of resistance, don't you see, ungracious if you like, but priceless—an unthinking and blessed stiffness before the outward and inward terrors, before the might of nature, and the seductive corruption of men—backed by a faith invulnerable to the strength of facts, to the contagion of example, to the solicitation of ideas. (*LJ*, 43)

Marlow would never have included women in this assessment if he were thinking solely of the merchant service. 'One of us' implies breeding and a sense of belonging to a particular social group: that of the English gentleman and the genteel classes. Furthermore, Marlow implies much more: these unintellectual, stoic individuals possess the qualities that the English public schools sought to encourage. In terms of the men Marlow is talking about they are like the late nineteenth-century protégés of Thomas Arnold who prefer winning cricket matches to Balliol scholarships. Jim appeals to Marlow because he seems to embody that spirit of 'solidarity', of communal effort that in Marlow's eyes, and in Conrad's, distinguishes the Merchant Service. For this reason Jim's case is, in Royal Roussel's words, so important because he is 'a test case for Marlow's allegiance to the group and the ethos defined by the phrase "one of us"' (Roussel, 80). Benita Parry points to the multiplicity of meanings and groups that the phrase suggests: 'The generality of this last phrase leaves it open to a number of constructions, and common to the possible interpretations which the text can support is the notion of a closed and elect group (the club, the regiment, the religious order, the guild, the masonic lodge)...' (Parry, 86). The white-clad imperial adventurer that Jim seems to epitomize thus represents his race and his breeding, a representative of the best that England can produce.

The romantic adventurer

Like the young Conrad, like Ballantyne's Ralph Rover and Marryat's Jack Easy, Jim is drawn to the sea, his desire fuelled by a course of 'light holiday literature', which no doubt contained illustrations like those in plates 11 and 12. Erdinast-Vulcan suggests that 'Jim's initial identification was the Stevensonian adventure story' (Erdinast-Vulcan, 19). Conrad probably had Stevenson's adventure mode in mind, but other, earlier writers of adventure fiction created the imperial fantasies on which Jim builds his daydreams. More plausible is the literature of Ballantyne, Marryat, Henty, and, given Jim's father's vocation, the publications of Kingston for the Religious Tract Society. For example Ralph Rover is fascinated with mariners' tales:

> I freely confessed that my heart glowed ardently within me as they recounted their wild adventures in foreign lands—the dreadful storms they had weathered, the appalling dangers they had escaped,

the wonderful creatures they had seen both on the land and in the sea, and the interesting lands and strange people they had visited … They told me of thousands of beautiful fertile islands … where summer reigned nearly all year round; where the trees were laden with a constant harvest of luxuriant fruit; where the climate was almost perpetually delightful; yet where, strange to say, men were wild, bloodthirsty savages … (*CI*, 23)

Even during training for the actual life in the mercantile marine Jim retreats into daydreams that resemble the adventures of plates 10 and 12:

On the lower deck in the babel of two hundred voices he would forget himself, and beforehand live in his mind the sea-life of light literature. He saw himself saving people from sinking ships, cutting away masts in a hurricane, swimming through a surf with a line; or as a lonely castaway, barefooted and half naked, walking on uncovered reefs in search of shellfish to stave off starvation. He confronted savages on tropical shores, quelled mutinies on the high seas, and in a small boat upon the ocean kept up the hearts of despairing men—always an example of devotion to duty, and as unflinching as a hero in a book. (*LJ*, 6)

Jim constructs his self-ideal through the images of adventure fiction; but just as the fantasies of Willems and Almayer are mercilessly undercut the moment they are articulated, so Jim's dream is interrupted by a real crisis. When presented with the actual possibility for heroism, in the form of a coaster running into a cutter, Jim is paralysed. Prefiguring his later failure on the *Patna*, Jim fails to fulfil his romantic ideal. As Hampson says, he deludes himself: 'Jim is immobilised by real danger [p. 7], but then, like Willems, preserves his self-ideal through a series of self-deceiving manoeuvres …' (*Betrayal*, 119).

   This isn't the first hint of Jim's less than romantic stature. The opening of the novel gives the first clue: 'He was an inch, perhaps two, under six feet' (*LJ*, 3). A small matter perhaps, two inches, but for the romantic hero it is a significant shortfall, and Conrad makes the point wryly. The mystery of Jim's 'incognito' and sudden departures retreating 'in good order towards the rising sun' (*LJ*, 4–5) alerts us to the fact that this foreshortened hero may have something to hide. It could be a question of loyalty to a lady's endangered reputation as in *Under Two Flags*, or it could be something more sinister. The tension is maintained until Chapter 4 when Jim's dishonour is gradually revealed. Yet despite the early warning signs, Conrad encourages a sympathetic reading of Jim's romantic aspirations so that initially there is an illusion of reading a romantic boys' adventure story. It is with the appearance of Marlow that the complex moral dimension enters the book, and the kaleidoscopic perspectives on Jim's character come into play.

A chance missed

Jim persists in his delusions, but finds that 'the regions so well known to his imagination' are 'strangely barren of adventure' (*LJ*, 10). The alternative to daydreams of romantic adventure are the 'exactions of the sea, and the prosaic severity of the daily task that gives bread—but whose only reward is the perfect love of the work' (*LJ*, 10). This is the voice of a narrator who knows the sea and its rigours, is alive to its romance, but who holds no boyish illusions about such a life. Transported to the East Jim maintains his illusions because they have never been put to the test. He appears, superficially, to be qualified for his vocation: 'He was gentlemanly, steady, tractable, with a thorough knowledge of his duties' (*LJ*, 10). These are the qualities of the romance hero of boys' adventures, but, as Conrad will show, they do not necessarily imply the mettle to endure a real trial of character. Jim becomes chief mate 'without ever having been tested by those events of the sea that show in the light of day the inner worth of a man, the edge of his temper, and the fibre of his stuff; that reveal the quality of his resistance and the secret truth of his pretences, not only to others but also to himself' (*LJ*, 10). The 'light holiday literature' Jim reads as a child provides the foundations for his idealization of adventure and the basis for his seafaring character, but Conrad cuts through the stereotype and points to the need for substance beneath the confident gentlemanly surface of the romance. The romantic heroism Jim imagines for himself is qualified three times within the first ten pages of the novel: he is shorter than the stereotypical hero; he becomes paralysed in the face of the first opportunity for heroism; and then Conrad questions his ability to withstand a genuine test of character.

When the test comes it has already been clearly hinted that Jim's imagination is stronger than his character. The deceptive peace of the tropical seas allows his imagination full rein:

> At such times his thoughts would be full of valorous deeds: he loved these dreams and the success of his imaginary achievements. They

were the best parts of life, its secret truth, its hidden reality. They had a gorgeous virility, the charm of vagueness, they passed before him with a heroic tread; they carried his soul away with them and made it drunk with the divine philtre of an unbounded confidence in itself. There was nothing he could not face. (*LJ*, 20)

As the *Patna* drifts along on the treacherously peaceful sea 'black and smouldering in a luminous immensity, as if scorched by a flame flicked at her from a heaven without pity' (*LJ*, 16), Jim is 'penetrated by the great certitude of unbounded safety and peace that could be read on the silent aspect of nature...' (*LJ*, 17). Yet there is, as Kenneth B. Newell says, 'a sense in the air that the universe was about to make a revelatory move' (Newell, 27).

Jim is boyishly amused by the *Patna*'s seedy crew, regarding them with indulgent superiority. They 'did not belong to the world of heroic adventure; they weren't bad chaps though' (*LJ*, 24). He 'rubbed shoulders with them, but they could not touch him; he shared the air they breathed, but he was different' (*LJ*, 24–5). During the drunken quarrel between the skipper and the engineer, who Jim dismisses with his schoolboy idiom as, 'not bad chaps', the would-be hero is practically dozing: 'The line dividing his meditation from a surreptitious doze on his feet was thinner than a thread in a spider's web' (*LJ*, 25). While Jim indulges his waking dream the *Patna* pilgrims sleep 'surrendered to the wisdom of white men and to their courage, trusting the power of their unbelief and the iron shell of their fire-ship' (*LJ*, 17). They, too, are victims of the myth of white superiority and trust the white tuan without seeing, as Marlow does, 'the subtle unsoundness of the man' (*LJ*, 89). Jim's middle-class English background, blond, blue-eyed Anglo-Saxon good looks, gentlemanly demeanour, and confidence seem to mark him out as the 'unflinching hero' of imperial romance. Yet his aloofness adds an ironic dimension to his being 'one of us' because, by leaping into the lifeboat, Jim becomes by association and in deed, 'one of them', the crew. His chance to prove himself a romantic hero is missed.

The jump: imagination and impulse

The characters in *Lord Jim* distinguish themselves from those they perceive as inferior by comparing the other to animals: the German captain refers to his passengers as 'dese cattle' (*LJ*, 15); the second engineer views them as 'vermin' (*LJ*, 25). In the delirium of alcohol poisoning, he calls them 'reptiles' (*LJ*, 51) and 'pink toads' (*LJ*, 52), creatures in a primeval swamp from a lower order of evolution. Marlow's impression of the captain is of a 'trained baby-elephant walking on hind-legs' (*LJ*, 37), and he wants to see him 'pierced through and through, squirming like an impaled beetle' (*LJ*, 42). Jim, however, is 'clean-limbed, clean-faced, firm on his feet, as promising a boy as the sun ever shone on' (*LJ*, 40). Yet Marlow knows more of Jim than his outward appearance and concludes that he 'had no business to look so sound' (*LJ*, 40). The outward appearance of promising white youth is held up to question: this challenges Jim's claim to gentlemanly status and confuses Marlow. Delving beneath the simple 'truths' of the imperial romance, Conrad exposes conflicts that strike at the heart of the self-satisfaction of Western civilizations.

Jim's public school exterior, his imperialist's uniform of clean white linen and immaculate pipe-clayed shoes is a deceptive surface beneath which lurks a more primitive self; his 'fixed from-under stare' made Marlow 'think of a charging bull' (*LJ*, 3). This impulsiveness and lack of 'sang-froid' is borne out by Jim's later behaviour: despite his daydreams of remaining cool in the face of imminent shipwreck, he fails to understand the desperate pleas of the father on the *Patna* for water for his sick child. Just as Amy Foster will later panic when Yanko Goorall, on his deathbed, pleads for water, Jim acts on impulse. At that moment of crisis Jim associates water with drowning, so he flings the lamp in the man's face. Even when recounting the story Jim displays no sense of compassion. His response is not that of the gentleman hero, but one of pure impulse reacting to panic. So much for romantic daydreams of keeping up 'the hearts of despairing men' like a hero in a book. When the officers call to the ship for the already dead George to jump, Jim hears a bleat, a scream, and a howl, and the instinct for self-preservation, the appeal to the animal in him, is stronger than the romantic illusion of heroism. It is also stronger than his sense of duty to the ship's passengers and crew. When Marlow is faced with the dilemma about whether to 'leap ashore for a howl and a dance' in *Heart of Darkness* he acknowledges the temptation, but gruffly explains how duty prevented him. Marlow denies that 'fine sentiments' prevented him from succumbing to the appeal of primitive urges in himself: 'Fine sentiments, be hanged! I had no time. I had to mess about with white-lead and strips of woollen blanket helping to put bandages on those leaky steam-pipes—I tell you' (*HD*, 97). Marlow's sense of duty protects him from disaster; Jim's lack of a sense of duty precipitates his own personal disaster. His impulsive leap is a jump from the romantic daydream of imperial heroism into the reality of his own fallibility.

The *Patna* crew have no thoughts of gentlemanly conduct when they send up their animal cries to the boat. Compare their desertion with the abandoning of the *Hispaniola* in *Treasure Island*. Captain Smollett, Squire Trelawney, and Dr Livesey abandon ship to evade the murderous mutineers. When the Captain calls to Abraham Gray to join them his appeal is to Gray's social instinct:

> 'Gray,' resumed Mr. Smollett, a little louder, 'I am leaving this ship, and I order you to follow your captain. I know you are a good man at bottom, and I dare say not one of the lot of you's as bad as he makes out. I have my watch here in my hand; I give you thirty seconds to join me in.'
> There was a pause.
> 'Come, my fine fellow,' continued the captain, 'don't hang so long in stays. I'm risking my life, and the lives of these good gentlemen every second.'
> There was a sudden scuffle, a sound of blows, and out burst Abraham Gray with a knife-cut on the side of the cheek, and came running to the captain, like a dog to the whistle. (*TI*, 90–1)

Gray obeys a code of Christian morality and gentlemanly solidarity; he acts according to the conventions of romance. Preserving his reputation as a 'good man' Gray can continue to participate in the adventure. Called to join the elect band of English gentlemen he rejects the base mutineers. For Jim, alone in an indifferent universe, the 'truths' of romance are not enough. Allying himself with the cowardly crew Jim makes the opposite choice to Gray, thus denying himself the opportunity of further adventure at sea. When he reassures Marlow that he would never do it again, he reveals, as Berthoud observes, both the cause and the consequence of his jump: 'The very glibness of the promise of good conduct tells us why the jump has been possible at all; and at the same time we are made to see that it won't happen twice, not because Jim has decided it won't, but because it can't' (Berthoud, 78). It can't because no one will ever again put Jim in the position of chief mate. Yet the next time Jim is given responsibility for the lives of others, Dain Waris and his men, he repeats his initial failure. Thus his glib remark has a double irony.

The trial: the English gentleman under scrutiny

Jim's trial spans ten chapters, ending in Chapter Fifteen with Chester's offer to effectively bury Jim alive on an island of guano. For nearly one hundred and fifty pages his time aboard the *Patna* is recounted, assessed, and judged by various personalities and from a multiplicity of angles. He confounds those who comment on him, Brierly and Marlow in particular, by breaking the code of honour that binds seamen and English gentlemen together, and then by turning to the very order that he violates and offering himself up for sacrifice to its rigours. Jim's existence brings the gentlemanly code of honour into question. At the centre of the debate surrounding Jim's 'soundness', his status as 'one of us', and of course Marlow's recognition of him as such, is the notion of what soundness and belonging actually mean. If Jim is, in Parry's terms, a member of that 'closed and elect group' that constitutes late nineteenth-century white imperial manhood, why does he not fit the model? Having fallen short of the ideal why does he not do the honourable thing and disappear without trace so as not to disturb those who have not incurred disgrace? Part of the answer lies in Jim's romantic self-conception, and part of it lies in what Jim symbolizes for those who judge him.

In physical peril Jim's instinct for self-preservation is too strong to be overcome by his training as a gentleman and his romantic belief in his own heroic possibilities. But, when his honour is in question, he does the gentlemanly thing and meets disgrace head on. The inconsistency of these two acts performed by the same man perplexes Marlow and ultimately destroys Brierly. Jim's symbolic status is part of the romance of Empire, a myth that Conrad explodes revealing fault lines in the system that created such men as Jim. The codes of honour that Jim breaks, the trust he betrays, are sacred rites vital to the imperial success of England. As Marlow says:

> He was a youngster of the sort you like to see about you; of the sort you like to imagine yourself to have been; of the sort whose appearance claims the fellowship of these illusions you had thought gone out, extinct, cold, and which as if rekindled at the approach of another flame, give a flutter deep, deep down somewhere, give a flutter of light ... of heat! (*LJ*, 128)

Jim appeals to the idealist and the romantic in Marlow, and Marlow, addressing his listeners, implies their acquiescence in his longing for that ideal. Jim's crime is in being, inadvertently, an iconoclast: his action destroys the romantic illusion of English youth that he had revived in the crusty old mariner Marlow. And Marlow resents the loss:

> [A]nd, looking at him, knowing all he knew and a little more too, I was as angry as though I had detected him trying to get something

out of me by false pretences. He had no business to look so sound. I thought to myself—well, if this sort can go wrong like that … (*LJ*, 40)

In Marlow's last words lies the despair of an imperial race faced with its failure to live up to its own ideal. Jim's leap exposes the fragility of the ideal and reveals Conrad's modernist vision: if 'this sort' can go wrong no moral value is exempt from challenge.

Jim's self-image, however, is still strong enough to affect his behaviour once out of physical danger. In schoolboy language, doggedly facing the trial he asserts: 'But I've got to get over this thing, and I mustn't shirk any of it or … I won't shirk any of it' (*LJ*, 154). Or? Perhaps he could no longer believe in himself? The illusory world of heroic achievement is his refuge. Jim's self-image proves to him that he is better than those with whom his jump allied him. Justifying his refusal to run away, he distances himself from the cowardly skipper. Clearing out was 'all very well for him', but Jim couldn't and wouldn't: 'They all got out of it one way or another, but it wouldn't do for me' (*LJ*, 79). This will not erase the fact that Jim jumped. As Marlow comments: 'He had tumbled from a height he could never scale again' (*LJ*, 112).

Jim's ego ideal is a deception arising out of the literary tradition of gentlemanly conduct and imperial adventure; but Conrad shows how an ideal must be bound to a moral conviction for it to have worth and substance. Jim's consciousness encompasses his own soul and reputation, but he misses the wider implications of his transgressions. The various stories within the frame narrative of the trial attempt to explore these wider implications, providing multiple perspectives on what is required of the would-be imperial hero. The different lenses under which Jim's predicament is examined are presented as Marlow's attempt to make some sense of the enigma. In a multi-angled examination of what constitutes honour and heroism, these layers of narrative illuminate a variety of responses to the code of honour and gentlemanly conduct that imperialist ideology imposes on its adventurers.

Brierly's self-doubt

Big Brierly, 'the captain of the crack ship of the Blue Star line', provides an example of what Jim might have become, just as Jim represents to Brierly a nightmare vision of his own potential actions. When Brierly's self-image as the ideal English sailor is challenged by Jim's failure to be just that, the foundation of Brierly's perceived superiority and rectitude is shaken. He reveals the hollowness of his philosophy to Marlow.

Having loftily dismissed the value of the whole Asian race, Brierly propounds his imperial ethic: 'We aren't an organised body of men, and the only thing that holds us together is just the name for that kind of decency' (*LJ*, 68). For Brierly Jim's real crime is not the betrayal of the *Patna* pilgrims: it is the betrayal of the idea of gentlemanly honour and heroism, the empty rhetoric of imperialism and imperialist fiction upon which Brierly's conduct is based. Like Brierly, no one in imperialist fiction could 'care a snap' for the colonized peoples: they care for the symbol of Empire and the belief in the rightness of English imperial rule. Jim is, as Parry says, 'recognisably the product of imperialism's Service classes':

> His idiom is reminiscent of a Boy Scout, his demeanour that of a disgraced subaltern eager for the chance to prove his true worth, and the youthful dreams which had set him apart from his more tractable companions on the training ship are taken chapter and verse from popular colonial fiction, retaining intact the veneration of endurance and leadership native to the genre. (Parry, 79)

Except, of course, the genre of imperialist fiction does not question the fitness of its heroes. Jim demonstrates 'unfitness' to lead, to rule, and an inability to disguise his primitive self beneath a veneer of white 'civilized' behaviour, despite the fact that he seems to stand for the very class he betrayed.

Rather than face the implicit emptiness of the idea on which his own reputation is based, Brierly wishes to hide the truth and perpetuate the illusion. 'If he went away all this would stop at once', he says to Marlow. 'I wish he had never come out here' (*LJ*, 67–8). Jim disturbs the peace of Brierly's belief in 'professional decency', just as the *Patna* disaster disturbed Jim's belief in a benign universe and his own potential for romantic heroism. Both men attempt to hide what Parry calls, 'a stance dependent on keeping up formal appearances and devoid of moral content' (Parry, 83) under a cloak of respectability. So Jim, with his English sense of duty and justice, faces the trial, and Brierly, outraged by the threat to the ideal that Jim's jump represents, wants him to 'creep twenty feet underground and stay there' (*LJ*, 66). When Jim refuses to disappear it is Brierly who is destroyed. His meticulous suicide anticipates Jim's ritual sacrifice; leaving the faithful dog under the care of Jones, Brierly prefigures Jim's entrusting of Jewel to Tamb' Itam before walking to certain death. In their inheritance, their dreams, and their deaths Jim and Brierly have much in common.

In his article 'Well Done', written for the *Daily Chronicle* in 1918, Conrad puzzles over what it was that made the British merchant seamen so special:

> But what was most difficult to detect was the nature of the deep impulses which these men obeyed. What spirit was it that inspired the unfailing manifestations of their simple fidelity? No outward cohesive force of compulsion or discipline was holding them together or had ever shaped their unexpressed standards. It was very mysterious. At last I came to the conclusion that it must be something in the nature of the life itself; the sea-life chosen blindly, embraced for the most part accidentally by those men who appeared but a loose agglomeration of individuals toiling for their living away from the eyes of mankind. Who can tell how a tradition comes into the world? We are children of the earth. It may be that the noblest tradition is but the offspring of material conditions, of the hard necessities besetting men's precarious lives. But once it has been born it becomes a spirit. Nothing can extinguish its force then. (*NLL*, 183)

'Deep impulses', 'spirit', 'simple fidelity', and 'unexpressed standards' are placed in opposition to an 'outward cohesive force of compulsion or discipline'. It is the former that Jim and Brierly lack and the latter on which Brierly bases his faith. Conrad values the 'simple fidelity' and points to the futility of imposed ideas. The idea of the English gentleman and the romantic illusions of imperial heroism are insubstantial because they are rigid codes of conduct and ideas imposed from without. A moral grounding is required for such notions to have real meaning.

Outward discipline cannot defeat an inner weakness, but the inner strength of a 'simple fidelity' gains the force of an indomitable tradition. Brierly lacks the inner conviction. When Jim fails to live up to the imposed code of gentlemanly behaviour by his lack of human decency in abandoning the pilgrims that code is revealed as a sham. This too throws some light on Jim's failure. He comes to the sea looking for the glamour and adventure of boys' adventure novels. Hence, he singularly fails to be absorbed into that community of sailors working together. He imagines himself too fine to be associated with the common sailor. When he fails to participate in the rescue on board the training ship Jim 'could detect no trace of emotion in himself', and 'unnoticed and apart from the noisy crowd of boys, he exulted with fresh certitude in his avidity for adventure, and in a sense of many-sided courage' (*LJ*, 9). But this is not good enough. As Robert Heilman says: 'Jim is the prototype of the boy who "makes good," but what Conrad does is to explode the popular stereotype by ultimately defining the "good" in qualitative and spiritual instead of quantitative terms' (in Kuehn, 108). Jim may dismiss his fellow trainees as a 'noisy crowd of boys' by quantifying his own imagined heroism, but, lacking the spiritual dimension required for true heroism, he is demonstrably 'not good enough'.

The English gentleman: the verdict

English, French, Malay, Australian: Marlow consults half the world on Jim's jump. But it is not just Jim who is under scrutiny: it is the whole idea for which he stands and the soundness of the 'elect' of the Empire that comes into question. When Jim says to Marlow, 'I am—I am—a gentleman, too' (*LJ*,131), he asks for an affirmation of his status. Marlow's hasty 'Yes, yes,' indicates more than a hint of doubt. After all, the gentlemanly code insists on honour and the protection of weaker souls. Jim lost his honour when he jumped and betrayed the *Patna* pilgrims. Thus Marlow expresses a deep anxiety about Jim's status as a representative of 'fit' Anglo-Saxon youth – and, by implication, about Anglo-Saxon youth generally. Jim's 'shadowy ideal of conduct' is based on nothing more substantial than a 'course of light holiday literature' and the rhetoric of nineteenth-century public schools. Once the hollowness of the ideal is revealed Brierly leaps into oblivion, his self-esteem in tatters, the faith of the Malays in the imperial system is revealed as misplaced when the system abandons them, and the would-be imperial gentleman hero is left prey to the degenerate outcast Chester.

The idea of the gentleman is as imaginary as the heroes of *The Coral Island*, *Mr. Midshipman Easy*, or even *With Clive in India*. Real-life heroism is as unglamorous as Bob Stanton's semi-comic altruism when he attempts to save the ladies' maid. It is as prosaic as the blind faith of the *Patna*'s Malay crew. The fantasy world of boys' adventure fiction is dangerous because it offers a rigid formula for success on the imperial stage, and a stereotyped ideal of male heroism and gentlemanly conduct. Jim is a victim of the ideal and the imperial ideology that such literature perpetuates. His presence in the East, and his failure, ripple out into the lives of others and challenge the soundness of their belief in the existence of a 'true gentleman' because that belief is based upon the same notions from which Jim created his own self-image.

An indulgent father and his chosen son

Without the reputation and tropes of heroic achievement Jim sinks into a pre-adult state within which he is even more reliant upon his imagination and infinitely more open to suggestion. Marlow, despite his scepticism, clings to the last vestiges of romantic heroism in Jim's imagination, somehow hoping that this romantic heroism can be achieved. For, if Jim, with all his symbolic power, disappears so does the romantic ideal. Jim's childlike demeanour at this point is suggestive of a possible salvation, and Marlow clings to this notion nearly as much as Jim does himself. He follows Marlow 'as manageable as a little child, with an obedient air' (*LJ*, 170). There is awakened in Marlow, the ironic old bachelor, a paternal feeling to which he must respond. He realizes that 'There was nothing but myself between him and the dark ocean. I had a sense of responsibility' (*LJ*, 174). Moreover, Marlow is not the first fictional surrogate father to have such a sense of responsibility for a floundering young protégé. When Marryat's Jack Easy comes to the notice of Captain Wilson, the Captain debates with his first-lieutenant, Sawbridge, how to educate the boy:

> 'But we must proceed a little further: suppose that you were to find that the lad was not all that you could wish,—that he had imbibed erroneous doctrines, which would probably, if not eradicated, be attended with consequences fatal to his welfare and happiness, would you therefore, on that account, withdraw your protection, and leave him to the mercy of others, who had no claims of gratitude to sway them in his favour?'
> 'Most certainly not, sir,' replied Sawbridge; 'on the contrary, I would never part with the son until, by precept or otherwise, I had set him right again ...' (*MME*, 49)

Marlow is too much of a cynic to believe that he can set Jim 'right again', but he is still loyal to the ideal that Jim represents, an ideal he cannot easily abandon to the schemes of the degenerate Chester. Envisaging Jim as if indeed stranded on Walpole Reef, Marlow's respect for the order from which Jim came is laid bare: 'My compassion for him took the shape of the thought that I wouldn't have liked his people to see him at that moment' (*LJ*, 173). Allan Hunter points to Marlow's and to Brierly's desire to gloss over Jim's failure, but outlines the cost of such compassion: 'Marlow helps Jim, and Brierly wishes to help him, both wishing to excuse his failings. To do so, however, they are both prepared to make concessions to their own established moral senses, and thus threaten to subvert their own integrity' (Allan Hunter, 52). Jim's refusal to accept Brierly's compromise, however, forces Brierly to confront his own potential for failure. The difference for Marlow is that he has no romantic illusions about himself; but he does have a desire to preserve the symbolic 'son'. Marlow's compassion, aligned with his scepticism, shows a depth of understanding that Brierly's introspection prevents and the French lieutenant's rigidity forbids. As he does with Kurtz's 'Intended', Marlow bolsters the illusion to protect the ideals of others. It is a chivalrous urge; it is also a conscious decision to keep at bay that vision of chaos that would prevail were the 'chosen son' to sink without trace.

Kipling's Kim is helped out of the squalor of his birth and childhood through the paternal intervention of Colonel Creighton; Alan Breck carefully nurtures Stevenson's David Balfour into heroic manhood; and Haggard's Leo Vincey is constantly under the watchful eye of Horace Holly.[5] Marlow, like Lingard, responds to the same paternal urges. At times it even seems as if the narrative will develop into the romantic mode, as when Marlow envisages a time when he would see Jim 'loved, trusted, admired, with a legend of strength and prowess forming round his name as though he had been the stuff of a hero' (*LJ*, 175). But Marlow's 'as though' gives the game away: this is not a romantic adventure yarn; it is a modernist tale of scepticism about the very values the imperial romance celebrates. Thus Jim's schoolboy idiom and naive belief that 'Some day one's bound to come upon some sort of chance to get it all back again' (*LJ*, 178) have a particularly hollow ring in the light of Brierly's suicide and Marlow's sombre musings.

Jim's failure to step out of the fictional future he imagines for himself is particularly evident in his language. His idiom is that of the boys' adventure hero: Marlow's room is 'jolly convenient—for a chap—badly hipped' (*LJ*, 178). Such schoolboy language makes him seem peculiarly two-dimensional, as when he tries to thank Marlow for his introduction to the 'cynical more than middle-aged bachelor':

> 'What a bally ass I've been,' he said very slow in an awed tone. ... 'You are a brick,' he cried next in a muffled voice. He snatched my hand as though he had just then seen it for the first time, and dropped it at once. 'Why! this is what I—you—I' ... 'I would be a brute now if I....' and then his voice seemed to break ... 'I must go now,' he said. 'Jove! You *have* helped me. Can't sit still. The very

thing…' He looked at me with puzzled admiration. 'The very thing…' (*LJ*, 184)

This is the language of Tom Brown or Henty's Charlie Marryat, the language of the public-school-educated imperial adventurer on his way to wrest glory and wealth from the outposts of the Empire. Its bluff naivety and assumptions of gentlemanly behaviour betray Jim's self-image as a superior sort of 'chap'. Even Marlow comments that 'he looked a dear good boy in trouble' (*LJ*, 180). The urgency and confidence of Jim's language naively suggests that life really can be lived like a novel: 'I always thought that if a fellow could begin with a clean slate…And now you…in a measure…yes…clean slate' (*LJ*, 185). Marching out of the room with the deliberation and self-confidence of an imperial hero, Jim has, with Marlow's help, wrapped himself in the mists of adventure fiction and subsumed his guilt beneath a self-created fantasy. Bruce Johnson explains that Jim 'believes he has an ordained identity as a hero, a predetermined self which, though experience may temporarily frustrate its appearance, will ultimately shine forth'. Johnson says that like Stephen Crane's hero, Henry Fleming, in *The Red Badge of Courage* (1895), 'Jim believes that some people are created courageous, others not' (Johnson, 60). That may be so, but Fleming learns to acknowledge his weakness and to move forward in the awareness that heroism is not inherent, but a learned response through hard experience. Jim refuses to accept his own fallibility; he cannot progress out of his self-made fictional destiny.

It is thus left to Marlow to strike the jarring note and remind us that actual existence is anything but romantic:

> But as to me, left alone with the solitary candle, I remained strangely unenlightened. I was no longer young enough to behold at every turn the magnificence that besets our insignificant footsteps in good and in evil. I smiled to think that, after all, it was yet he, of us two, who had the light. And I felt sad. A clean slate, did he say? As if the initial word of each our destiny were not graven in imperishable characters upon the face of a rock. (*LJ*, 185–6)

This is a Marlow who is deeply sceptical about the possibilities of romantic heroism for a 'son' who has already proven that he is 'not good enough'. Even so, Marlow betrays his own yearning for the 'flutter of light' (*LJ*, 128) that Jim rekindles in his imagination. His sadness at the thought of Jim's possession of that light is the sadness of the indulgent parent who knows that innocence is but the first stage in human psychological development. As the Marlow of *Heart of Darkness* knows only too well, disillusion inevitably follows.

The very thing

Jim, like Ouida's Bertie Cecil, hides his shame beneath an incognito and embarks upon a nomadic existence. There is a difference, however: Cecil assumes his brother's guilt to protect a woman's reputation, Jim's guilt is real, and it is his own reputation that he is trying to resurrect. Believing Marlow has provided him with the 'very thing' to 'wipe his slate clean', Jim resumes his self-created role as the romantic hero. Marlow's friend, like Marlow himself, responds to the ideal of English youth that Jim appears to represent:

> Had he been a girl—my friend wrote—one could have said he was blooming—blooming modestly—like a violet, not like some of these blatant tropical flowers. He had been in the house for six weeks, and had not as yet attempted to slap him on the back, or address him as 'old boy,' or try to make him feel a superannuated fossil. He had nothing of the exasperating young man's chatter. He was good-tempered, had not much to say for himself, was not clever by any means, thank goodness—wrote my friend. (*LJ*, 187)

This Jim could have been the creation of Thomas Hughes. Arnold would have been proud of him and Tom Brown not ashamed to shake his hand and own him as a friend. Jim has a girl's 'freshness' and aspect of purity; he is self-confident without arrogance; he has a proper veneration for his elders. Marlow's friend cannot imagine him 'guilty of anything much worse than robbing an orchard' (*LJ*, 188). But Jim is capable of much worse: when he metaphorically 'jumps', abandoning his position to avoid detection, he exposes the consciousness of his crime and his inability to face it.

Thus, when his past threatens to burst in on the fantasy and sully its purity Jim plunges into another adventure mode: Egström's plucky and enterprising errand boy whose star is rising. He has the vigour, good humour, and competence of Ballatyne's Jack Martin; his seamanship rivals that of Jack Easy. Ships' captains remark: 'Never saw a boat handled like that in all my life' (*LJ*, 194). Egström is overjoyed at his good fortune: 'Can't get a man like that every day, you know, sir; a regular devil for sailing a boat; ready to go out miles to sea to meet ships in any sort of weather...I tell you, Captain Marlow, nobody had a chance against us with a strange ship when Jim was out' (*LJ*, 194–5). But beneath the surface of his ephemeral success in these Eastern ports lies another narrative: Jim's 'formal little note of apology, which is either silly or heartless' (*LJ*, 188), and probably both, according to Marlow's friend, reveals the egotism and fear at the centre of his motivations.

Jim's jump from the *Patna* lurks ominously behind the story of his attempts to 'bury' it. As Marlow observes: 'The truth seems to be that it is impossible to lay the ghost of a fact' (*LJ*, 197). The 'clean slate' is a figment of Jim's romantic imagination. Tanner remarks that it is as if Jim thought 'it was possible to separate the deed from the man who did it' (Tanner, 39). His quest for heroism may in itself amount to a kind of courage but it is, nevertheless, also a kind of cowardice. This is the paradox that Marlow either cannot grasp or refuses to accept when he says of Jim's 'ghost':

> You can face it or shirk it—and I have come across a man or two who could wink at their familiar shades. Obviously Jim was not of the winking sort; but what I could never make up my mind about was whether his line of conduct amounted to shirking his ghost or to facing him out. (*LJ*, 197)

Cloaking himself in a romantic ideal, Jim claims superiority to the likes of the second engineer and avoids the fact of his own failings, the fact that he is capable of leaping down to the level of the cowardly crew. For, as Egström complains: 'And what the devil is he—anyhow—for to go on like this?' (*LJ*, 196). What he imagines himself to be is revealed when he announces his intention of leaving: 'Good-bye,' he says, nodding at me like a lord; 'you ain't half a bad chap, Egström. I give you my word that if you knew my reasons you wouldn't care to keep me' (*LJ*, 195). Egström can only laugh at the absurd self-importance of such a statement. Were he eloquent enough, Egström might well have borrowed Tadeusz Bobrowski's words concerning what he regarded as Conrad's father's self-destructive idealism: 'I assert only that in general poets, men of imagination and ideals, are not capable of clearly formulating the concrete postulates of existence'.[6]

Romance and reality are poised at opposite ends of the narrative: this is part of Conrad's strategy for subverting the romantic imagination. The minute Jim's disgrace surfaces within the romantic construct it propels him in pursuit of another fantasy existence where he can submerge the trembling frailty at the core of his being. He is, as Tanner says, 'attempting to get away from the world of facts altogether', and 'straining somehow to leave the earth' (Tanner, 40). Steadily retreating towards the setting Eastern sun, Jim relentlessly pursues the romantic ideal back to the place where it is most potent. As he moves further and further away from the West, the birthplace of his gentlemanly ideal, he penetrates deeper and deeper into the exotic location of the imperial romance. In the bustling centres of seaports Jim remains vulnerable; buried in the depths of a Malay village he is as far away from the destructive force of the fact as it is possible to be – or so Marlow and Stein believe.

'Something practical': Stein's solution

Marlow considers Stein an 'eminently suitable person to receive [his] confidences about Jim's difficulties' (*LJ*, 203), perhaps because, unconsciously, Marlow recognizes that Stein's romantic past is exactly the sort of history Jim desires for himself. Stein's revolutionary activities in 1848 prevent his return to Europe; Jim's jump forever exiles him to the imperial East. Furthermore, Marlow is aware that Stein's Malay trading posts would be isolated enough from white commercial activity to protect Jim from the scrutiny of his own race. Jim requires a romantic opportunity and Marlow does his best to provide it. For Parry Jim's 'romantic conscience', 'innocent individualism', and 'yearnings after an ideal' are 'at variance with his outward image as the very model of colonial manhood' (Parry, 80). Yet Jim's conscience, ideals, and yearnings constitute the myth created by imperialist literature. They are the fantasies that grown men put aside as they engage with the hard realities of life as a sailor or an imperial officer; Jim never progresses beyond these fantasies.

The remnants of Marlow's romantic yearnings linger beneath his cynical surface, still open to the suggestiveness of Jim's romantic idealism. As he consults Stein Marlow associates the German's romantic past with Jim's idealistic longings. Patusan is, as Jacques Darras observes, a 'mysterious island, on the kind of Treasure Island where two ageing adolescents, Marlow and Stein, have intended, through Jim, to restore their faith in their own devalued dreams' (Darras, 25–6). But we should not overlook the evident warning signs even as the romantic adventure is being conceived: Stein says 'incomprehensibly', 'And the woman is dead now', leaving Marlow to conclude that 'once before Patusan had been used as a grave for some sin, transgression, or misfortune' (*LJ*, 219). Furthermore, Stein's romantic career is over: he left the land of romance, Patusan, and now lives in a kind of limbo land.

Stein is often regarded as a combination of various mythic romantic types. For Hunter it is 'all too tempting to regard him as a holy man, who sits in a circle of light, devoted to the pantheism of insects' (Allan Hunter, 45). He has too something of the Merlin-like wizard, or the Prospero figure.[7] But he is also the imperial adventurer. The narrative of his mytho-romantic past reads like a brief account of a novel by Haggard. This, for example, is how in *Allan Quatermain* Nyleptha bids farewell to Curtis as he goes to war:

> Good and Umslopogaas had gone on with the army, but Nyleptha accompanied Sir Henry and myself to the city gates, riding a magnificent white horse called Daylight. ... Her face bore traces of recent weeping, but there were no tears in her eyes now, indeed she was bearing up bravely against what must have been a bitter trial to her. At the gate she reined in her horse and bade us farewell. (*AQ*, 229)

Stein recounts to Marlow how he left his wife and child at the fortified house:

> He described how she came with him as far as the gate, walking with one hand on the neck of his horse; she had on a white jacket, gold pins in her hair, and a brown leather belt over her left shoulder with a revolver in it. 'She talked as women will talk,' he said, 'telling me to be careful, and to try to get back before dark, and what a great wickedness it was for me to go alone'. (*LJ*, 208–9)

Stein, like Curtis, marries his 'native' princess and becomes a romantic hero. Quatermain comments how 'it was a marvellous thing that a man, who but little more than one short year before had entered a great country as an unknown wanderer, should to-day be married to its beautiful and beloved Queen, and lifted, amidst public rejoicings, to its throne' (*AQ*, 268). All of the trappings of the romance genre accrue around Stein: he wanders the Empire, a superior white man in pursuit of the treasures of the East (in Stein's case the treasure is rare butterflies); he is adopted by a wealthy father figure, and inherits a fortune and a prominent position; he marries a beautiful Eastern princess; he has a faithful 'native' friend/servant, Mohammed Bonzo; and he becomes involved in bloody skirmishes with unscrupulous 'native' chieftains. Henty, Marryat, Ballantyne, even Haggard could not have conceived a more stereotypical imperial romance.

But underlying the narrative of Stein's past glory is the poignancy of a present pervaded with a sense of loss, of sadness for the heroism and romance of the past. For as Stein says at the end of his story:

> Yes, my good friend. On that day I had nothing to desire; I had greatly annoyed my principal enemy; I was young, strong; I had friendship; I had the love' (he said 'lof') 'of woman, a child I had, to make my heart very full—and even what I had once dreamed in my sleep had come into my hand, too! (*LJ*, 211)

This could almost be Jim's future in Patusan. The ideal, however, cannot endure; as Saveson observes: 'Stein's recognition of the illusory nature of happiness stems from his own loss' (Saveson, 174): '"Friend, wife, child," he said, slowly, gazing at the small flame—"phoo!" The match was blown out. He sighed and turned again to the glass case. The frail and beautiful wings quivered faintly, as if his breath had for an instant called back to life that gorgeous object of his dreams' (*LJ*, 211).

Marlow's interview with Stein lies at the centre of the novel, bridging the gap between the *Patna* disaster and its aftermath, between the trial in the world of white commercial enterprise, and the misty romantic world of Patusan. He is also, as Michiel Heyns notes, 'the transitional figure between two sets of narrative terms, that of literary realism and that of the romance' (in Fincham and Hooper, 82). The 'consultation' with Stein takes place in a world suspended between the bustle of life in European capitals and the elusive world of dreams and ideals as symbolized by the butterflies, frozen as it were, in time. Hampson remarks that Chester and the French lieutenant are at opposite poles but that both define Jim as 'no good': 'Marlow's task is to find a *tertium quid*, a middle way between these extremes, to match his sense that there is more to Jim than either Chester or the French Lieutenant can perceive' (*Betrayal*, 127). Thus it is to Stein, a man who understands romantic ideals, that Marlow turns. Stein's famous advice, a 'man that is born falls into a dream', is uttered while to Marlow he seems to be carried 'out of this concrete and perplexed world':

> His tall form, as though robbed of its substance, hovered noiselessly over invisible things with stooping and indefinite movements; his voice, heard in that remoteness where he could be glimpsed mysteriously busy with immaterial cares, was no longer incisive, seemed to roll voluminous and grave—mellowed by distance. (*LJ*, 213)

He becomes insubstantial, his physical self giving way to a disembodied voice and pronouncing his enigmatic solution about the nature of existence. It is a much argued over, much analysed statement: for Watt the difficulty of interpreting what he calls 'Stein's parable', lies in the fact of its basic contradictions; Berthoud suggests that Stein 'dislocates our normal sense of the relationship between living and dreaming', and that his declaration is 'only partly endorsed by the novel as a whole' (Berthoud, 87–8). Tanner also points to the deliberate opacity of Stein's statement: 'vaguely, tantalisingly, Stein seems to be trying to synthesise his realism and his romanticism' (Tanner, 43).[8] Stein, as Marlow recognizes, 'had known how to follow with unfaltering footsteps, that life begun in humble surroundings, rich in generous enthusiasms, in friendship, love, war—in all the exalted elements of romance' (*LJ*, 217). But Stein is a realist too: he sees the essential paradox of Jim's position as a romantic and comments that it is both 'very bad' and 'very good' (*LJ*, 216). After the romantic vision Stein asserts that they must now 'do something practical' (*LJ*, 217).

Conrad, Clifford, and Kipling: how to make a man

In consulting Stein, Marlow fulfils his role as surrogate father to the romantic hero. Kipling's *Kim* generates similar paternal feelings in Mahbub Ali and Colonel Creighton, who consult over Kim's future much as Stein and Marlow do over Jim's. But while Kim is sent into rural India to prove himself suitable for recruitment into 'The Great Game', Jim is sent to Patusan as a final attempt to salvage his own ego ideal. Like Hugh Clifford's Gervaise Fornier, the young hero of 'In the Heart of Kalamantan' (1900), Jim is exiled to the heart of the Malay Archipelago. In Clifford's story the headquarters Resident discusses Fornier's future with his chief.[9] They agree that the young man is 'not the cut of youngster for any station'. The chief, however, concludes that 'it is about the only chance I can see of making a man of the fellow—an off-chance, I admit, but it's fair to give it to him' (*Tales from the Outposts*, 74).[10] As in *Kim*, these men are concerned with making a good imperial officer out of the boy; they are not concerned with his soul, as Marlow is with Jim's. It is a point of difference that Conrad clearly recognized in a letter to Clifford while he was working on *Lord Jim*. Conrad admires Clifford's style in 'Father Rouellot', published in *Blackwood's* in December 1899, but points to his own preoccupation with moral dilemmas: 'As to *Your* sketch (for it is that) in last B'wood, it has pleased me immensely. The simplicity of treatment is effective. Of course you are favoured by the subject while I have always to struggle with a moral horror of some sort' (*Letters 2*, 227). At the end of Clifford's story the unpromising youngster confounds expectations and becomes a minor imperial hero. He abandons his imagination and confronts rebellious Mûruts with a blind belief in his European superiority. Jim's exile, however, provides scope for the free rein of his imagination and the final judgement on his success or failure remains a contentious point, 'a moral horror'.

Clifford's and Kipling's heroes are overseen by successful imperial officers for whom the fate of the individual is subordinate to the needs of Empire. These men know, to borrow Stein's adaptation of Hamlet's predicament, 'how to be'. Assimilating their individual needs with the needs of the Empire, they both present a behavioural model, and are reliable judges of the actions of the hero; in *Lord Jim* Conrad makes no such clear-cut distinctions. When Marlow consults Stein it is Jim, the man, he is concerned with, not Jim the potential imperial representative, despite Jim's self-image as such. There is no absolute truth in *Lord Jim*, no rigid code to which the narrative urges adherence. The nearest the story comes to proposing a *modus vivendi* is through the tale of Bob Stanton, and that is hardly a lesson on how to live. Imperialism and the expectations placed on the Empire's enforcing officers emerge out of Jim's story as a complex web of externally imposed ideals and fragile romantic yearnings fraught with dangerous assumptions.

Still envisaging *Lord Jim* as a sketch rather than a novel, Conrad explained his 'patchwork' of characters to Clifford:

> I want to put into that sketch a good many people I've met—or at least seen for a moment—and several things overheard about the world. It is going to be a hash of episodes, little thumbnail sketches of fellows one has rubbed shoulders with and so on. I crave your indulgence; and I think that read in the lump it will be less of a patchwork than it seems now'. (*Letters 2*, 226–7)

Just as the whole of Europe contributed to the making of Kurtz, so half the world is brought in to comment on Jim's situation, on what makes a 'man'. The solutions of the self-deceived idealist (Brierly), the degenerate runaways (the *Patna* crew), and the realist (Chester) must be rejected: only Stein offers an answer acceptable to Marlow. As Marlow realizes, what Stein throws upon Jim's possibilities is a 'charming and deceptive light' (*LJ*, 215). He presents Jim with the opportunity to be a romantic imperial knight, like a hero in a book, like Sir Henry Curtis, or like Stein himself.

A leap into romance

Patusan is a remote world beyond the knowledge of western civilization. More than once Marlow compares it to a distant planet, as if by going there Jim were stepping outside of earthly existence altogether:

> Nobody, however, had been there, and I suspect no one desired to go there in person, just as an astronomer, I should fancy, would strongly object to being transported into a distant heavenly body, where, parted from his earthly emoluments, he would be bewildered by the view of an unfamiliar heavens. (*LJ*, 218)

Romance, as Gillian Beer says, 'invokes the past or the socially remote' (Beer, 2). Marlow invokes both in his initial description of Patusan. The sense of the unfamiliarity of the place is drawn directly from the romance tradition. In the works of H. G. Wells, the notion of travelling to the stars was as romantic as Hawthorne's evocation of moonlight in *The Scarlet Letter*.[11] While writing *Lord Jim*, Conrad was in close contact with Wells, who had just published *The War of the Worlds* (1898). He frequently refers to Wells's scientific romance in his letters and his admiration is made clear in this comment to Aniela Zagorska: 'H. G. Wells published this year *The War of the Worlds* and *The Invisible Man*. He is a very original writer, romancier du fantastique, with a very individualistic judgement in all things and an astonishing imagination' (*Letters 2*, 138). It is thus quite likely that Conrad had Wells in mind in making his allusion to space travel in his own novel.

Patusan is also the realm of Haggard's African romances: its split mountains recall the twin peaks of Sheba's Breasts in *King Solomon's Mines*. They symbolize the boundary between the world of struggle and survival and the world of heroic romantic adventure. Sheba's Breasts first appear to the travellers gloriously illumined by the rising sun: 'There not more than forty or fifty miles from us, glittering like silver in the morning sun, soared Sheba's Breasts; and stretching away for hundreds of miles on either side of them ran the great Suliman berg' (*KSM*, 88). Marlow sees the split hills of Patusan with the romantic, nearly full, moon rising behind: '[I]ts diffused light at first throwing the two masses into intensely black relief, and then the nearly perfect disc, glowing ruddily, appeared, gliding upwards between the sides of the chasm, till it floated away above the summits, as if escaping from a yawning grave in gentle triumph' (*LJ*, 220–1).[12]

But Conrad also makes Patusan into a '*tableau vivant*' just as he had with Karain's kingdom. The timelessness and immobility of the Patusan of Marlow's memory conjures up the painted immobility of the shore in 'Karain'. Marlow describes Patusan as 'like a picture created by fancy on a canvas': it 'remains in the memory motionless, unfaded, with its life arrested, in an unchanging light' (*LJ*, 330). Patusan is, as Heyns says, 'almost explicitly acknowledged as a creation of the artistic imagination' (in Fincham and Hooper, 85). Further parallels with the overt romance of 'Karain' are apparent when Marlow, like the crew of the schooner in 'Karain', leaves romance behind and heads for the world of Western commerce: 'I had turned away from the picture and was going back to the world where events move, men change, light flickers, life flows in a clear stream, no matter whether over mud or over stones' (*LJ*, 330). Marlow seems to question the validity of the life Patusan offers, preferring instead the struggle of the real world. Patusan is, for Marlow, a claustrophobic prison, but one from which he, unlike Jim, can escape at will.

It is as difficult for the adventurer of imperial romance to enter the romantic kingdom as it is to leave. Its glories and mysteries are only revealed after a long and arduous journey has tested the determination of the hero. In *King Solomon's Mines* an arid desert must be crossed and mountains conquered before entering Kukuanaland. In *She* Holly and Leo face death many times before descending into the caves of Kôr. In *Allan Quatermain* Zu-Vendis is reached by a death-defying journey on a sulphurous underground river. No ordinary mortal can penetrate the mysteries of the remote land of romance; only the adventure hero gains access. Many lesser men perish in the attempt, their corpses littering the path as a warning to the would-be intruder. Jim reaches Patusan after a long sea journey and a hot, uncomfortable trip up river. He takes a heroic leap out of the Rajah's stockade before truly beginning to build his mythic reputation among a trusting and simple people. Patusan is the 'clean slate' for which Jim yearns: 'He left his earthly failings behind him and that sort of reputation he had, and there was a totally new set of conditions for his imaginative faculty to work upon. Entirely new, entirely remarkable. And he got hold of them in a remarkable way' (*LJ*, 218). 'Earthly failings' suggests that, once in Patusan, Jim is no longer of the earth that Marlow and his assumed audience belong to. In Patusan childhood dreams can be realized; it is like the escapist domain of Jack, Ralph, and Peterkin's coral island. Jim, having failed in the world of men retreats back to the world of childish adventures like a Tom Sawyer or Jefferies's Bevis. He is at this point, according to Marlow, 'The youngest person now in existence' (*LJ*, 219).

Kuehn argues that 'Jim's early adventures in Patusan require little comment' (Kuehn, 11). Yet to fully understand Jim's fate his earlier exploits and his responses to them must be examined. Redmond O'Hanlon and Allan Hunter argue convincingly that Jim takes a step back in evolutionary time when he enters Patusan. Hunter says that 'Jim retreats towards the rising sun in the same way that the journey in *Heart of Darkness* takes Marlow back into primeval time, and Patusan is seen as: "in the original dusk of [its] being"' (Allan Hunter, 38). By this Marlow means that Patusan is on the threshold of existence in the modern imperial world; he invokes the primeval to emphasise the distance of Patusan from Western civilization. The area had, in fact, acquired some 'glory' in the seventeenth century through the pepper trade. But since then 'civilization' had left it behind, and its current Sultan is, according to Stein, 'an imbecile youth with two thumbs on his left hand' (*LJ*, 227). Far from emerging into civilization, Patusan is an older, degenerative form of civilization, having been bypassed by the progress of the nineteenth century, as Marlow makes clear:

> The stream of civilisation, as if divided on a headland a hundred miles north of Patusan, branches east and south-east, leaving its plains and valleys, its old trees and its old mankind, neglected and isolated, such as an insignificant and crumbling islet between the two branches of a mighty, devouring stream. (*LJ*, 226)

Jim is sent, as if back in time, to rebuild a once-glorious Empire, the pure-blooded English boy come to rescue a decadent and declining culture. By the power of his imperialist vision and his 'fitness' as an imperial representative, Jim, like a fictional hero, goes to Patusan to bring light to one of the 'dark places' of the earth. As Padmini Mongia says: 'Stein diagnoses Jim as "romantic"; the cure for that condition requires the imperialist backdrop to find expression. It seems that for Jim to express his nature, a region such as Patusan needs to be available' (Mongia, 179).

Marlow emphasizes the distance between Jim's exotic existence in Patusan and the comfortable firesides of England to which Marlow was returning. Of Jim he says bluntly: 'He would never go home now' (*LJ*, 222). His betrayal of the code is too much for the genteel English society that Marlow sentimentalizes. The return to this haven of peace and stability is the reward for hard work and fidelity:

> There are the girls we love, the men we look up to, the tenderness, the friendships, the opportunities, the pleasures! But the fact remains

that you must touch your reward with clean hands, lest it turn to dead leaves, to thorns, in your grasp. I think it is the lonely, without a fireside or an affection they may call their own, those who return not to a dwelling but to the land itself, to meet its disembodied, eternal, and unchangeable spirit—it is those who understand best its severity, its saving power, the grace of its secular right to our fidelity, to our obedience. (*LJ*, 222)

Jim's hands are unclean and thus he is barred from the 'saving power' of the land that created him.

Once Patusan and its romantic possibilities take hold of him, Jim's behaviour undergoes a transformation. His boyish excitement is, to Marlow, absurd:

He tossed his head fearlessly, and I confess that for the first and last time in our acquaintance I perceived myself unexpectedly to be thoroughly sick of him. Why these vapourings? He was stumping about the room flourishing his arm absurdly, and now and then feeling on his breast for the ring under his clothes. Where was the sense in such exaltation in a man appointed to be a trading-clerk, and in a place where there was no trade—at that? Why hurl defiance at the universe? This was not a proper frame of mind to approach any undertaking; an improper frame of mind not only for him, I said, but for any man. (*LJ*, 235–6)

But at this point Jim is no longer a man; he is the boyish hero of an adventure story, 'voluble like a youngster on the eve of a long holiday with a prospect of delightful scrapes' (*LJ*, 234). His schoolboy idiom is evidence of the regression to childhood. Shakespeare, Jim avers, is the 'Best thing to cheer up a fellow' (*LJ*, 237). His speech is peppered with expressions like 'Jove' (*LJ*, 235), 'bally' (*LJ*, 253), and the public school oath 'Honour bright!' (*LJ*, 269). Watt points to the contrast in Marlow's view of honour and Jim's unquestioning acceptance of the code. Marlow's doubts, Watt argues, reflect 'the whole modern intellectual and psychological outlook, which tends to view the code of honour as rigid, inhumane and retrograde'. Jim's 'old schoolboy oath of fidelity', says Watt, 'suggests the stuffy and hypocritical moralism of the Victorian public school' (Watt, 354). This moralism is the foundation stone of the romantic adventure fiction Jim reads and tries to recreate in his actions. Marlow, in fact, is at times drawn into Jim's fictional behavioural mode: as he takes his leave of Jim they both fall into the speech of the stereotype, Marlow calling Jim 'dear boy' and Jim responding with the words 'old man' (*LJ*, 240–1). Marlow's friend had respected Jim for his reserve in not using such familiar forms of address, but that was another Jim, one who was trying to be a 'man'.

The extent to which Jim has adopted the fictional mode is now clear. In the European world of commerce his behaviour is a conscious attempt to conform, to 'play the white man' and prove his jump to be a temporary aberration. Once in the world of romance he slips naturally into the idiom of schoolboy fiction and the gestures of fictional heroes. He wholly embraces the world of romance and misses or refuses to hear Marlow's more sombre warnings.

The ring and the gun: tools of the trade

Even before departing for Patusan Jim imaginatively immerses himself in the romance. Stein provides the 'magic' talisman, 'a silver ring, such as natives use, worn down very thin and showing faint traces of chasing' that he gleefully shows Marlow (*LJ*, 233). The ring is a 'sort of credential—("It's like something you read of in books," he threw in appreciatively)' (*LJ*, 233–4). Its evident age and native origins give the ring a romantic quality that fires Jim's imagination and reminds him of the adventure fiction he read as a boy. The ring and the letter to Cornelius represent Jim's passport to the land of romance, and he guards it like a treasure: 'Jove! Wouldn't do to lose the thing' (*LJ*, 234). For Erdinast-Vulcan it is emblematic of the very language of Patusan: 'In the world of Patusan, where the poetic or metaphoric is the culturally ascendant language, *the ring is friendship*. It is, in this sense, a charm through which, as in a myth or a fairy-tale, Jim is gifted with the quality of friendship' (Erdinast-Vulcan, 43).

His childish enthusiasm and faith in the symbolic importance of the ring denote a state of mind that is 'a little mad, dangerous, unsafe' (*LJ*, 234). Dangerous, too, to trust in the absolute power of the talisman of friendship, for in the end that very ring becomes the symbol of betrayal of the friendship. But Jim is too wrapped up in his romantic future to contemplate failure. 'I'll show yet…I'll…I'm ready for any confounded thing…. I've been dreaming of it…Jove! Get out of this. Jove! This is luck at last…. You wait,' he confidently tells Marlow, and then forgets to take the box of cartridges (*LJ*, 235). The revolver and its cartridges are the means by which white men demonstrate 'superiority' over the 'native'. Confident of his fiction, Jim forgets the necessary tools of his trade. The silver trinket, as a romance trope, has more value to Jim than the life-saving weapon. The division between the imaginary world of romance and the actual world of the struggle for survival is defined in Jim's failure to fully understand the conditions of the existence he is entering. He is indeed, as Cornelius recognizes, like a little child requiring constant supervision so as not to make mistakes that could prove fatal. Thus Marlow rushes after him to give him the cartridges, and later Jewel guards him against the assassins, putting into his hand the lethal weapon.

Allan Hunter stresses the use of technology in *Lord Jim*, that is, the use of superior firearms by the white men, to show that the success of their enterprise is ensured not by superior intelligence, but by superior weaponry.[13] Jim fails, at first, to recognize this fact. Were he a 'true' fictional hero he would appreciate, as do Henty's Hardy family in *Out on the Pampas*, that the prerequisite for any venture into unknown territory is the scrupulous preparation of weaponry. The Hardys equip themselves with the latest breech-loading rifles before embarking on their farming venture in South America; they undergo rigorous training to become expert shots. The 'Indians' have little chance against such advanced technology, being armed mainly with bows and arrows. Their outmoded muskets are sluggish and ineffectual, whereas the latest breech-loader wreaks havoc amongst the unsuspecting native South Americans: 'The Indians in front, surprised and confused, were mown down by the long rifles like grass before the mower, and those behind, after one moment's hesitation, broke and fled' (*OP*, 289). Jim dreams of romance, but has not even grasped its fundamental tenets. He embarks upon his romantic adventure ill prepared for what awaits him but brimful of confidence and belief in his own potential. Like Willems, Jim relies too heavily on his own ego ideal without assimilating the practicalities of his situation into his projected future.

A cast of colourful characters

'It's well worth seeing'

Marlow hands Jim over to the master of the brigantine that will deliver him to Patusan. If Jim and Marlow's parting words are taken straight out of a romantic adventure, then the skipper of the boat is a stereotype of the same genre: he chatters absurdly; Marlow says that his 'flowing English seemed to be derived from a dictionary compiled by a lunatic' (*LJ*, 238). O'Hanlon deems it 'biologically fitting that a half-caste, proud of his mastery of the language of an advanced society, should take the degenerate Jim to degenerate Patusan and should himself, in reality, speak a degenerate English …' (O'Hanlon, 129). But the ship's master is no fool: he has no intention of going all the way up the river, and he cryptically predicts Jim's death, declaring that 'the gentleman was already "in the similitude of a corpse"' (*LJ*, 240). A sinister suggestion of doom surrounds Jim's departure, created by the master's imp-like appearance. Marlow could 'see the little wretch's face, the shape and colour of a ripe pumpkin, poked out somewhere under Jim's elbow' (*LJ*, 241). Jim seems to be entering an enchanted world of witches and goblins, or one of Haggard's African kingdoms where ancient hags like Gagool possess dark unnatural powers. This is a land unknown to white men: when Marlow visits him nearly two years later the old fisherman pilot tells him that he is only the second white man he has ever seen; the first one presumably being Jim. Colourful characters people Patusan: beautiful butterflies like Jewel; creeping beetles like Cornelius. Jim's first real encounter with the inhabitants suggests dark suspicions of treachery. The paddlers of the canoe carrying him up river have hatched a secret plan to hand him over to the Rajah rather than take him to Doramin and relative safety: enter the 'cunning native'.

Rajah Allang is as colourful and bloodthirsty a character as any created by Henty or Haggard. Marlow tells us that his 'cruelty and rapacity had no other bounds than his cowardice':

> He hung over the town of Patusan like a hawk over a poultry-yard, but he devastated the open country. Whole villages, deserted, rotted on their blackened posts over the banks of clear streams, dropping piecemeal into the water the grass of their walls, the leaves of their roofs, with a curious effect of natural decay as if they had been a form of vegetation stricken by a blight at its very root. (*LJ*, 257)

Such is the effect of the reign of Allang 'till Jim came'. The wholesale slaughter attributed to him is a familiar romance theme: the 'Herculean' yellow-haired chief in *The Coral Island* thinks nothing of ripping a baby from its mother's arms and hurling it into the sea. Cannibalism and unmotivated slaughter are the hallmarks of the 'savage' in Ballantyne's novel. The wicked Indian ruler Tippoo in *The Tiger of Mysore*, for example, exhibits a similar bloodlust. Dick's uncle recounts how Tippoo will 'ravage the plains for weeks'. He is a 'bad native'. Hyder in comparison gains some respect since his slaughter has good economic motives: 'Hyder, no doubt, slaughtered many, but he was not cruel by nature. He carried off enormous quantities of people, with their flocks and herds, but he did this to enrich Mysore with their labour, and did not treat them with unnecessary cruelty' (*TM*, 84–5). Tippoo, 'on the other hand, is a human tiger', delighting in 'torturing his victims', and slaying 'his prisoners from pure love of bloodshed' (*TM*, 85). In the same way, Haggard's evil native ruler, Twala in *King Solomon's Mines*, relishes bloody witch-hunts. Ignosi declares that 'The land groans at the cruelties of Twala the king; it is wearied of him and his red ways' (*KSM*, 163).

Drawing on this romance tradition of brutal 'native' villains, Conrad presents Allang as a stereotype. He is old and frail, but decidedly powerful and threatening. Filth and neglect surround him, as much evidence of his degeneracy as the 'tangled strings of his mop' of hair through which his eyes fix menacingly on Jim. He smokes opium, an unmistakable sign of degeneracy. He displays the stereotype's childlike naivety in the presence of Western devices. Jim is requested to mend a clock, and expresses his 'superiority' through the disdain with which he undertakes the task: 'The Rajah wanted to know whether the white man could repair a watch? They did actually bring out to him a nickel clock of New England make, and out of sheer unbearable boredom he busied himself in trying to get the alarum to work' (*LJ*, 252).

Doramin is an elected headman, fair and thoughtful. In contrast to Allang's squalid stockade Doramin lives with his motherly wife and noble son in domestic orderliness. His appearance nevertheless evokes the exoticism of the East. He is 'one of the most remarkable men of his race [Marlow] had ever seen':

> His bulk for a Malay was immense, but he did not look merely fat; he looked imposing, monumental. This motionless body, clad in rich stuffs, coloured silks, gold embroideries; this huge head, enfolded in a red-and-gold head-kerchief; the flat, big, round face, wrinkled, furrowed, with two semicircular heavy folds starting on each side of wide, fierce nostrils, and enclosing a thick-lipped mouth; the throat like a bull; the vast corrugated brow overhanging the staring proud eyes—made a whole that, once seen, can never be forgotten. (*LJ*, 259)

Sherry identifies two real-life sources for Doramin, his wife, and entourage. He indicates the Rajah of Goa and his Queen as described in Wallace's *The Malay Archipelago* as likely originals. He also suggests as originals, Nakhoda Trong and Inche Maida, Princess of Perak, in McNair's *Perak and the Malays*. The engraving of Nakhoda, plate 7 in Sherry's book, could certainly have provided the inspiration for

Doramin's immense bulk.[14] But Conrad makes Doramin larger than life: with his massive bulk and 'ponderous movements' aided by 'two short, sturdy young fellows, naked to the waist, in white sarongs and with black skull caps on the backs of their heads' he barely escapes the grotesque (*LJ*, 259). He becomes almost comic in Jim's description of his demeanour at the top of the hill watching the debacle with Sherif Ali. Jim calls him an 'amazing old chap—real old chieftain...with his little fierce eyes—a pair of immense flintlock pistols on his knees' (*LJ*, 264). Doramin rarely speaks: his presence and exotic accoutrements sufficiently create the required romantic effect.

Doramin's 'motherly' little wife is described with the condescending affection reserved for mothers, particularly 'native' mothers, in the romance. She is the foil to Doramin's imposing bulk and taciturnity: 'They were wonderfully contrasted: she, light, delicate, spare, quick, a little witch-like, with a touch of motherly fussiness in her repose; he facing her, immense and heavy, like a figure of a man roughly fashioned of stone, with something magnanimous and ruthless in his immobility' (*LJ*, 260). They enhance Jim's fictional existence: they are 'like people in a book', and he shows them off like curiosities. 'It's well worth seeing', he tells Marlow (*LJ*, 260).

Cornelius: a beetle among the butterflies

The formula of imperial romance demands a villain: Brown performs that function, aided by Cornelius. A Malacca Portuguese, Cornelius is one of Stein's beetles, something of a cross between Almayer and Babalatchi, but without the former's pathos or the latter's eloquence: 'He reminded one of everything that is unsavoury. His slow laborious walk resembled the creeping of a repulsive beetle, the legs alone moving with horrid industry while the body glided evenly' (*LJ*, 285). With his 'little yellow face, all crumpled as though it had been squeezed together' (*LJ*, 328), and his wheedling voice, Cornelius is an archetypal villain, cowardly and repulsive. When Marlow assures him that Jim will never leave Patusan, Cornelius affects a seizure:

He leaned his forehead against the fence, and in that position uttered threats and horrible blasphemies in Portuguese in very weak ejaculations, mingled with miserable plaints and groans, coming out with a heave of the shoulders as though he had been overtaken by a deadly fit of sickness. It was an inexpressibly grotesque and vile performance, and I hastened away. (*LJ*, 329)

Like Mr Hyde, Cornelius is the underside of the human animal, venomous and destructive. Utterson is repulsed by Hyde's mixture of 'timidity and boldness'. Hyde speaks with a 'husky, whispering, and somewhat broken voice' (*Jekyll and Hyde*, 37). In the 'healthy' air of the romance Cornelius, like Hyde, is an infection, associated with illness and insanity: beetles, after all, were thought to carry disease, especially cockroaches. He speaks 'like a man in the cold fever of a fit', and Jim declares that he must 'have been off his chump in some way' (*LJ*, 292–3). His yellow skin signifies his 'unhealthiness', and when plotting to murder Jim he appears like some sick madman:

> His good-night came huskily from under the table. Jim was amazed to see him emerge out with a dropping jaw, and staring, stupidly frightened eyes. He clutched at the edge of the table. 'What's the matter? Are you unwell?' asked Jim. 'Yes, yes, yes. A great colic in my stomach,' says the other; and it is Jim's opinion that it was perfectly true. (*LJ*, 296)

Like Willems's wife, Joanna, Cornelius is half-Portuguese and carries the suggestion that 'interbreeding' weakens the race. The traits of cowardice, sickness, and imbecility are attributed to those of 'mixed blood' whose racial 'strengths' have been 'diluted' and who are consequently descending down the evolutionary scale, rather like the Beast people in Wells's *The Island of Doctor Moreau* (1896). Cornelius's slinking, cringing sideways movement suggests a dog or a beetle, associated with slums and degenerate life. Patusan is populated with romance stereotypes and Cornelius is part of that colourful cast of characters.

Dain Waris: the 'noble savage'

Marlow admits to being 'captivated' by Dain Waris. Doramin's adored only son, Dain, like Uncas in *The Last of the Mohicans*, commands respect through his reserve of manner, nobility of bearing, beauty, and his 'European mind', which singles out the noble savage of the romance. Thus Alice Munro gazes at the 'free air and proud carriage' of Uncas as she would have 'looked upon some precious relic of the Grecian chisel, to which life had been imparted by the intervention of a miracle' (*LM*, 63). Uncas proves 'a brave and noble friend' to the white colonists, as the pious Duncan Heyward had hoped (*LM*, 63). The same dignity and reserve characterizes Ignosi in *King Solomon's Mines*. He has a 'proud, handsome face', and Quatermain remarks that he had never seen 'a finer native', as if he were some kind of scientific specimen (*KSM*, 48). Ignosi, like Uncas, has something of the European about him: Quatermain is struck by the fact that he was 'very light-coloured for a Zulu' (*KSM*, 44); and he is impressed by Ignosi's refined 'mode of speech'. A prince, like Uncas and like Dain, Ignosi instinctively befriends the white men, evidence that his intelligence and moral awareness are further developed than those of his 'savage' fellow Africans. When Ignosi stands beside Sir Henry Curtis, Good comments that 'they make a handsome pair' (*KSM*, 48); and, admiring Curtis's stature, Ignosi claims kinship with him: 'We are men, thou and I' (*KSM*, 48). These traits of the 'noble savage' are threaded through the literature of the romance genre. In Buchan's *Prester John* (1910), the Kaffir Laputa (depicted in plate 16) is a 'born leader of men, and brave as a lion'. He has the 'heart of a poet and a king'. Arcoll says of him that it is 'God's curse that he has been born among the children of Ham' (*PJ*, 138).

This is the tradition out of which Dain Waris emerges. He has 'a proud carriage, a polished, easy bearing, and a temperament like a clear flame'. His silent, courteous demeanour 'seemed to hint at great reserves of intelligence' (*LJ*, 262). Being Malay, Dain is necessarily of 'small stature', but this makes him an even more suitable companion for Jim since Jim himself is 'an inch, perhaps two, under six feet'. While Jim wants to believe he is participating in a heroic romance, Dain Waris is in fact the formulaic romantic 'native' friend. In his enigmatic way Marlow senses that the romance hanging around the figure of Dain Waris hints at the deep mystery of the East: 'Such beings open to the Western eye, so often concerned with mere surfaces, the hidden possibilities of races and lands over which hangs the mystery of unrecorded ages' (*LJ*, 262). Dain is a 'being', romantically half-removed from the 'real world'. He is seen, not clearly, but vaguely suggested by gestures that hint at the poise and pride of the aristocrat.

Never heard speaking directly in the novel, Dain becomes an extension of Jim's ego, adding glamour to his position. It was 'Jim, who in consultation with Dain Waris, appointed the headmen' (*LJ*, 273). The heir apparent, Dain, steps aside and allows the white man to govern and administer a province that by rights should be his role. Jim's dazzling white presence obscures Dain's political power and allows only the romantic shimmer to be seen. According to John McClure: 'Jim monopolises the sunshine of his adopted community, hoards the whiteness of all virtues, the energy of power. Beside him, because of him, everyone else is put in the shadow, diminished' (McClure, 125–6). In contrast to Kurtz, Heyns says that Jim's imperialism is 'enlightened': 'Instead of succumbing to the lawlessness of Patusan, he imposes the structures of the society he has left...' (in Fincham and Hooper, 78–9). The dark vision of *Heart of Darkness* where the imperial hero becomes corrupt and insane is set against that of *Lord Jim* where Conrad explores a more overtly naive imperial intention.[15]

Nevertheless, the success of Jim's imperial enterprise in Patusan is tragically undercut by his betrayal of Dain and by his own sacrificial death which leaves the political stability of the area in the balance. Jim's monopoly of the Patusan community recreates the people around him. They exist in the novel only in their relationship to the white man, seen through the romantically tinted lens of Jim's vision. From being the son of the old ruler Doramin Dain becomes, more importantly, Jim's faithful and trusting friend, his presence in Patusan at once diminished and transformed. Dain acquires the romance of Jim's imagination and is seen in terms of his exotic presence, his heroic actions, and his friendship with Jim. He is in fact even less substantial than his namesake, Dain Maroola. We are allowed glimpses of Dain Maroola's inner life; he has a distinct physical presence in *Almayer's Folly* and contributes substantially to the action. Dain Waris possesses the exotic aura of Maroola, but he is more of a fictional stereotype than his predecessor. Living in the shadow of Jim's glorious reputation he is an active participant in the myth making but, like the stereotypical noble native of romance, he is subordinate to the white man.

The jewel in Jim's crown

Jewel arrives in the novel as a 'flitting white form within the house'. Her 'child-like but energetic little face with delicate features and a profound, attentive glance peeped out of the inner gloom, like a bird out of the recess of a nest' (*LJ*, 278). This is not the sexually powerful presence of Aïssa in *An Outcast of the Islands*, nor the threatening but magnificent presence of Kurtz's African lover. For the boys' adventure story tones of the second half of *Lord Jim* a more naive and physically insubstantial female presence is required. Jewel is a delicate heroine, childlike, birdlike, complementing the boyish nature of Jim's newborn character. She anticipates W. H. Hudson's heroine Rima in *Green Mansions* (1904), also associated with birds fleetingly glimpsed through the foliage of the South American forest.[16] Jewel and Rima are child-women, combining childish innocence with a soft femininity. Jewel, like Rima, is associated with the natural world of the forest which collaborates with the female to protect the male: 'The land, the people, the forests were her accomplices, guarding him with vigilant accord, with an air of seclusion, of mystery, of invincible possession' (*LJ*, 283). But 'accomplices' alludes to a crime: Marlow cannot resist ascribing to the woman the desire to fully possess the man, to imprison him. For Inniss Jewel's 'fiercely possessive love is one aspect of the familiar tropical enchantment that holds Jim where he does not belong' (Inniss, 41). Jewel is the embodiment of the land Jim has chosen for his own and which in turn limits him within its boundaries: 'There was no appeal, as it were; he was imprisoned within the very freedom of his power, and she, though ready to make a footstool of her head for his feet, guarded her conquest inflexibly—as though he were hard to keep' (*LJ*, 283).

In a new development on the love theme within Conrad's fiction Jim becomes Jewel's precious treasure, just as she is his. Jewel retains Jim's devotion to the end: it is not the world of harsh reality that comes between Jim and Jewel, rather, the world of romantic male idealism separates them. Aïssa comes to be regarded by Willems as a threat to his manhood; but, while Jim is 'jealously loved', he is also lovingly protected. The selfishness and destructive passion that dominate *An Outcast* have no place in the Patusan episodes of *Lord Jim*. Jewel's innocence and slender, youthful grace supplant the sensual details of *An Outcast* where Aïssa's suggestive poses and womanly roundness imply an active and destructive sensuality.

Jewel has the typical long black hair of the 'native' heroine, but she acquires a new romantic dimension by the addition of the boyish cap. Marlow makes specific reference to its effect: 'What I remember best is the even, olive pallor of her complexion, and the intense blue-black gleams of her hair, flowing abundantly from under a small crimson cap she wore far back on her shapely head' (*LJ*, 282). The cap, reminiscent of a public schoolboy's cap worn jauntily on the back of the head, identifies Jewel as the counterpart of the 'schoolboy' Jim. They address each other in terms that testify to the newness and freshness of youth and of childlike romantic love, untainted by the 'corrupting' eroticism of an Ayesha or an Aïssa.[17] Jim addresses Jewel with a cheery 'Hallo, girl!' and she, 'with amazing pluck', answers, 'Hallo, boy!' (*LJ*, 321). Theirs is the innocence of a boys' adventure story where sexuality is studiously avoided, and where girls are respected only if they display the 'pluck' of a boy. For example, in *The Tiger of Mysore* Dick rescues Annie, the child heroine, from slavery in an Indian harem (see plate 15). Having escorted her across the desert, referring to her always as 'child', Dick admits to his mother that Annie is a 'very plucky girl' (*TM*, 292).

Jewel is a vulnerable heroine in need of protection, but she also possesses knowledge about Patusan that is vital to Jim's survival. She watches over him like a guardian angel. When his life is threatened by Ali's assassins Jim sleeps soundly: '"But *I* didn't sleep," struck in the girl, one elbow on the table and nursing her cheek. "I watched." Her big eyes flashed, rolling a little, and then she fixed them on my face intently' (*LJ*, 294). Her knowledge seems unnatural and comic in such a childlike creature. At times she acquires the birdlike watchfulness and sagacity of Jenny Wren in *Our Mutual Friend*. When Jim realizes the trouble she has taken to protect him he 'thought he had been an awful brute somehow, and he felt remorseful, touched, happy, elated' (*LJ*, 299). No such gratitude touches Willems when Aïssa saves him from her father's murderous attack. Jim's are the simple emotions of the boy hero in response to the devotion of the plucky girl-woman. Jim loves Jewel too, for her unbounded belief in him. Jewel affirms that the assassins know Jim to be 'big, strong, fearless', and her faith in him forces Jim to confront the would-be murderers.

Jim new-creates Jewel: he names her 'Jewel' and thus bestows her identity. She becomes, in her reliance upon him, a vague reflection of Jim, almost a kind of double:

> Her mother had taught her to read and write; she had learned a good bit of English from Jim, and she spoke it most amusingly, with his own clipping, boyish intonation. Her tenderness hovered over him like a flutter of wings. She lived so completely in his contemplation that she acquired something of his outward aspect, something that recalled him in her movements, in the way she stretched her arm, turned her head, directed her glances. (*LJ*, 283)

Inniss also sees Jewel as the heroine of schoolboy literature and identifies her subtle merging of childish innocence with exotic allure: 'She represents that "dash of Orientalism on white" which Conrad once confessed, was far more likely to excite him than "the genuine Eastern"' (Inniss, 42). The 'olive pallor' of her skin and her long black hair add an Oriental mystery to Jewel's presence so that she becomes a kind of Eastern princess, but sufficiently European to merit Jim's devotion.

Her mother, a beautiful 'half-caste' woman, seduced and abandoned by her white lover and ending her days in a loveless marriage with the seedy Cornelius, contributes a romantic quality to Jewel's story. The motherless girl, abused and kept in poverty by the wicked stepfather, is a nineteenth-century Cinderella rescued by her prince, Jim. After a battery of verbal abuse Cornelius would hound her about the compound:

> Thereupon he would begin to abuse the dead woman, till the girl would run off with her hands to her head. He pursued her, dashing in and out and round the house and amongst the sheds, would drive her into some corner, where she would fall on her knees stopping her ears, and then he would stand at a distance and declaim filthy denunciations at her back for half an hour at a stretch. (*LJ*, 288)

Finally he would fling mud into her hair. It falls little short of the traditional pantomime. Jim rescues Jewel from this squalid life and elevates her to the status of wife of the powerful white lord. The fairytale elements of Jewel's story are exactly the kind to fire Jim's romantic imagination: 'He sympathised deeply with the defenceless girl, at the mercy of that "mean, cowardly scoundrel"' (*LJ*, 288). Marlow even evokes medieval legends of knights and damsels, lending their romance a mythic quality: 'I don't know so much about nonsense, but there was nothing lighthearted in their romance: they came together under the shadow of a life's disaster, like knight and maiden meeting to exchange vows amongst haunted ruins' (*LJ*, 311–12).

Jewel and Jim are frequently pictured together as soul mates deep in conversation:

> More than once I saw her and Jim through the window of my room come out together quietly and lean on the rough balustrade—two white forms together very close, his arm about her waist, her head on his shoulder. Their soft murmurs reached me, penetrating, tender, with a calm sad note in the stillness of the night, like a self-communion of one being carried on in two tones. (*LJ*, 284)

Marlow's description has the romance of William Morris, or the brief pastoral idyll of Tess Durbeyfield and Angel Clare. But whereas Inniss suggests that Jim 'dreams' this romance, it is more to the point to say that Conrad creates in Patusan exactly the conditions in which Jim's imagination can flourish, thus emphasizing his complete retreat from the complexities of the 'real' world. Jewel, then, is a deliberate romance stereotype, created to complement Patusan's 'otherworldliness'.

Yet Jewel apparently threatens Jim's heroic potential with her possessiveness; hence Marlow's nervousness as he listens to her fears. Clinging to Jim's symbolic status, Marlow expects of Jewel the nineteenth-century ideal of womanhood, the total faith of Ruskin's 'queens', and the perfect love of Ursula Halifax: 'She should have made for herself a shelter of inexpugnable peace out of that honest affection' (*LJ*, 313). But, says Marlow, she didn't have the 'knowledge', or perhaps the 'skill'. Jewel is not the 'perfect' wife because she is no middle-class English woman. McCracken speaks of the dominant masculine tone within Conrad's 'modernist textual strategy':

> Conrad's novels constantly stress the nature of the identity of the speaking subject, contrasting a subject position privileged by 'race,' gender or class against other, often marginalized subject positions. The 'boy's own' nature of Conrad's narratives constructs a romance of lonely masculinity, where ultimate self-sufficiency, the ideal of Heyst's island in *Victory*, is an unattainable utopia. (McCracken, 18)

Jim's 'lonely masculinity' demands that he stay within the enchanted world of Patusan, the only place where his heroic ego ideal can be sustained. Jewel fears his departure is a certainty. Her mother had told her, 'They always leave us' (*LJ*, 309). Aïssa's experience with Willems rings through Jewel's fears just as her mother's experience proves its repetitive pattern: white men never stay with their 'native' lovers.[18] Jewel, with the wisdom of her Malay inheritance, expects Jim to desert her.

Marlow, with his prejudices about the female intelligence, could never be equal to explaining why Jim stays in Patusan. As Jewel recounts her mother's dying words, Marlow has a vision of woman as unfathomably chaotic:

> For a moment I had a view of a world that seemed to wear a vast and dismal aspect of disorder, while, in truth, thanks to our unwearied efforts, it is as sunny an arrangement of small conveniences as the mind of man can conceive. But still—it was only a moment: I went back to my shell directly. One *must*—don't you know?—though I seemed to have lost all my words in the chaos of dark thoughts I had contemplated for a second or two beyond the pale. (*LJ*, 313).

Marlow wonders why Jewel should care for the 'world beyond the forests' (*LJ*, 318) placing her firmly back into the romantic stereotype and dismissing the chaos of dark thoughts that threaten his peace of mind. Jim's heroic ambitions cannot be realized in the 'world beyond the forests'. Jewel believes in the perfection of her 'white lord' vehemently denying Marlow's assertion that Jim 'is not good enough'. Berthoud pinpoints the paradox that ensures Jim's continuance in Patusan when he asks 'how can she believe that the truth of her irreproachable knight is guaranteed by his falsity?' (Berthoud, 91). The romantic idyll, however, is poised to collapse: Jim will leave Jewel, but not in the way she expected. Jim's utopia, built with Jewel's help, is about to come in violent contact with 'the world beyond the forests', and the truth of Marlow's assertion that Jim is 'not good enough' will be proven.

Jim the imperial hero

Doramin hopes that Dain will one day become ruler of Patusan, but this ambition relies heavily on Jim's continued presence there: 'He, too, as he protested, had an unbounded confidence in Tuan Jim's wisdom. If he could only obtain a promise! One word would be enough!' (*LJ*, 274) Doramin's fears are based upon experience of white imperialists; but he is also duped by Jim's ego ideal, believing in the heroic persona Jim creates. The 'course of light holiday literature' that prompted Jim's seafaring life also provides the model of the imperial knight on which to base his behaviour in Patusan. Apart from Marlow's occasional grim warnings, and until the arrival of Brown, Jim's Patusan experience is the stuff of imperial romance, and he is thus equal to any of the challenges he encounters.

Armed with the talismanic ring, having befriended the powerful Doramin and his son, Jim possesses all the trappings of the hero of imperial romance. Jim is 'one of us'; he never becomes 'one of them', as his failure to protect Dain Waris proves. Faced with the ultimate choice, Jim keeps faith with a degenerate member of his own race and betrays his adopted Malay family. It is a narrative pattern that recurs in *The Rescue* (1920). Despite his failures, Jim never ceases to believe in what Parry calls 'a continuing tradition embodied in unchanging mores commanding fidelity to agreed purposes ... binding on all classes and through the ages'. Parry argues that Jim remains 'one of us' by virtue of the fact that he 'never ceases to pay homage to the precepts of this commonwealth' (Parry, 88). This is the behavioural code for the imperial adventurer. Unlike Willems, Jim maintains his impeccable imperial uniform with scrupulous care. Its very rigidity inflames Brown: 'And there was something in the very neatness of Jim's clothes, from the white helmet to the canvas leggings and the pipe-clayed shoes, which in Brown's sombre irritated eyes seemed to belong to things he had in the very shaping of his life contemned and flouted' (*LJ*, 380). For Marlow Jim was like a 'figure set up on a pedestal, to represent in his persistent youth the power, and perhaps the virtues, of races that never grow old, that have emerged from the gloom' (*LJ*, 265). This is the symbolic Jim: he represents a 'superior' race which, with its Christian morality, sanctions the imperial cause believing that its representatives 'bring light' to the dark corners of the globe. It is also 'Gentleman' Jim: a personification of the chivalric order that provided the behavioural values for English manhood – the values that Brown had 'contemned and flouted'.

Hunter remarks that 'Jim may go back in time, but he does not degenerate, as his clothing shows, and he never ceases to have all the characteristic marks of a white man' (Allan Hunter, 41). But through Jim's character nothing is endorsed: rather, everything is questioned because of his failure to achieve the ideal in the 'real' world. His white uniform is a facade behind which hides a man who is 'not good enough'. Through the romance world of Patusan Conrad thus offers an ironic comment on the assumptions of white superiority in the 'real' world. The symbolic signifiers of the white man only work as a protection in the simple world of imperial romance where there are no tribunals, and where the imperial adventurer can create a utopia in the knowledge that his is the most powerful voice for miles around. Marlow knows that Jim was 'in every sense alone of his kind there':

> There was nothing within sight to compare him with, as though he had been one of those exceptional men who can be only measured by the greatness of their fame; and his fame, remember, was the greatest thing around for many a day's journey. You would have to paddle, pole, or track a long weary way through the jungle before you passed beyond the reach of its voice. (*LJ*, 272)

This type of reputation is built by feats such as the Rajah Brooke accomplished. Dragging 'two rusty iron 7-pounders' up a steep hill by use of his ingenuity with cables, Jim recreates one of Brooke's famous escapades. Gordan notes how in 1844 Brooke, when asked for help in defeating the rebels, encamped in forts on the Sarambo mountains, 'brought up guns, including two six-pounders, and bombarded the rebel strongholds until they were ready to fall apart' (Gordan, 627). In another attack by Brooke on the fortified villages of the Saribas and Paddi, Runciman recounts how the Saribas fled into the jungle and how 'Paddi was then easily taken and consigned to the flames'. Rembas resisted attack, but it too 'was stormed with little loss and looted and burnt, the inhabitants fleeing to the jungle' (Runciman, 77). This resembles Jim's description of the rout of Sherif Ali's fortifications:

> Jim told me that from the hill, turning his back on the stockade with its embers, black ashes, and half-consumed corpses, he could see time after time the open spaces between the houses on both sides of the stream fill suddenly with a seething rush of people and get empty in a moment. (*LJ*, 271)

Brooke's exploits could certainly have contributed to Conrad's vision of Jim's romantic adventures in Patusan. For, as Gordan says:

> The romance of the man and his achievement liberates the imagination from the confines of ordinary life in the fashion of a novel of adventure. There is about it, indeed, a quality reminiscent of fiction. The East, the little principality on its river back from the sea, the European protagonist, native intrigue and violence, all suggest a particular kind of novel and a particular novelist … Brooke might have stepped from the pages of a Conrad novel. (Gordan, 615)

Brooke's life was the stuff of myth and legend, the substance of romance. It belonged to the past when the possibilities for romance and adventure were available to the imperial hero. Brooke lived in a time when the East was still mysterious and unknown, and susceptible to the greater firepower of European weapons. The relative isolation of Patusan suggests the early nineteenth century when adventurers like the real-life Brooke could build romantic reputations in the exotic East.

In the still 'primitive' domains of the East the domestic disputes of 'simple natives' seem petty. For Jim a dispute over cooking pots is the infantile squabble of 'a lot of silly villagers' (*LJ*, 268). Jim's imagination reduces the Malays and Bugis to the stereotypes of imperial fiction like Haggard's gullible Africans awed by the power of a rifle, or duped by Good's use of an eclipse of the sun. The imperial romance uses the different knowledge and weaponry of European travellers to reveal the 'ignorance' of the 'native'. Thus Henty's Mr Hardy deters the 'Indians' with breech-loading carbines and the latest in war technology – rockets. Having scattered the 'black mass' of 'Indians' who were rounding up his cattle, Mr Hardy was not worried about pursuit: 'he felt sure that the slaughter of the day by the new and mysterious firearms, together with the effect of the rockets, would have too much terrified and cowed them for them to think of anything but flight' (*OP*, 164). Nearer the beast than the human, Henty's 'natives' react purely on instinct, lacking the rational faculties of their English colonizers. The English out-think their adversaries and have the weapons appropriate to an advanced society; this apparently gives them the right and the power to acquire the land inhabited by the native South Americans.

Jim acquires mythic status by virtue of his whiteness which makes him appear 'like a creature not only of another kind but of another essence' (*LJ*, 229). Like Kipling's Dravot and Carnehan or Haggard's adventurers, Jim's 'otherness' endows him with a godlike quality. The local population 'might have thought he had descended upon them from the clouds' if they had not seen him arrive in a canoe (*LJ*, 229). Just as Curtis is 'looked on throughout Kukuanaland as a supernatural being' because of his valour in battle (*KSM*, 268), the legend of Jim's defeat of Sherif Ali 'had gifted him with supernatural powers' (*LJ*, 266). Brian Street sees Curtis as exemplifying the growing mythological status of white men in the Empire: 'Such examples, while confirming white superiority, also reflect the growing myth, emphasised by the popularisation of the discovery of Livingstone, of white travellers who would be accepted as kings or gods among "savages"' (Street, 45).

Jim could 'settle the deadliest quarrel in the country by crooking his little finger' (*LJ*, 269). Although he claims annoyance at his mythic status, he clearly delights in it. When the 'simple folk of outlying villages' believe that he carried the guns up the hill two at a time, on his back Jim stamps his foot in irritation and, with the arrogance of the hero of imperial romance and an 'exasperated little laugh', exclaims, 'What can you do with such silly beggars? They will sit up half the night talking bally rot, and the greater the lie the more they seem to like it' (*LJ*, 266). Such reputation, glory, and apparent superior political skill are exactly the 'balm' required for Jim's wounded reputation. The fictional qualities of his life in Patusan, enable him to act like the hero he had always dreamed of being. Describing his triumph to Marlow, Jim looks remarkably like one of Haggard's heroes: 'He stood erect, the smouldering brier-wood in his clutch, with a smile on his lips and a sparkle in his boyish eyes' (*LJ*, 264).

Jim slides easily into the glib language of the imperial adventurer. The dispute over the cooking pots is 'the dashedest nuisance':

> Every bally idiot took sides with one family or the other, and one half of the village was ready to go for the other half with anything that came handy. Honour bright! No joke! … Instead of attending to

their bally crops. Got him the infernal pots back of course—and pacified all hands. No trouble to settle it. Of course not. (*LJ*, 269)

His dismissive tone indicates the 'contemptuous tenderness' (*LJ*, 248) of Jim's regard for these people.[19] Jonah Raskin sees Jim as 'a kind of Peace Corps volunteer' (Raskin, 164). Certainly on the surface his rule is benevolent and paternal, like a less self-congratulatory Lingard. Yet despite Raskin's claim that 'he does not fight savages to the death' (Raskin, 162), we should not forget the 'half-consumed corpses' in Sherif Ali's burnt-out stockade. Jim ascends to his position as nominal ruler of Patusan just as other imperial 'benefactors' do: he wipes out the opposition. Brooke's libertarian regime was only established after a series of bloody battles in which thousands died. Runciman asserts that 'no one was more determined than he that native races should not be exploited or oppressed' (Runciman, 97); but the political stability of Sarawak was achieved through a bloody rout of pirates and rebels.

Jim holds views similar to those of Brooke, and he establishes peace and stability in a previously divided community. He creates an imperial utopia where he, the only white man for miles around, holds the balance of power. Having liberated the 'slaves' of Sherif Ali, Jim assumes the mantle of the protector of the people, recognizing their reliance on his presence to preserve the peace. He says that 'for generations these beggars of fishermen in that village there had been considered as the Rajah's personal slaves'; Jim had 'changed all that'. Jim foresees political chaos if he were to leave: 'Jove! Can't you see it? Hell loose' (*LJ*, 333). He assumes a proprietorship over the people – 'my people' he calls them – as he settles their domestic disputes and keeps Sherif Ali and Rajah Allang at bay. This is his racial 'right', his historically pre-scribed role; it is at once romantic and rehabilitating, for Jim at least.

'[E]verything redounded to [Jim's] glory' because, once he has proven that he can fulfil the white man's role, power and reputation follow naturally in his wake. Patusan is, as Mongia says, not only a world of escape for Jim, but also 'a convenient space in which to achieve the heroic stature only possible in romance':

The encounter between the white man and the native 'other' sug-gests the necessity for the white man to regulate a chaotic world torn by internal strife. Jim's childish fearlessness serves him well; he quickly becomes Lord Jim by regulating the internal strife of the region in such a way that he manages the tensions between the war-ring factions of Doramin and the Rajah. Jim's dream, to play the schoolboy hero, the fearless rescuer, is realised for a time. (Mongia, 182–3)

In its romantic isolation Patusan is, as Stein realizes, the ideal place for Jim. His white imperial uniform, his public school idiom, his yearning for a world of simple choices and clear-cut morality, achieve a mythic, romantic power in such a place. Embracing the fictional stereotype of his romantic imagination and playing out his boyhood dreams, Jim becomes like a character in a book.

'So fine as he can never be'

The Patusan episode of *Lord Jim* marks a shift in tone from the sobriety of the *Patna* disaster and the subsequent inquiry. The overt romance of Jim's early adventures in Patusan confirms the power of the imperial myth. At times Conrad even seems to revel in his romantic creations. O'Hanlon suggests that Conrad overworks the stereotype, creating in Cornelius an unintentional grotesque (see O'Hanlon, 144). Marlow, too, is keenly conscious of Patusan's characters, and of its mythic qualities:

> The immense and magnanimous Doramin and his little motherly witch of a wife, gazing together upon the land and nursing secretly their dreams of parental ambition; Tunju Allang, wizened and greatly perplexed; Dain Waris, intelligent and brave, with his faith in Jim, with his firm glance and his ironic friendliness; the girl, absorbed in her frightened, suspicious adoration; Tamb' Itam, surly and faithful; Cornelius, leaning his forehead against the fence under the moonlight—I am certain of them. They exist as if under an enchanter's wand. (*LJ*, 330)

The inhabitants of Patusan are immobilized in Marlow's imagination. Frozen in time and place, like Stein's butterflies, they are the stereotypes of imperial romance. Jim, however, 'the figure round which all these are grouped—that one lives'. As a 'real' person Jim is more complex than the stereotype whose actions and thoughts are dictated by the formula of imperial romance: as such Marlow is not 'certain of him' (*LJ*, 330). Jim belongs to the 'real' world: 'No magician's wand can immobilise him under my eyes. He is one of us' (*LJ*, 330–1). If he is 'one of us' he cannot also be 'one of them', the people of romance. Marlow consigns Jim to the world of romance, but he also claims him for the 'real' world of teeming multitudes. Such duality of identity cannot endure, and the tension points to inevitable catastrophe. Jim cannot remain part of the motionless canvas of Patusan which, as Tanner says, 'partakes of that stillness and permanence which is the prerogative of a work of art' (Tanner, 49). Jim is too real to be a stereotype, too flawed to be a genuine hero, and yet possessed of too romantic an imagination to succeed in the world to which Marlow is returning: it seems to be an irreconcilable dilemma.

The 'world beyond the forest' is a release from the fetters of romance, offering the freedom to be 'not good enough' so long as you willingly join 'in the ranks of an insignificant multitude'. Marlow's sense of freedom as he leaves Patusan belies the romantic illusion of Jim's history revealing the danger inherent in the ideal:

> I breathed deeply, I revelled in the vastness of the opened horizon, in the different atmosphere that seemed to vibrate with a toil of life, with the energy of an impeccable world. This sky and this sea were open to me. ... I let my eyes roam through space, like a man released from bonds who stretches his cramped limbs, runs, leaps, responds to the inspiring elation of freedom. 'This is glorious!' I cried, and then I looked at the sinner by my side. (*LJ*, 331–2)

Jim is caught in a paradox: his romantic aspirations have been realized, but he cannot effect the imperial hero's triumphant return home. Said observes that imperial romance narratives 'serve to confirm and celebrate' the success of the 'imperial undertaking': 'Explorers find what they are looking for, adventurers return home safe and wealthier, and even the chastened Kim is drafted into Great Game'. But, 'against this optimism, affirmation, and serene confidence, Conrad's narratives ... radiate an extreme, unsettling anxiety' (*Culture and Imperialism*, 227). 'Well Done' expresses Conrad's belief that the 'simple fidelity' binding the toiling masses together is not created by an 'outward force of compulsion or discipline'. Conrad identifies an impalpable 'spirit' arising out of the 'hard necessities besetting men's precarious lives' (*NLL*, 183). This is at odds with the 'serene confidence' of the imperial romance that assumes its hero is rewarded for adherence to a strict code of conduct. In Conrad's vision the romance of Empire is a dangerous fiction that sets up unattainable and simplistic ideals of individual heroism.

Unable to accept his human ordinariness and fallibility, Jim embraces a fictional identity that is concretized in his imagination by his 'course of light holiday literature'. He resists 'the hard necessities' besetting his life in the real world of tribunals and dishonour by retreating into the childhood land of adventure fiction. In Patusan, he can rise above the masses and be unique. When Marlow superimposes the image of the very mortal, very flawed Jim upon the Patusan fantasy the dream is emptied of meaning. Jim's pauses, his gloomy mutterings, and his moody remarks indicate his yearning to accompany Marlow back to the 'world of grown men'; but Jim must remain, Peter-Pan-like, in a world where he can never grow up. He will be as Cornelius says 'just like a little child', and like a child he remains vulnerable.

Sailing back to the world of real and constructive activity, Marlow sees Jim's symbolic figure poised between the shore of Patusan and the brink of the sea leading to Europe. He is forlorn and isolated, diminishing as Marlow moves further away and swallowed up by the darkness that surrounds him. The dazzling whiteness of Jim's figure is opposed to the darkness that engulfs him. This 'whiteness', both racial and symbolic, will be no proof against what Brantlinger calls 'the cold, destructive emptiness at the heart of empires' (*Bread and Circuses*, 140). The romantic idyll is about to be invaded by the forces of darkness that reveal the shallowness of ideals based upon externally imposed codes of behaviour. With the arrival of Brown, Marlow's dimly recognized misgivings about the substantiality of Jim's heroic reputation are tested and proven. Jim, Jewel, Doramin, his wife: all those who had based their future happiness upon Jim's reputation are about to discover a truth learned by Hardy's Elizabeth-Jane in *The Mayor of Casterbridge* (1886), that 'happiness is but an occasional episode in the general drama of pain' (*Mayor of Casterbridge*, 411).

The 'real' world: breaking the dream

Erdinast-Vulcan observes that time and memory invade the world of Patusan 'in the person of Gentleman Brown' (Erdinast-Vulcan, 45). The intrusion of time is made evident as Marlow ends his tale. The romantic spell is broken and the narrative shifts briefly to a busy Western city. The 'privileged man' who reads the end of Jim's story lives in one of those countless European cities where the 'slopes of the roofs glistened, the dark broken ridges succeeded each other without end like sombre, uncrested waves, and from the depths of the town under his feet ascended a confused and unceasing mutter' (*LJ*, 337). Real life is here in the grey and thronged city. Despite its resemblance to London, Conrad leaves this city nameless and it thus represents the whole of Western Europe, Jim's birthplace, and the home of Conrad's prospective readers.

Shifting the narrative to the 'real' world, Conrad forces a reminder that Jim does not belong in the imaginary world of romance.

The opening of this chapter also jerks the narrative into the present where 'real' lives are lived. The 'privileged man' draws the curtains and locks out the 'driving rain' which 'mingled with the falling dusk of a winter's evening' and 'the booming of a big clock on a tower striking the hour'. He sighs as he sits down to read, reflecting that 'his wandering days were over' (*LJ*, 337–8): he is an adventurer who did return home. This man reads Marlow's narrative 'like one approaching with slow feet and alert eyes the glimpse of an undiscovered country' (*LJ*, 338), and the fictional nature of Jim's story is thus emphasized. It is an imperial romance, the type of story that 'England told itself as it went to sleep at night' (Green, 3).

Marlow's deliberations include a juxtaposition of Jim's life in 'The Fort, Patusan' and his father's parsonage where he is still 'dear James'. Conrad thus contrasts the romance of Jim's tale with the ordinariness of everyday life where 'placid, colourless forms of men and women' live in that 'quiet corner of the world as free of danger or strife as a tomb, and breathing equably the air of undisturbed rectitude' (*LJ*, 342). Tanner notes how the inflexible morality of Jim's father's words indicates the source of Jim's 'excessive self-concern and egoism' (Tanner, 51). His father's exhortation to never 'do any thing which you believe to be wrong' (*LJ*, 342) echoes Ben Hadden's motto, 'Do right, whatever comes of it'. It is the hollow rhetoric of the late nineteenth-century parsonage that could never provide young men like Jim with a sound philosophy for dealing with the complexities of modern life. It has the hollow ring of Farrar's moralistic *Eric*, and looks forward to the perplexity of Somerset Maugham's hero in *Of Human Bondage* (1915), who is similarly duped by the empty phrases of his parson uncle. As Tanner observes, this is a 'typical Protestant trait' (Tanner, 51).

Marlow finds it 'amazing' that Jim should belong to that world. His romantic yearnings surface when he imagines Jim returned home, like the hero of imperial romance, not as 'a mere white speck at the heart of an immense mystery', but 'of full stature, standing disregarded among their untroubled shapes, with a stern and romantic aspect, but always mute, dark—under a cloud' (*LJ*, 342). However much he may taint his narrative with ironic comments, Marlow has difficulty himself in letting go of the ideal. His abiding image of Jim acquires a symbolic force: 'It's difficult to believe he will never come. I shall never hear his voice again, nor shall I see his smooth tan-and-pink face with a white line on the forehead, and the youthful eyes darkened by excitement to a profound, unfathomable blue' (*LJ*, 343). Jim's healthy, youthful face with its blue eyes epitomizes an ideal of English youth, and the sadness of Marlow's tone reflects his sense of bereavement: he has lost a surrogate son, but, more significantly, he has lost his belief in the ideals of conduct exhibited by the heroes of imperial romance. Jim and the romantic ideals he stood for are gone.

Undercutting the narrative is a deep anxiety about the imperial venture. In his fatal encounter with Brown, Jim comes face to face with the facts of his own cultural heritage. He has to make choices that cannot be denied or glossed over. Marlow's yearning to see Jim returned home 'with a stern and romantic aspect' ignores the fact of Jim's jump from the *Patna*, his betrayal of his 'adopted' community and of Dain, and his desertion of Jewel. The 'privileged man's' belief that 'we must fight in the ranks or our lives don't count' (*LJ*, 339) is predicated on the fact that he is a racist and an imperial apologist. This man's conviction that giving one's 'life up to them (*them* meaning all of mankind with skins brown, yellow, or black in colour) was like selling your soul to a brute' (*LJ*, 339) acquires a subtle irony when one considers that Jim actually 'sold his soul' to a brute who happened to be white man named Brown. In sending the final chapter of Jim's story to this man Marlow seems to be sending out a challenge to the man's racial and imperial prejudices. Marlow's tone is often notoriously difficult to gauge – here it could be read as aggressive. Sitting in his comfortable flat, in a dreary European city, with his ideas about the 'morality of ethical progress', and reading a tale of imperial adventure this 'privileged' man appears to represent the popular late nineteenth-century consciousness. The end of Jim's story could thus be read as an invitation to the reader and to the 'privileged man' to question whether the imperial paradigm ever existed. In ascribing these ideas to the 'privileged man' Conrad effectively distances himself, and Marlow, from the racist and jingoistic implications of the man's statements. Where Conrad and Marlow stand on the issue of imperialism is thus, as ever, left unclear.[20]

Marlow reaches a sombre conclusion concerning Jim's fate:

> The imprudence of our thoughts recoils upon our heads; who toys with the sword shall perish by the sword. This astounding adventure, of which the most astounding part is that it is true, comes on as an unavoidable consequence. Something of the sort had to happen. (*LJ*, 342–3)

Marlow finally gives in to the fact that 'there is no disputing its logic' (*LJ*, 343). Despite the fact that his adventure is 'romantic beyond the wildest dreams of his boyhood', a flaw in Jim's character that under-mines the imperial ideal dictates the logic of its conclusion. As such Ernest Bevan sees similarities with Hardy in Conrad's belief that charac-ter is 'largely fixed; no amount of reflection or experience can conquer or alter, fundamentally, who one is, as men are destined to live out the private and social effects of their psychologies' (Bevan, 91). The dream was bound to be broken because only in the dream could Jim be as ideal as he imagined himself to be. As Andrzej Gasiorek observes, *Lord Jim* 'dis-closes the way that popular literature translates a life like Brooke's into a mythic idiom and then shows what can happen when a naïve reader like Jim tries to translate myth back into reality' (Gasiorek 99–100). In Conrad's fiction ideals such as Jim's are insubstantial, even dangerous.

'Something of the sort had to happen'

As though beginning a new romantic narrative altogether Marlow commences the last chapter of Jim's existence with the swashbuckling exploits of Brown: 'It all begins with a remarkable exploit of a man called Brown, who stole with complete success a Spanish schooner out of a small bay near Zamboanga' (*LJ*, 344). It all begins romantically enough too, but the sordid details of Brown's final days cast a shadow over the narrative with a grim foreboding of tragedy. The 'ugly yellow child, naked and pot-bellied like a little heathen god' (*LJ*, 345) perched at the foot of Brown's couch adds the same sense of the grotesque to the ensuing story as the captain of the brigantine that conveyed Jim to Patusan.

The bloodthirsty, piratical history of this 'son of a baronet' is recounted with relish. He is a reckless desperado in the tradition of romance villains like Long John Silver. An unscrupulous, if likeable, rogue, Silver thinks of himself as a 'gentleman of fortune'. When Jim Hawkins considers the meaning of this term he concludes that it 'meant nothing more nor less than a common pirate' (*TI*, 63). Then there is the villain Elzivir of John Meade Falkner's *Moonfleet* (1898), a cunning and manipulative scoundrel to the last. Conrad, of course, used actual men as well, as indicated by Sherry and suggested by Lieutenant-Cdr Andrew K. M. Browne, who identify possible originals from the colourful personalities Conrad may have heard of in his voy-ages in the Malay Archipelago and Australia.[21] Brown's bungled inva-sion of Patusan is recounted with the pace and romantic detail of Stevenson's adventure classic. By the time he and his band of cut-throats are stranded up river in Patusan they are established as a des-perate troupe equal to any atrocity they feel it necessary to commit: Jim's nemesis is at hand.

In rehabilitating his ego ideal by assuming leadership of the Patusan community, Jim renders defenceless the very people he purports to protect. The irony of this is apparent when Marlow recounts how Dain Waris fails to move his people: 'He had not Jim's racial prestige and the reputation of invincible, supernatural power. He was not the visible, tangible incarnation of unfailing truth and of unfailing victory. Beloved, trusted, and admired as he was, he was still one of *them*, while Jim was one of *us*' (*LJ*, 361). Dain Waris, the rightful heir to power in Patusan, is rendered politically powerless by Jim's legend: the people have bought the myth so far as to believe Jim little short of a god. His fiction has become so powerful that he can no longer control its proportions. Just as he has benefited by the 'native' tendency to create legend out of actual events so he will suffer by it.

In accordance with the demands of imperial romance Brown had to be defeated, wiped out. Jewel and Dain as bona fide romance types argue for this course of action. But Jim is a fabricated romance type and a false god. It is ironic that Jim 'was the only one in Patusan who possessed a store of gunpowder' and the only one not prepared to use it. The forces of darkness manifest in Brown, his cronies, and the venomous Cornelius are now in the ascendance, and Jim is not 'good enough' to counter their power. Cornelius, like Caliban, tells Brown, the latter-day Stephano, that all he has to do is to kill Jim (who has assumed Stein's Prospero role) 'and then you are king here' (*LJ*, 368). Prospero makes the conscious choice to abandon his magic and rejoin the band of ordinary mortals, albeit in the elevated position of Duke of Milan. Jim is unequal to such a renunciation: he can never return to the land of his birth. Jim's 'magic' rests in his white imperial uniform, and the 'racial prestige' that guarantees his reputation among the Malays: it is not enough.

Emerging from the 'knot of coloured figures', Jim is the epitome of the English adventuring hero: wearing 'European clothes, in a helmet, all white' (*LJ*, 379) he stands out against the brown bodies surrounding him. When Jim meets Brown across the creek where he leapt into romance, it is like the meeting of two separate worlds. Brown's antagonism at the sight of Jim underscores the impossibility of the merging of the universe of the romantic and the sordid underside of the actual, and indicates, as Roussel says, the impossibility of Jim's 'attempt to free himself from the life of men' (Roussel, 98). Jim, with child-like naivety, attempts the impossible and precipitates the tragedy that engulfs the lives of all those who had trusted in him. For Marlow their conversation 'appears now as the deadliest kind of duel on which Fate looked on with her cold-eyed knowledge of the end' (*LJ*, 385). Describing the shooting of the Bugis villager Brown demonstrates an awful ruthlessness. Yet Jim fails to see the implications: Brown is not to be trusted. Appealing to their common racial identity Brown clouds Jim's judgement. A dead 'native' is of less importance than Brown's dead white comrade in this discourse. Having suggested their racial bond, Brown presses the point home:

> He asked Jim whether he had nothing fishy in his life to remember that he was so damnedly hard upon a man trying to get out of a deadly hole by the first means that came to hand—and so on, and so on. And there ran through the rough talk a vein of subtle reference to their common blood, an assumption of common experience; a sickening suggestion of common guilt, of secret knowledge that was like a bond of their minds and of their hearts. (*LJ*, 387)

For some critics it is enough to comment that Brown claims kinship through racial identity, unknowingly touching Jim's most vulnerable point, his desertion of the *Patna*; but in fact several things are happening. The 'common guilt' is also the guilt of Adam. Erdinast-Vulcan centres her argument upon the parallels between *Lord Jim* and the myth of Eden and argues that 'Jim tries to regain the wholeness of Adam in the garden of Eden', but, being human, he 'cannot erase the mark of Cain' (Erdinast-Vulcan, 45). Jim has not, in fact, murdered anyone, but his betrayal of the *Patna* pilgrims is a significant transgression, and his rout of Sherif Ali's stockade clearly resulted in many deaths. Brown appeals not only to racial identity but to a common Christianity that apparently 'elevates' them above the Bugis natives. A simple Christian logic is evoked when Brown argues that the death of the Bugis was 'a life for a life' (*LJ*, 386). Jim, the parson's son, cannot annihilate Brown, another Christian soul, as he annihilated Sherif Ali's Muslims. The imperialist discourse is dominant here: Jim is so intensely caught up in the romantic notions of the imperial venture that Brown's insinuations are particularly apt.

Brown is also Jim's evil other, the doppelgänger. Like Dostoevsky's underground man or Stevenson's Hyde, Brown is the evil side of the human personality, pure malevolence, in contrast to Jim's symbolic status as the spirit of moral correctness and white superiority. He appeals to Jim's understanding of human nature just as the degenerate trio of the *Patna* had appealed to the instinct for self-preservation. Brown touches the nerve of Jim's recognition of their common human impulses and Jim implicitly acquiesces in the logic that when 'it came to saving one's life in the dark, one didn't care who else went—three, thirty, three hundred people' (*LJ*, 386). The animal impulse in Jim made him desert the three hundred *Patna* pilgrims to what he believed was certain death, and unknowingly Brown confronts Jim with his own 'original sin'.

Brown also appeals to Jim's romantic imagination. In the world of imperial romance a very simple code is enforced: whites are superior and one remains loyal to one's own race. Brown's insinuation that Jim has 'gone native' suggests that he had committed one of the worst possible crimes for the imperial adventurer: given in to the alluring temptations of the 'barbarous' and the 'primitive'. At Jim's suggestion that he would kill him Brown appeals to Jim's racial identity: 'I told him that sort of game was good enough for these native friends of his, but I would have thought him too white to serve even a rat so' (*LJ*, 381). Brown 'had a satanic gift of finding out the best and the weakest spot in his victims' (*LJ*, 385). Jim's weak spot is his romantic idealism. When Brown says, 'We don't ask you for anything but to give us a fight or a clear road to go back whence we came....' (*LJ*, 382), he invokes Tom Brown's English sense of fair play, of playing by the rules laid down in the boys' adventure story and in public school education. When Jim responds with 'Will you promise to leave the coast?' (*LJ*, 387), he could almost have added his schoolboy oath, 'Honour Bright!' Jim remains 'true' as Stein says, true to his role as romantic adventure hero: he responds to the appeal to racial identity, to Christian morality, and to the white man's romantic code of honour: Brown has defeated him.

The 'real' world tracks Jim down in the form of 'Gentleman' Brown, who is, of course, no gentleman; and we should not miss Conrad's irony in presenting him as an impostor. If, like his later counterpart, 'Gentleman' Jones in *Victory* (1915), this degenerate, murderous 'son of a baronet' can call himself a gentleman then the notion of what constitutes a gentleman is called into question. In the 'real' world where Jim belongs, where Marlow has claimed him as 'one of us', there are no certainties. As an 'agent of darkness' Brown bursts upon Jim's utopia, confronting him with the 'real Jim' lurking beneath the projected heroic image. For Hampson 'Brown has the same effect on Jim as Jim has on Brierly: he represents a secret fear and a secret guilt, the self-mistrust that is part of a personality constructed on identification with an alterated identity' (*Betrayal*, 125–6). Brown's identity as 'gentleman' is as false as Jim's identity as romantic hero. His arrival in Patusan disrupts the peaceful fabric of Jim's romantic existence there just as the *Patna*'s collision with the unidentified object jerked him out of his confidence in a benign universe. The placid surface in which Jim trusts contains hidden depths: the catastrophe that Brown precipitates, like the unforeseen object on which the *Patna* foundered, is a reminder that, in the dawn of the twentieth century, the certainties and optimism of nineteenth-century imperial literature can no longer be taken for granted.

The end of romance

In the imperial romance a white man's word should guarantee his honour. But, as Marlow observes: 'It is evident that he did not mistrust Brown; there was no reason to doubt the story, whose truth seemed warranted by the rough frankness, by a sort of virile sincerity in accepting the morality and the consequences of his acts' (*LJ*, 394). That Jim does not sense the 'almost inconceivable egotism of the man' signifies his complete trust in the formula of boys' adventure stories. Brown is a conventional villain and as such must be treacherous; but this man has compromised Jim's heroic status, his soundness of judgement. No hero of imperial romance could be made to wince, as Jim does, by the villain's words. Brown causes him to doubt his position in Patusan. When Jim says, 'I don't know whether I have the power' (*LJ*, 388), he admits his human fallibility. His wavering over whether to give Brown a 'clear road' or a 'clear fight' is the moral dilemma of the 'real' world, not the clean choice of romance. The true romance hero knows what course of action to take: Brown should have had a clear fight in which Jim would have emerged victorious; but Brown and his cronies are 'the emissaries with whom the world he had renounced was pursuing him' (*LJ*, 385). Convincing the sceptical Doramin to let Brown go, Jim steps out of the role of romantic hero and makes a fatal error.

Brown's act of vengeance demythologizes Jim, revealing the fallible human being cloaked in the garb of a romance hero: Jim will never be equal to the 'opportunity which, like an Eastern bride, had come veiled to his side' (*LJ*, 416). In the end it is Tamb' Itam, the faithful retainer of the romance tradition, who alone is capable of positive action. Tamb' Itam describes the death of Dain, that princely son, who like Uncas, should have ensured the continuance of his line. With the grim deliberation of a Chingachgook, he dispatches Cornelius; it is more than Jim is capable of. When Jim tries to exact revenge upon Brown, Tamb'

Itam indicates the gravity of his situation. 'It is not safe for thy servant to go out amongst the people,' he says, and then 'Jim understood. He had retreated from one world, for a small matter of an impulsive jump, and now the other, the work of his own hands, had fallen in ruins upon his head' (*LJ*, 408). To the last Jim fails to recognize the enormity of his failure aboard the *Patna*: it is still 'a small matter', and he misses the connection between that betrayal of trust and the present one. Enveloped in his fantasy of heroism, Jim commits his last act of betrayal. Jewel reminds him of his commitment: 'Do you remember you said you would never leave me? Why? I asked you for no promise. You promised unasked—remember' (*LJ*, 412). When Jim replies, 'Enough, poor girl...I should not be worth having', he has already committed himself to his 'romantic' self-sacrifice.

The closing scenes underscore Jim's deliberate romantic gestures: the logical conclusion to his particular romance is death. The stoicism of his final departure from Jewel is self-conscious melodrama, with the hollow and superficial gestures of the romance novel, such as we see in plates 6 and 15:

> She ran after them a few steps, then fell down heavily on her knees. 'Tuan! Tuan!' called Tamb' Itam, 'look back;' but Jim was already in a canoe, standing up paddle in hand. He did not look back. Tamb' Itam had just time to scramble in after him when the canoe floated clear. The girl was then on her knees, with clasped hands, at the water-gate. She remained thus for a time in a supplicating attitude before she sprang up. 'You are false!' she screamed out after Jim. 'Forgive me,' he cried. 'Never! Never!' she called back. (*LJ*, 413–4)

Romance is at an end: Jim's decision to meet death at the hands of Doramin is a final romantic flourish. The glance he sends 'right and left' is 'proud and unflinching', recalling how he had imagined himself as 'always an example of devotion to duty, and as unflinching as a hero in book' (*LJ*, 6). The novel begins and ends with Jim projecting himself as a fictional stereotype. In his final gesture, the romantic suicide, Jim believes he fixes an idealized version of himself in the memories of those he leaves behind. In his pride and evident self-satisfaction in this 'heroic' death Jim believes he has finally achieved the romantic proportions of the hero like the dying Quatermain of plate 6. But Quatermain has the equally heroic and romantic Curtis to sound the final note on his life; in *Lord Jim* the last words are spoken by an altogether different sort of man, the sceptic Marlow.

Jim's version of himself is not the final verdict of the novel. In his closing words Marlow presents the reader with an insoluble puzzle. Jim may well, in his last moments, have seen the face of the 'veiled' opportunity and realised his romantic ideal. But that is not enough for Marlow: Jim has also left 'a living woman to celebrate his pitiless wedding with a shadowy ideal of conduct' (*LJ*, 416). Marlow is unable to make a conclusive judgement on Jim: all he can say is, 'Who knows?', closing his narrative with the picture of the living woman Jim left behind 'leading a sort of soundless, inert life in Stein's house' (*LJ*, 416–17). Like some latter-day Guinevere, Jewel retreats to a nunlike existence, cloistered in Stein's house. This legacy of Jim's departure is also a reminder that the simple choices of the romance are inadequate when applied to actual lives. Jewel's claim that he was 'false' and Stein's rejoinder 'No! no! Not false! True! true! true!' (*LJ*, 350) are opposing views of Jim that the narrative refuses to reconcile. As C. B. Cox argues, if we try to 'sort out the enigma, we fall into simplification. The last word on Jim can never be said' (Cox, 44).

Roussel argues that the 'conception of a work of art as a self-contained, imaginative and harmonious world' is the foundation for the careers of Jim and Stein. This, says Roussel, is a 'nostalgic echo of a time when art could address itself to the ideal harmony which men thought existed beneath the phenomenal surface of events' (Roussel, 99). In death Jim believes he is affirming that harmony, but Marlow's inconclusive 'Who knows?' undercuts that belief. Conrad, the modernist writer, speaks through Marlow, indicating the questioning sensibility of the sceptic who assumes no such harmony. Marlow's perplexity is an expression of the 'moral horror' of which Conrad speaks to Hugh Clifford. Jim may, momentarily, realize his romantic aspirations in Patusan, but through his death and the conflicting responses to it of Jewel, Stein, and Marlow, Conrad questions the simple values of the romance genre. Thus, while Jim dies in the belief that he is fulfilling his role as prescribed by the imperial romance, Marlow casts doubt on the notion of heroism and indicates a more complex world in which there is no absolute truth.

As the novel closes it becomes clear that romance is at an end. When Marlow tells us that Stein, the German romantic, 'has aged greatly of late' and is 'preparing to leave all this' (*LJ*, 417), we are left to conclude that Jewel, the romantic heroine, will end her days in the frigid atmosphere of Stein's house where the corpses of beetles and butterflies are all that is left of romantic adventure. We are also left to conclude that the Patusan of the latter part of the novel, the utopia which Jim regarded as 'the work of his own hands', will disintegrate into the political chaos of the days before his arrival. With Dain Waris dead, Doramin stricken by grief, and the white Tuan no longer there to protect the people with his mythic reputation, there is nothing to prevent a return to the strife and tyranny that Jim had ended. The romance of the mythic kingdom of Patusan is, like Camelot, a fleeting glimpse of a utopia that will descend again into the dark ages.

Conclusion:
Subverting the Imperial Romance

In *Lord Jim* the motifs and formula of the imperial adventure story are self-evident, much more so than in *Almayer's Folly* or *An Outcast of the Islands*. Yet even in his earliest fiction it is clear that Conrad was concerned with many of the preoccupations of the romance and adventure genre. As Millais's painting suggests, for the late nineteenth-century British consciousness the Empire was romantic; it was the location of exoticism, and it was the location of adventure. The conquest and retention of the Empire was also perceived to confirm the 'greatness' of Britain and the superiority of her people. No writer of fiction set in the Empire could ignore these perceptions; most chose to perpetuate them. Conrad was one of the first novelists who began to question the values and assumptions underpinning imperialism at the end of the century. In some subtle and some not so subtle ways, Conrad consciously manipulated the genre of imperial romance to force a reassessment of the imperial cause and its heroes. At times, in doing so, he also managed to problematize the conventional response to the subject peoples of the Empire; yet there are occasions when he also seems to have endorsed assumptions about 'native' subjects, especially women. The effect of all this on Conrad's early Malay fiction has been the subject of this book.

Comparing the later work of Robert Louis Stevenson to that of Conrad, Andrea White observes that both writers see 'the native as the victim of imperial intrusions', but she argues, Conrad presents a more complex view of the imperial encounter:

> Imperial intrusions in Conrad's modernist texts enact a complex reality in which the intruder is associated with a cause of purported benevolence and is often a failed idealist himself, a kind of victim of

his own desires that have been shaped in complicated ways, and the native, while indeed subjugated, even brutalized, is often not innocent and rarely romanticized' (White, 197–8).

Jim intrudes upon the imperial East with benevolent intentions and realizes, briefly, his dream; however, when the real world intrudes upon the fantasy he departs as the dream collapses around the lives of those to whom he had pledged fidelity. His loyalty is ultimately only to his own 'shadowy ideal of conduct'. For, as Marlow says, 'no one is good enough'. Through his narratives of failed attempts to wrest glory, reputation, and wealth from the imperial East Conrad offers no solutions to the questions he raises; but the fact that he raises those questions is in itself a significant departure from the conventional fiction of empire. The ideals of empire and heroism that the imperial romance presents are the very ideals that Conrad takes apart, examines, and reveals as a late nineteenth-century yearning for a time past when the Empire was young.

The collapse of the imperial ideal never happens in the romance of empire. Haggard's heroes, for example, take decisive action to exclude the outside world from their imperial utopias. Sir Henry Curtis, having married a white African Queen and risen to the role of absolute ruler of Zu-Vendis, is determined to exclude all foreigners from the land: 'I do not say this from any sense of inhospitality, but because I am convinced of the sacred duty that rests upon me of preserving to this, on the whole, upright and generous-hearted people the blessings of comparative barbarism' (*AQ*, 276). Curtis goes on to say: 'Where would all my brave army be if some enterprising rascal were to attack us with field guns and Martini-Henrys?' (*AQ*, 254). Conrad provides the answer in *Lord Jim*: Brown, the 'enterprising rascal' slaughters Dain Waris's 'brave army' and precipitates the collapse of Jim's fragile utopia. In Haggard's romances the Empire is 'protected', its 'innocence' preserved; Conrad, the realist, knows that the Empire is repeatedly under threat. By dramatizing the cultural and political consequences of white intrusion he provides a perspective on imperialism that is not available in the imperial romance. The working-out of these consequences in Conrad's Malaya challenges the simple truths of the imperial romance and the 'moral horror' that he mentioned to Clifford emerges. Haggard kept the Empire firmly in the world of fantasy for the purposes of creating best-selling romance that celebrated the white imperial adventurer. Conrad, in foregrounding the conflict between the romantic aspirations of his heroes and the realities of their existence, was concerned with subverting the myth of imperial adventure in such fiction as Haggard's and questioning the very basis of assumptions about imperialism and English manhood. Such achievements as Jim yearns for belong to a previous heroic generation of Rajah Brookes, or the fantasy world of imperial fiction. In Conrad's modernist vision the individual is both beetle and butterfly, and the yearned for romantic hero of the fledgling twentieth century is only 'such stuff as dreams are made on'.

Conrad's opinion of Marryat's writing helps to explain some of his own critical perspective on the imperial romance. He says, in 'Tales of the Sea' published in *Outlook* in 1898, that for Marryat's young heroes 'the beginning of life is a splendid and warlike lark, ending at last in inheritance and marriage'. Conrad viewed the action of Marryat's novels as 'the disclosure of the spirit animating the stirring time when the nineteenth century was young. There is an air of fable about it'. He acknowledges the legacy of the events of this remote period since 'its reality affected the destinies of nations', but he avers that 'in its grandeur it has all the remoteness of an ideal'. Marryat's characters live for Conrad because they have in them 'the truth of their time' (*NLL*, 53). It was a time of 'a headlong, reckless audacity, an intimacy with violence, an unthinking fearlessness, and an exuberance of vitality which only years of war and victories can give' (*NLL*, 54). For Conrad, Marryat offered an 'insight into the spirit animating the crowd of obscure men'. This is the same spirit about which he wrote in 'Well Done'. It is the spirit that is singularly absent in Jim, in Willems, and in Almayer. Marryat, says Conrad, 'is really a writer of the Service. What sets him apart is his fidelity. His pen serves his country as well as did his professional skill and his renowned courage. His figures move about between water and sky, and the water and sky are there only to frame the deeds of the Service' (*NLL*, 54).

Jim's desertion of the *Patna* exemplifies Conrad's scepticism about the possibility of romantic heroism in the late nineteenth century. The fidelity and courage evident in Marryat's heroes is part of that 'stirring time when the nineteenth century was young'. Conrad has a sentimental attachment to the simple adventure stories he read in his youth that prompted him, like Jim, to seek a life of ocean-going adventure. But Conrad, the mature sailor and struggling writer, also recognizes the distance between the imperial adventure narrative of the early nineteenth century and the actual experience of late nineteenth-century imperialism. Like Marlow, Conrad longs for the positive action and fidelity of the time long past when romance was evident in real-life exploits such as Marryat's sea life and Brooke's imperialism. But like Marlow, too, his romantic yearnings are tempered by a deep-rooted scepticism about achieving that romantic ideal.

The hero of imperial romance is an idealist, like Haggard's Sir Henry Curtis, and always destined for glory, wealth, and power. The only 'heroes' in Conrad's early fiction are ordinary men: MacWhirr, Singleton, the Malay crew of the *Patna*, even Marlow. These men represent a new kind of hero, as celebrated in Marianne Moore's poem, 'The Steeple-Jack', who ensures that

> It could not be dangerous to be living
>   in a town like this, of simple people,
> who have a steeple-jack placing danger-signs by the church
> while he is gilding the solid-
>   pointed star, which on a steeple
> stands for hope.
>
> (*Salt and Bitter and Good*, 239)

Such men have no romantic ego ideal. Stoic, unimaginative individuals, dogged in the performance of their jobs, Conrad's 'heroes' work to save lives while never seeking, nor achieving glory. These unremarkable individuals are as essential to the safety of the ships in which they serve as the very bolts that hold the hull together: the vessel could not exist without them. In Conrad's view, modern heroism exists in the performance of the prosaic tasks of everyday life. Those men and women in Conrad's fiction who strive for a romantic ideal find only disillusionment, and death becomes a welcome escape from a world in which the idealist has no place. This is the truth of Conrad's time.

At the close of the nineteenth century and the dawning of the twentieth Conrad saw little cause for optimism. In 1905 he wrote 'Autocracy and War' for the *Fortnightly Review*. Within this sombre meditation on European struggles for democracy he reveals a profound cynicism in his perception of modern life. Recalling an 'early Victorian, or perhaps a pre-Victorian, sentimentalist', who wept for joy at the sight of 'so much life' (*NLL*, 84) in a London street, Conrad reflects that the contemporary response to teeming multitudes would be quite different:

> Wept for joy! I should think that now, after eighty years, the emotion would be of a sterner sort. One could not imagine anybody shedding tears of joy at the sight of much life in a street,

unless, perhaps, he were an enthusiastic officer of a general staff or a popular politician, with a career yet to make. And hardly even that. (*NLL*, 85)

The 'early Victorian', says Conrad, shed 'arcadian tears' worthy of the 'golden age', unaware of the 'series of sanguinary surprises held in reserve by the nineteenth century for our hopeful grandfathers' (*NLL*, 85). In the shadow of approaching war the value of human life is diminished. Thus the romantic past radiates a naive optimism about the future. The years intervening between the 'Victorian sentimentalist's' tears of joy and Conrad's article taught bitter lessons. In the gulf between the romantic imagination of the past and the modernist sensibilities of the present of his protagonists lie the tensions that Conrad's early Malay stories expose.

Notes

Introduction

1. Zdzislaw Najder, for example, describes *An Outcast* as a 'dress rehearsal' for *Lord Jim* (*Polish Background*, 23). R. A. Gekoski calls it 'the novel of an author not quite ready to write *Lord Jim*' (Gekoski, 57).
2. See Heliéna Krenn, *Conrad's Lingard Trilogy: Empire, Race, and Women in the Malay Novels*.
3. For example, Ian Watt in *Almayer's Folly in Conrad in the Nineteenth Century*, pp. 44–7; Martin Green, *Dreams of Adventure, Deeds of Empire*, p. 309; and Jonah Raskin *The Mythology of Imperialism*, pp. 162–9, are among those who have paid attention to the romance elements in Conrad's work. Andrea White, in *Joseph Conrad and the Adventure Tradition*, traces the influence of boys' adventure fiction and travel writing upon Conrad's early work.
4. Hereafter cited in the text as *TI*.
5. The two boys are in fact Millais's sons, Everett and George (see *World's Greatest Paintings*, T. Leman Hare, ed. [no page numbers]).
6. In his 'Author's Note' to *The Mirror of the Sea* Conrad speaks of his love of the sea and compares his passion to a love story (*MS* [Gresham], x).
7. See Wendy Katz, pp. 161–2 for a list of Haggard's non-fiction.
8. Hereafter cited in the text as *AQ*.
9. Many critics have commented on how Haggard stereotypes his female characters and frequently 'feminizes' the geography of Africa. See for example Ann McClintock, 'Maidens, Maps, and Mines: The Reinvention of Patriarchy in Colonial South Africa' in *South Atlantic Quarterly* 87, pp. 147–92. For a discussion of how this relates to Conrad's characterization of women and the East in *Lord Jim* see Padmini Mongia 'Ghosts of the Gothic: Spectral Women and Colonized Spaces in *Lord Jim*' in *The Conradian* vol. 17.2, pp. 1–16.
10. Hereafter cited in the text as *KSM*.
11. I use the term English instead of British in this discussion quite deliberately. As will become clear in Chapter 1, although the Empire was British it was primarily the English who administered it and who assumed superiority even over the Welsh, Irish and Scottish.
12. The assumption that because they are white these imaginary people would be permanently under siege underscores the racism inherent in attitudes towards the Africans in the late nineteenth century.
13. Hereafter cited in the text as *MR*.
14. Hereafter cited in the text as *CI*.
15. Hereafter cited in the text as *OP*.
16. For more information on Clifford see A. J. Stockwell 'Sir Hugh Clifford's Early Career' in the *Journal of the Malay Branch of the Royal Asiatic Society* 49.1, and H. A. Gailey, *Clifford: Imperial Proconsul*.

17. See J. de V. Allen, 'Two Imperialists: A Study of Sir Frank Swettenham and Sir Hugh Clifford,' *Journal of the Malayan Branch of the Royal Asiatic Society*, 37.1, for a discussion of Swettenham.
18. See Norman Sherry, *Conrad: The Critical Heritage* for some early responses. Detailed examples of reviews will be given in subsequent chapters.
19. Gene Moore cites Orson Welles and V. S. Naipaul as admirers of the 'filmic quality of Conrad's fiction. For Naipaul, "The Conrad novel was like a simple film with an elaborate commentary"' (*Conrad on Film*, 3).
20. Catherine Dawson and Gene Moore also note that 'Scholars have generally failed to appreciate the political aspects of Conrad's depictions of the lives of native people except insofar as these aspects can be linked directly with Western colonial imperialism' (*Conrad on Film*, 104).
21. See *the Pall Mall Magazine*, January–March, 1902.
22. I have an early French edition of 'Typhoon' (*Typhon*, traduit par André Gide, illustrations de Émilien Dufour. Paris: Hachette, 1923), which contains very stylized black and white illustrations. Greiffenhagen was also an illustrator for Haggard's books. See note 29 below. My copy of *Romance* (1903), published by Thomas Nelson and Sons, has a frontispiece by Dudley Tennant. This appears to be an early edition but there is no publishing date. See Gene M. Moore *Conrad on Film* (1997) for further discussion of the early films of Conrad's work and for reproductions of images from some of these films.
23. *The Oxford Companion to English Literature* states that the SPCK was founded in 1698:

> One of its primary objects was the setting up of charitable schools for the instruction of poor children in reading, writing, and the catechism, with the addition of arithmetic for boys and sewing for girls. The Society is also a publishing agency for the dissemination of works of a Christian character. (*Oxford Companion*, 925)

The English Catalogue of Books Vol. III, January 1872 to December 1880 lists nearly one hundred books published by Kingston.
24. Hereafter cited in the text as *BH*.
25. Hereafter cited in the text as *ES*.
26. Hereafter cited in the text as *PJ*.
27. Hereafter cited in the text as *TM*.
28. Hereafter cited in the text as *S*.
29. It seems that Charles Kerr and Maurice Greiffenhagen did most of the illustrations for the Longman versions of Haggard's novels. However, Percy Muir notes, in *Victorian Illustrated Books* (1971), that R. Caton Woodville 'made 32 drawings to illustrate the serial version' of *Nada the Lily* (1892) which was published in *the Illustrated London News* (Muir, 206).
30. There is not space here to discuss the production costs and prices of individual volumes; that really is beyond my scope in this study. Muir gives a good deal of attention to these issues (see Muir, 6–10).
31. Rick Gekoski, speaking at the 24th International Conference of the Joseph Conrad Society (UK) in 1998, lamented the fact that no dust jackets for Conrad's novels prior to around 1902 appear to have survived, but those dating from the early twentieth century are indeed plain and unadorned.

T. J. Wise gives a detailed account of the first editions of Conrad's work noting how they were issued in plain dark-coloured cloth boards with contrasting lettering, sometimes in gold. He seems to suggest that early print-runs, except for American editions, did not have dust jackets. See, for example, p. 9.

32. The footnote to this comment in *Letters 2* says: ' "Youth", according to Quiller-Couch (*Speaker*, 17 September 1898, p. 343) "might be one of the ordinary stories told by ordinary writers for ordinary boys at Christmas. But the framework goes for little; for the story contains an idea" '. See *Letters 2*, p. 417.

Chapter 1   Making the imperial hero

1. Hereafter cited in the text as *MME*.
2. *Allan Quatermain* opens with Quatermain mourning the death of his only son. In a tragic and ironic twist Haggard's own son died in 1891 which gives a poignancy to the dedication and the opening of the story that Haggard could not have foreseen. Opposite the dedication in the 1901 Longman edition is, in fact, a photograph of Haggard's son, Arthur.
3. This signed portrait is designed to give a stamp of authenticity to the book. Authenticating novels with signed portraits is part of a Victorian convention. The desire for verisimilitude and authentication influenced the promotional tactics of publishers. Thus, as Gerard Curtis notes, the Maclise portrait of Dickens in *Nicholas Nickleby* (1838–9) is 'used to market the real man instead of the formerly "pseudonist" caricature' – Dickens had decided to change his name from 'Boz'). Thus the 'signature and portrait were coming to be a trademark feature for certain products in the period, acting as stamps or seals to protect against fraudulent imitators'. See Curtis, 'Dickens in the visual market' in *Literature in the Marketplace*, Jordan, John O. and Robert L. Patten, eds, pp. 213–49 for a fuller discussion of the use of illustrations in nineteenth-century books.
4. Hereafter cited in the text as *IK*.
5. It was essentially Englishness that was the question, not Britishness. Where Welsh, Scottish, or Irish gentlemen were concerned they were token 'Englishmen' if they behaved accordingly. This I see as a symptom of the perceived superiority of the English and their social codes.
6. See Girouard, pp. 87–110, for a fuller discussion of the Eglinton Tournament.
7. See Girouard, pp. 116–20, for images of Albert dressed up as a chivalric knight.
8. T. S. Eliot, 'The Wasteland' in *Selected Poems* (1973), p. 67.
9. This is expressed most clearly in the characters of Twemlow and Eugene Wrayburn in *Our Mutual Friend* (1864–5). Twemlow is a gentleman by birth and by nature; Wrayburn assumes himself to be a gentleman by birth alone and must learn to be a gentleman by nature through suffering before he receives authorial approval through the voice of Twemlow. See *Our Mutual Friend*, p. 52, where Twemlow defends Wrayburn's marriage to Lizzie Hexam saying that Wrayburn is 'the greater gentleman for the action'. In *Great Expectations* (1860–1) Pip's final awareness of the background of violence

out of which his status as a gentleman comes highlights some complex ironies. For Gilmour *Great Expectations* 'taps a deep source of uneasiness in the Victorian cult of the gentleman' (Gilmour, 144). Indeed the only type of behaviour that the novel unequivocally affirms is that of Joe, the 'gentle Christian man'. As John Lucas says, through Magwitch's attempt to 'out-do' the respectable society of which he is a victim, 'Dickens exactly nails the absurdity that fed the Victorian idea of being or becoming a gentleman' (Lucas, 302). We have come a long way from Digby's definition of the gentleman: in a development of the early nineteenth-century ideal of the gentleman the classless notions of the gentleman became infused with chivalric values.

10. Hereafter cited in the text as *TBS*.
11. Hereafter cited in the text as *JH*.
12. Robin Gilmour provides an illuminating study of John Halifax and the mid-century version of gentlemanly behaviour in terms of the guidelines set down in Samuel Smiles manual *Self-Help* (1859). See Gilmour, pp. 99–103.
13. The idea of manliness will be discussed at length later. Claudia Nelson, in 'Sex and the Single Boy: Ideals of Manliness and Sexuality in Victorian Literature for Boys' provides a study of nineteenth-century notions of sexuality in children's literature. She argues that in the mid-century sexuality was perceived as dangerous, to be suppressed for the benefit of the purity of the spirit. Thus the assumption that women lacked libido led to an ideal fusion of the feminine quality with the male. This made androgyny the ideal physical state for the male prior to marriage, and hence the ideal for the boy hero. In Martha Vicinus, ed., *A Widening Sphere*, Carol Christ puts similar arguments concerning androgyny and male sexuality using the examples of the poetry of Tennyson and Patmore. See the chapter 'Victorian Masculinity and the Angel in the House'.
14. Carol Christ cites Ruskin as locating 'moral qualities in woman to compensate for man's naturally aggressive temperament'. Christ says that Ruskin even implies that women are at fault if they do not curb male aggressiveness. See Vicinus, ed., p. 159. This links in with the notions of female passivity as discussed by Claudia Nelson (see note 13). But women, specifically middle-class women, were increasingly claiming independence from the restrictive role placed upon them, and Ruskin was no doubt aware that his view was becoming untenable. Ruskin's is a specifically middle-class definition of roles. As Martha Vicinus explains: 'It is within the context of middle-class feminism that we can best understand the limitations a class-ordered society imposed upon women' (Vicinus, ed., p. xvi). Vicinus qualifies this statement by citing the lack of research into the organizations of working-class women. That situation has no doubt changed since 1977; however the problems of working-class women are outside the scope of this study.
15. Hereafter cited in the text as *LH*.
16. See her chapter 'Imperialism and Textuality', pp. 12–59, for a lucid and full discussion of the imperial novel and its social and political concerns.
17. Hereafter cited in the text as *Athleticism*.
18. Hughes's and Kingsley's Christian Socialism is expressed in *Tom Brown's Schooldays* where the school is a mixture of boys from the middle classes. Hughes even has a dig at the decadence of the aristocracy when he defends

Tom's consorting with the village boys: 'the village boys were full as manly and honest, and certainly purer, than those in a higher rank' (*TBS*, 53–4).

19. In fact Thomas Arnold was far from being a staunch advocate of games. Girouard states that he certainly would not have made games compulsory and was actively hostile towards chivalry, believing 'it set personal allegiances before God, and the concept of honour before that of justice' (Girouard, 164). It was actually masters such as Cotton who emphasized the importance of team games.

20. Jeffrey Richards points to Hughes's distortion of the Arnoldian educational philosophy that put intellectual ability at the top of his list of achievements for boys. See Richards, p. 31.

21. This is a curious citing of Kipling since he was not in favour of the games ethic: he was more an advocate of nurturing individual qualities to bring to the service of Empire in the late nineteenth century when there were serious questions being raised about the 'fitness' of the troops, and the imperial venture in general, as is shown in *Stalky & Co.* (1899).

22. I have discussed this issue more fully in connection with *Heart of Darkness* in my paper, '*Heart of Darkness* and *Allan Quatermain*: Apocalypse and Utopia', in *Conradiana* 31.1 (1999), 3–24.

23. Jeffrey Richards also outlines the victory of athleticism in the popular mind: 'The stiff upper lip had triumphed, the result partly of the exaltation of athleticism, with its concomitant need for self-control, team spirit, modesty in victory and defeat, partly the needs of the empire for administers able to display *sang-froid* in the face of tight corners and the excesses of excitable natives, and partly the decline of Evangelicalism with its exuberant displays of emotion' (Richards, 99).

24. Hereafter cited in the text as *K*.

25. In *Manliness and Morality*, 'Symbols of Moral Superiority: Slavery, Sport and the Changing World Order, 1800–1950', pp. 242–60, Walvin makes the point that the English based much of their claim to moral superiority over every other race upon the fact that Britain had abolished slavery early in century.

26. Hereafter cited in the text as *Games Ethic*.

27. J. A. Mangan in *The Games Ethic and Imperialism* also makes this point citing the 'Myth of the African as Child' argument, pp. 111–12.

28. In *Masterman Ready* Marryat applies the idea of a parent nurturing a child to the notion of colonialism. In response to his son's questions about English colonialism Mr Seagrave explains: 'In infancy, the mother-country assists and supports the colony as an infant; as it advances and becomes more vigorous, the colony returns the obligation; but the parallel does not end there. As soon as the colony has grown strong and powerful enough to take care of itself, it throws off the yoke of subjection, and declares itself independent; just as a son who has grown up to manhood leaves his father's house and takes up a business to gain his own livelihood' (*MR*, 140–41). It is a convenient and patronizing argument to justify colonialism and Mr Seagrave links it to the economic benefits for the 'mother-country' and the supposed future economic benefits for the colonies themselves.

29. See Rebecca Stott, p. 24, for a discussion of this view of women and Africans.

30. James Walvin also points out that it is hardly surprising that the British were better at games since they were the 'pioneers' and 'originators' of those games (Walvin, p. 249).

31. In his note on Baden-Powell's comment John Springhall states that he often quoted prominent Tory MPs who made the same comparisons (Springhall, 66, n. 31). Patrick Brantlinger, for example, in *Bread and Circuses* discusses at some length the analogies with the Roman Empire amongst writers, philosophers and politicians during the nineteenth century and into the twentieth century. See pp. 113–53.
32. In the introduction to *The Conradian* 17:2. Achebe's lecture 'An Image of Africa', delivered at the University of Massachusetts in February 1975, and was first published in *The Massachusetts Review* 18 (1977), pp. 782–94, and later revised as 'An Image of Africa: Racism in Conrad's *Heart of Darkness*'. *Research in African Literature* 9 (Spring 1978), pp. 1–15.

Chapter 2   The possibilities of romance

1. Stevenson's essay was first published in *Longman's Magazine*, May 1884. It was a response to James's essay 'The Art of Fiction', which was itself a response to Walter Besant's lecture of the same name.
2. J. P. Stern in *On Realism* argues that all realist fiction is necessarily selective. See in particular p. 67. For further discussions of realism and its relationship to romance see George Becker, *Documents of Modern Realism* (1963), Christopher Cauldwell, *Romance and Realism* (1970), Maurice Larkin, *Man and Society in Nineteenth Century Realism* (1977), and Roland Stromberg, *Realism, Naturalism, and Symbolism* (1968).
3. See Peter Keating, *The Haunted Study*, pp. 16–18 for an account of Haggard's success.
4. Many critics comment on how Africa is presented in Haggard's novels, *She* in particular, as a female body to be invaded, penetrated, and explored. This feminizes Africa in ways that suggest a mysterious and dangerous sexuality as well as a female sexual passivity. See for example, Daniel Bivona, *Desire and Contradiction*, pp. 80–4, and Rebecca Stott, *The Fabrication of the Late-Victorian Femme Fatale*. These arguments can also be linked to some readings of *Heart of Darkness*.
5. Karl Miller in *Doubles* (1985) gives a detailed outline of this formulaic relationship in the romance.
6. Hereafter cited in the text as *UTF*.
7. Immediately after her death Flaubert describes Emma with pitiless realism:

> Her mouth hung open, the corner of it showing like a black hole at the bottom of her face; her thumbs were still crushed into the palms of her hands; a sort of white dust bestrewed her lashes, and her eyes were beginning to disappear in a viscous pallor that was like a fine web, as though spiders had been spinning there. (*Madam Bovary*, 343)

Almayer's corpse receives similar realistic treatment:

> Ford glanced in through the doorway. In the dim light of the room he could see Almayer lying on his back on the floor, his head on a wooden pillow, the long white beard scattered over his breast, the yellow

skin of the face, the half-closed eyelids showing the whites of the eye only.... (*AF*, 205)

8. I am indebted to John Lester for his comments on the satirical nature of Haggard's romances.

9. These novels are clearly aimed at boys and reflect a patriarchal society where women are confined to the domestic sphere and regarded by men as being constantly in need of protection. The attitude of the male Seagraves to the mother in *Masterman Ready* is a typical example of this stereotyping.

10. Patrick Dunae points out that it is not surprising that Henty emphasized the material interests of the Empire since 'he was himself a shareholder in several overseas consortiums' (Dunae, 110).

11. Henty clearly knew very little about the native South American: he describes them as wearing moccasins and wielding tomahawks, a distinctly North American characteristic. Perhaps this lack of authenticity merely reflects how unimportant he thought them.

12. Henty details the military blunders committed by English officers, partly to draw attention to the 'historical accuracy' of his books, and to glorify such 'heroes' as Clive who make very few mistakes.

13. In her 1907 preface Ouida states that the story was originally written for a military periodical.

14. Cecil's morally feeble brother is eventually brought to a recognition of his weaknesses. The central male characters' moral and racial purity is even stressed in their 'nicknames', Seraph and Beauty.

15. See Gissing's *Demos* (1886), and *The Nether World* (1889), and Arthur Morrison, *A Child of the Jago* (1896), for examples of the pessimistic preoccupations of the English naturalist school of writers in the late nineteenth century.

16. Hereafter cited in the text as *NL*.

17. Interestingly the young Kipling was inspired by 'reading Haggard's *Nada the Lily*' (Boehmer, 47).

18. Of course in Stevenson's 'The Beach of Falesá' and Conrad's early Malay novels miscegenation does occur, but these unions are problematic and mark a new departure in imperial fiction, a point I will come to later when discussing Conrad.

19. This goes further than Patrick Brantlinger who says, 'Although they sometimes criticize the violence, exploitation, and racism of imperialism, Conrad's stories more consistently express the diminution of chances for heroism in the modern world, the decline of adventure' (*Rule of Darkness*, 42).

20. For a more detailed discussion see specifically her chapter, 'The Shift toward Subversion: the Case of H. Rider Haggard', pp. 82–99.

Chapter 3   *Almayer's Folly*: when romance collides with reality

1. Hereafter cited in the text as *CH*.

2. This is an odd claim since romance by definition deals with the remote and unfamiliar. Noble is in fact, unconsciously, being self-deconstructive.

3. Both of these devices will be discussed in detail in the chapters dealing with 'Karain' and *Lord Jim*.

4. As Allan Simmons notes, his 'vision of Europe is based upon his mother's memories of the "lost glories" of Amsterdam' (*Conradian* 14: 1 and 2, 6). Nina's dreams too are fuelled by *her* mother's tales of glorious Malay chiefs. According to Mrs Almayer she is the 'granddaughter of Rajahs!' (*AF*, 67).

5. But, as Allan Simmons has pointed out to me, Wiltshire's sense of 'duty' is a code imported from the 'civilized' society that is now closed to him, and this is also Jim's problem in *Lord Jim*. Each is bound by laws that (properly) belong to the civilization from which they are ostracized. This dilemma receives fuller treatment in Stevenson's fiction in *The Ebb-Tide*.

6. Haggard's feelings about the white invasion of Africa find their clearest expression in Sir Henry Curtis's closing remarks in *Allan Quatermain* where he vows to keep out any white men in order to protect the Zu-Vendis: 'I have no fancy for handing over this beautiful country to be torn and fought for by speculators, tourists, politicians and teachers, whose voice is as the voice of Babel' (*AQ*, 276). Such statements provide White with the proof that 'Haggard's fiction subverted genre expectations by questioning home values'. Yet what Quatermain and Co. create in Zu-Vendis is a civilization and culture modelled very much upon utopian ideas of a pre-industrial, pastoral England. No challenge is made to the class system and the aristocracy remains the ruling class. Haggard thus yearns for an England of the past and has Curtis recreate this bygone age in the African land of Zu-Vendis. Far from subversive, such a vision is deeply conservative.

7. In his 'Note on the Text' in the World's Classic's edition of *Almayer's Folly* Berthoud charts the history of the 'Author's Note' and includes a comment in a letter of 4 January 1895 to W. H. Chesson where Conrad suggests that it could be 'dispensed with'. See Berthoud, World's Classics edn, 'Note on the Text', xlix–l, and 'Explanatory Notes', 209, for more details.

8. Peter Keating gives some interesting figures for the publication of novels in the late nineteenth century which would seem to back up Conrad's claim about the number of novels being published: 'By 1894, the year when the circulating libraries announced the death of the three-decker because they could no longer keep up with the amount of fiction being published, 1315 new adult novels appeared, an average of 3.5 per day, "Sunday included"'. And he notes how in one peak year, 1897, the number rose to 1618. See Keating, 32–3.

9. This comment may also be symptomatic of Conrad's characteristically deferential and self-deprecating tone when writing to his aunt.

10. See *Letters 1*, 158, to Marguerite Poradowska, 17 May 1894.

11. David Finkelstein has pointed out to me that this was a standard line taken by publishers at that time. Conrad, of course, as a novice, was probably unaware of this.

12. I am not suggesting that this was his only reason: Conrad was clearly drawing upon his own experiences in the Merchant Service.

13. In *Joseph Conrad: a Personal Remembrance* Ford relates, in his typically inflated style, how Conrad 'in his misty youth that seemed to pass in great houses or in the prison-yards of the exiled child, and mostly at night or at nightfall, read with engrossment Marryat and Fenimore Cooper, and so

sowed the seeds of his devotion to England' (Ford, 68). Watt discusses the genre and Conrad's knowledge of it in *Conrad in the Nineteenth Century*, p. 43.

14. See Norman Sherry, *Conrad's Eastern World*, pp. 89–138, for a full discussion of both Lingard and Almayer.

15. Hereafter cited in the text as *Betrayal*.

16. White makes a similar point but links it to the 'native voice' of Almayer's wife, who perceives her 'capture' by Lingard in quite different terms than Lingard himself. See White, pp. 125–6.

17. Hereafter cited in the text as *LM*.

18. Although he implies that both men and women were engaged in this quest for 'Oriental sex', the writers Said mentions are exclusively male: Flaubert, Nerval, Burton, Lane, Gide, Maugham, and even Conrad. There thus seems to be some confusion as to who was actively seeking this experience.

19. See Berthoud ed., *Almayer's Folly* (Oxford: Oxford UP, 1992), Explanatory Note to pp. 72, 231. Berthoud also points out that the 'labial kiss' was an unusual experience for Malays at that time.

20. Ted Boyle mentions the fairy-tale in connection with Nina. See Boyle, pp. 31–3.

21. By contrast, Ayesha's white robe coyly disguises the fact that she is a 'sexually predatory' female.

22. Hampson notes how Nina learns her mother's lesson and gives a lucid account of how 'the representation of sexual passion as male enslavement elides into sexual passion as demonic possession'. See Hampson in *Tenggara* 32 (1994), pp. 108–9.

23. Berthoud, Explanatory Notes, 220. He explains that by 'European standards, Eastern houses are underfurnished, and their owners sit on mats or rugs'.

Chapter 4 *An Outcast of the Islands*: echoes of romance

1. In a letter to Marguerite Poradowska dated Saturday [18th? August 1894] Conrad outlines his vision for the novel and says: 'I am calling it "Two Vagabonds"'. See *Letters 1*, p. 171.

2. See Norman Sherry, *Conrad: the Critical Heritage*, pp. 62–81 for a selection of early reviews.

3. It is also a cliché that Conrad was fond of using: in a letter to Spiridion Kliszczewski in 1885 he expressed the hope that the Kliszczewski boys would 'walk straight in the path traced by their parents ... for in the path of rectitude lies the true happiness!' (*Letters 1*, 17). In an article for the *Daily Mail* in 1910 Conrad recognizes that the temptation to stray from the path is a common human predicament: 'Most of us, if you will pardon me for betraying the universal secret, have, at some time or other, discovered in ourselves a readiness to stray far, ever so far, on the wrong road'. Reprinted in *Notes on Life and Letters*, p. 61.

4. It is interesting to note that as early as *The Tempest* (1623) there is reference to how travellers thus beguiled native peoples. Frank Kermode gives details of such instances in his introduction to the Arden edition (1994), p. xxxvii.

5. White notes the distinction between Willems and Almayer, commenting that while 'Almayer was unheroic in a pathetic sort of way, Willems is corrupt'. She goes further in suggesting that Willems is a 'contributing cause' to the 'disease imperialism proliferates' (White, 137).

6. The drooping mouth, of course, prefigures Willems's own much later in the novel when he is but a shadow of his former self. It also looks forward to Winnie Verloc's drooping lower lip, indicating her 'degeneracy' as she murders her husband in *The Secret Agent* (1907).

7. The comma here before 'white' is a curious inclusion perhaps designed to emphasize, or make an ironic comment upon, the fact that Leonard identifies himself with 'whites'. Or perhaps it suggests a hesitancy Leonard's part. But, as John Stape and Hans van Marle indicate in the Explanatory Notes to the World's Classics edition of *An Outcast*: 'in the Netherlands East Indies colony no legal distinctions were made between white and Eurasian inhabitants, all classified as Europeans from 1854'. See p. 374, note to p. 28.

8. White argues that Ignosi's comment is evidence of Haggard's 'insistence on the natural differences' that 'comfortingly, asserts the white man's superiority' (White, 79). Note how Ignosi's analogy is curiously close to the butterflies and beetles analogies in *Lord Jim*.

9. The Glossary to the World's Classics edition defines Sirani as 'Nazarene', in other words, Christian. This serves to further highlight the complex cultural conflicts in *An Outcast*.

10. In *The Mirror of the Sea* Conrad recalls a real-life character called Hudig who he describes as 'a big, swarthy Netherlander, with black moustaches and a bold glance' (*MS*, 51).

11. In a letter to Marguerite Poradowska dated Monday morning [29 October or 5 November 1894] [London] Conrad says: 'Mrs M. Wood has stolen my title. She has just published a book called *The Vagabonds* and now I am really furious. No! You would pity me if you knew how that annoys me'. See *Letters 1*, p. 185.

12. I give a fuller discussion of this comment in my paper '*Heart of Darkness* and *Allan Quatermain*: Apocalypse and Utopia' in *Conradiana* 31.1 (1999) pp. 3–24.

13. Letter dated Saturday [18? August 1894]. See *Letters 1*, p. 171.

14. Hereafter cited in the text as *BR*.

15. It should be recognized that the Islamic morals of the Malay Archipelago were extremely strict. They have their own rationale and their own internal validity, a fact of which Conrad was aware.

16. In *Allan Quatermain* the adventurers settle in Zu-Vendis where Quatermain eventually dies. But by this time they have created a democratic Christian paradise amongst a race of white Africans.

17. Robert Hampson goes further by exploring the psychological reasons for Willems's betrayals. Willems, says Hampson, 'lives in an amoral world where actions are dissociated from their consequences, whereas Lingard inhabits a world of responsibilities'. See *Betrayal and Identity*, p. 46, for further discussion of Willems's lack of conscience. For a fuller examination of Willems's struggle with his own identity see 'The Unshared Idea of Self', in *Betrayal and Identity*, pp. 32–66.

18. Andrea White also points to the multiple tellings of the story, which she says 'effectively distances Conrad's work from the genre so many read him in' (White, 149).
19. The most celebrated and successful English translation of this is by Sir Richard Burton (1885–8). E. W. Lane had previously published his version in 1838–40.

Chapter 5 'Karain': constructing the romantic subject

1. I am grateful to Laurence Davies for his perceptive insights and suggestions on this matter. Much of what I have written here is inspired by his ideas. His private remarks to me are also worth noting:

> In commercial terms, you might say that Conrad (and Ford in the period of *Romance*) had crossover dreams of writing novels and stories that both conformed closely enough to certain features of popular fiction to be highly saleable and yet were artistically serious. Whether one sees Conrad as an inspired subverter of imperial attitudes from within the premier imperialist magazine or as a cynical collaborator with the forces of racism, reaction, etc., this doubleness (literary / popular) would play a significant part. To anyone in the business, such as Garnett, 'Karain' would seem perfect, 'destined for' Maga, a match made in Heaven so to speak. Conrad had assimilated the codes so thoroughly that he wrote a story that was a natural for *Blackwood's* (and as Garnett suggests, perhaps only for *Blackwood's*) without realising it. Then he woke up and found himself a *Blackwood's* author.

2. Laurence Davies's comments here, and the ones that follow, are from our private correspondence. I am also indebted to David Benyon for his insightful comments about Conrad and Cunninghame Graham.
3. T. J. Wise includes this information in his description of *Tales of Unrest*:

> Upon the flyleaf of a copy of the First Edition of *Tales of Unrest* Mr. Conrad has written the following interesting statement:
>
>> *'This volume contains the first set of short stories I ever wrote. 'The Lagoon' is the earliest, and 'Karain' the latest, 1895–1897 ... With the exception of 'The Return' they were all serialised; 'Karain' beginning my connection with Blackwood's Magazine.'* (Wise, 15)

4. See, for example, the unsigned review in the *Daily Telegraph* on 9 April 1898, reprinted in Norman Sherry, *Conrad: the Critical Heritage*, pp. 101–2.
5. Lawrence Graver says that this narrator's voice 'belongs to Charlie Marlow'. See Graver, p. 31. But, as Michele Drouart points out, 'this narrator lacks Marlow's perception and discernment; he has far fewer doubts and misgivings about his own approach to the world he enters'. See Michele Drouart, 'Gunrunning, Theatre and Cultural Attitude in Conrad's "Karain"', *Span*, 33, p. 137.
6. Hereafter cited in the text as *Tenggara*.
7. Compare this description to the image of Dick Holland dressed in Indian attire in plate 15.

8. Robert Hampson suggests that the narrator's 'inadequacies are fore-grounded' and draws comparisons with Marlow's 'clinging to "surface truth"' in *Heart of Darkness*: 'It might also be seen as that European fetishization of science that Vladimir intends to attack through the bombing of the Greenwich Observatory in The Secret Agent' (*Tenggara*, 115).
9. See Douglas Kerr, 'Crowds, Colonialism and Conrad's *Lord Jim*', *The Conradian* 18.2, pp. 49–64, for an informative discussion of Western reactions to the Oriental crowd in the nineteenth century.
10. Again it is worth referring to Edward Said, *Orientalism*, for his assessment of Western interpretations of the Orient as 'a kind of second-order knowledge – lurking in such places as the "Oriental" tale, the mythology of the mysterious East, notions of Asian inscrutability – with a life of its own, what V. G. Kiernan has aptly called "Europe's collective day-dream of the Orient"' (*Orientalism*, 52).
11. See Andrzej Braun, 'The Myth-Like Kingdom of Conrad' in *Conradiana* X:1, p. 3. Braun identifies the diaries and letters of James Brooke as the source for Conrad's information about this area.
12. The first time is at the beginning of Karain's narrative (*TU*, 30).
13. See Patrick Brantlinger, 'Imperial Gothic', in *Rule of Darkness*.
14. Robert Hampson notes that the conferral of the 'charm', the image of Victoria which is 'the most powerful thing the white men know' (*TU*, 49), is 'the meeting of the ideas and artifacts of the West with a "more primitive" culture: this is a version of the "instrumental marvellous" that relates not to different times but to different cultures' (in Caracciolo, 222). The 'instrumental marvellous' is Tzvetan Todorov's term for 'that species of the marvellous which resides in technological feats which were not possible at the time of writing' (in Caracciolo, 221).
15. I am grateful to Professor Cedric Watts for bringing this to my attention.
16. Robert Hampson has noted the 'immense popularity of the *Nights*' in the mid to late nineteenth century and how the book influenced writers during that time: 'The British Library Catalogue includes thirty different editions of the *Nights* published between 1850 and 1890. For writers, the *Nights* provided a pool of images and allusions and a compendium of narrative techniques' (in Caracciolo, 218).
17. Robert Hampson also makes the point that the fact that Jackson picks out 'Bland's window "like a man looking for landmarks" betrays the disorientation he experiences, while the recurrent use of nautical metaphors (as at the end of *The Nigger of the Narcissus*) registers that these sailors on shore are out of their true element'. See Gene M. Moore ed., *Conrad's Cities*, pp. 161–3, for further discussion of the London of 'Karain'.

Chapter 6 *Lord Jim*: the limitations of romance

1. Wise seems to have acquired a personally inscribed American edition of *Lord Jim*. He notes that on 'the fly-leaf' of an American edition Conrad wrote:

   This is the first American edition, set up probably from English proofs, but neither revised nor in any other way corrected by me. It is probably much nearer the text of Blackwood's Magazine than the first English Edition. (Wise, 19)

2. See John Batchelor, ed., *Lord Jim* (OUP [World's Classics edn] 1996, 'Note on the Text'.
3. See Norman Sherry, *Conrad: the Critical Heritage*, pp. 111–28, for a fuller account of the book's reception.
4. See, for example, the representation of the Dutch officers in *Almayer's Folly*.
5. Not all of Stevenson's work is of the same pattern as the early adventure novels. Later with such works as 'The Beach of Falesá', *The Ebb-Tide* and *Weir of Hermiston* he moved into a quite different mood, and mode, of storytelling.
6. Quoted by Eloise Knapp Hay, 'Lord Jim: From Sketch to Novel' in *Twentieth Century Interpretations of Lord Jim*, p. 29.
7. Tony Tanner sees Stein thus: 'While he is talking Stein takes on a curious stature, an odd remoteness, some indefinable air of the white magician. He becomes something of a Prospero. He seems to be "out of this concrete and perplexed world" and, like Prospero, preoccupied with "high charms" and heavenly arts. "He hovered noiselessly over invisible things" and he seems "mysteriously busy with immaterial cares". This is the man, the magician, who is to help Jim' (Tanner, 43).
8. See also for example Bruce Johnson, *Conrad's Models of Mind*, pp. 56–8, Benita Parry, *Conrad and Imperialism*, p. 93, Redmond O'Hanlon, *Joseph Conrad and Charles Darwin*, pp. 118–28.
9. '[H]eadquarters Resident' is the term Clifford uses for this character. See my article, 'Conrad and Hugh Clifford: "An Irreproachable Player on the Flute" and "A Ruler of Men"' in *The Conradian*, Spring 1998, vol. 23.1, pp. 51–72, where I trace the relationship of Conrad and Clifford and discuss Clifford's story in more detail. There is some suggestion that Clifford was comparing his story with *Lord Jim* and that there was a degree of literary rivalry between them.
10. Hugh Clifford, 'In the Heart of Kalamantan' was first published in *Blackwoods Magazine*, vol. 168 (October 1900), pp. 511–35.
11. In fact Wells's *The First Men in the Moon* was published in 1901, and it is thus possible that he had also discussed this story with Conrad while he was writing *Lord Jim*.
12. Padmini Mongia cites Ann McClintock's analysis of the feminizing of Africa in *King Solomon's Mines* and says McClintock reveals how 'the novel crudely makes explicit the connections between the colonial map and the native female body which must be plundered by white male scientist-explorers in order to yield its hidden "treasure"'. See Mongia, 'Empire, Narrative, and the Feminine in *Lord Jim* and *Heart of Darkness*' in Fincham and Hooper, p. 122, n. 4.
13. See Allan Hunter, *Joseph Conrad and the Ethics of Darwinism*, pp. 45–8.
14. See Norman Sherry *Conrad's Eastern World*, pp. 158–61, for a discussion of these sources for Doramin. Sherry also indicates an original for Rajah Allang and suggests the names Doramin, Tamb' Itam and Tunku Allang were taken from McNair.

15. See my paper '*Heart of Darkness* and *Allan Quatermain*: Apocalypse and Utopia' in *Conradiana* 31.1 (1999) 3–24, for a fuller discussion of Conrad's use of the romance tradition in *Heart of Darkness*.
16. Conrad and Hudson in fact became friends. He refers to Hudson in a letter to Cunninghame Graham in December 1897 calling him 'a most loveable man'. Karl and Davies affirm that 'Although Conrad almost certainly corresponded with Hudson, none of the letters has turned up'. See *Letters 1*, p. 419.
17. Mongia sees Jewel's sexuality as problematic and ultimately diminishing of her impact in the novel:

> For Jewel pays a price for her amalgamated role as wife / mistress. Retaining only the external features of sensuality – her dark hair, her exotic Malay background – Jewel is inscribed as 'boyish' (*LJ*, 283) and a 'child' (*LJ*, 289). Located between the poles of Kurtz's Intended (who lacks even external features of sexuality and desire) and his African mistress, Jewel is a combination of the angel and the demon. However, since the only vocabulary for desire in these two novels is the gothic, Jewel's sensuality is sacrificed in order to inscribe her as domestically viable. Often dressed in virginal white, Jewel is at odds with the sexual promise and fulfilment she is also asked to represent. (in Fincham and Hooper, 128)

18. Although this is usually assumed to mean that white men always leave their 'native' lovers, Jewel's statement could also be taken to mean that men always leave women. It could even be interpreted in a more general imperial sense: the imperial adventurer always leaves the 'native' people he has subjugated. But in whatever sense we interpret this statement it carries the bitterness of experience and a sense of betrayal by white men.
19. This also recalls the 'tender contempt' that Willems feels for his own sickly child.
20. I am grateful to Allan Simmons for helping me to clarify some ideas on the 'privileged man'. One or two of his private comments to me are also worth including. He suggests that since the attitude of the 'privileged man' towards the masses echoes his own earlier attitude, Marlow may be addressing a former self in the light of what he has learned from Jim's experience. Simmons also commented that *Lord Jim* starts by addressing the issue of whether Jim is a hero and ends by asking whether there is such a thing as heroism.
21. See Norman Sherry, *Conrad's Eastern World*, 155–6 and Lt-Cdr Andrew K. M. Browne, RN (Ret.) 'An Original for "Gentleman" Brown' in *Conradiana* 26: 1, 1994, pp. 76–9.

Bibliography

Primary sources: Conrad

Conrad, Joseph. *Almayer's Folly and Tales of Unrest,* 1895 (London: J. M. Dent, 1947).
———. *Almayer's Folly: The Story of an Eastern River,* ed. Jacques Berthoud (Oxford: Oxford University Press, 1992).
———. *An Outcast of the Islands,* 1896 (London: J. M. Dent, 1949).
———. *An Outcast of the Islands,* ed. Stape, John H. and Hans van Marle (Oxford: Oxford University Press, 1992).
———. *The Nigger of the 'Narcissus': A Tale of the Sea,* 1897 (London: J. M. Dent, 1956).
———. *Lord Jim: A Tale,* 1900 (London: J. M. Dent, 1946).
———. *Typhoon, Pall Mall Magazine,* January–March, 1902.
———. *Typhoon,* 1903, in *The Nigger of the Narcissus, Typhoon, The Shadow-Line* (London: J. M. Dent, 1956).
———. *Typhon,* trans. André Gide (Paris: Hachette, 1923).
———. *Nostromo: A Tale of the Seaboard,* 1904 (London: J. M. Dent, 1947).
———. *The Mirror of the Sea: Memories and Impressions,* 1906 (London: J. M. Dent, 1946).
———. *The Mirror of the Sea: Memories and Impressions* (London: Gresham, 1925).
———. *The Secret Agent: A Simple Tale,* 1907 (London: J. M. Dent, 1946).
———. *Chance: A Tale in Two Parts,* 1913 (London: Hogarth Press, 1984).
———. *Victory: An Island Tale,* 1915 (London: J. M. Dent, 1948).
———. *The Rescue: A Romance of the Shallows,* 1920 (London: J. M. Dent, 1949).
———. *Notes on Life and Letters,* 1921 (London: J. M. Dent, 1949).
———. *Last Essays,* ed. Richard Curle (London: J. M. Dent, 1926).
Conrad, Joseph and Ford Madox Heuffer. *Romance: A Novel* (Thomas Nelson, n.d.).
Blackburn, William ed., *Joseph Conrad: Letters to William Blackburn and David S. Meldrum* (Durham, North Carolina: Duke University Press, 1958).
Garnett, Edward ed., *Letters from Conrad 1895 to 1924* (Bloomsbury: Nonesuch Press, n.d.).
Karl, Frederick, R. and Laurence Davies, eds. *The Collected Letters of Joseph Conrad, Volume 1 1861–1897* (Cambridge: Cambridge University Press, 1983).
———. *The Collected Letters of Joseph Conrad, Volume 2 1898–1902* (Cambridge: Cambridge University Press, 1986).

Secondary sources: fiction

First editions of these texts have been used when available, but this has not always been possible.

Ballantyne, R. M. *The Coral Island,* Intro. Margaret W. J. Jeffrey (London: Collins, 1960).

Black, E. L. ed. *1914–18 in Poetry* (London: University of London Press, 1970).

Braddon, Miss. *Lady Audley's Secret* (London: Thomas Nelson, n.d.).

Buchan, John. *Prester John* (London: Thomas Nelson, n.d.).

Clifford, Hugh. 'In the Heart of Kalamantan', in *'Blackwood' Tales from the Outposts: Jungle Tales,* ed. L. A. Bethel (London: William Blackwood, 1946).

Cooper, James Fenimore. *The Last of the Mohicans* (London: Thomas Nelson, n.d.).

Crane, Stephen. *The Red Badge of Courage and Other Stories,* ed. Pascal Covici (London: Penguin, 1991).

Defoe, Daniel. *Robinson Crusoe* (London: Daily Sketch Publications, n.d.).

Dickens, Charles. *Great Expectations* (London: Penguin, 1971).

——. *Our Mutual Friend,* ed. Stephen Gill (London: Penguin, 1971).

Eliot, T. S. *Selected Poems* (London: Faber and Faber, 1973).

Falkner, John Meade. *Moonfleet* (London: Jonathan Cape, 1934).

Farrar, Frederic W. *Eric, or Little by Little: A Tale of Roslyn School* (London: Ward, Lock, n.d.).

Flaubert, Gustav. *Madame Bovary: A Story of Provincial Life,* trans. Alan Russell (London: Penguin, 1950).

Forster, E. M. *A Passage to India,* ed. Oliver Stallybrass (London: Penguin, 1989).

Gissing, George. *Demos: A Story of English Socialism,* ed. Pierre Coustillas (Brighton: Harvester Press, 1972).

——. *New Grub Street,* ed. Bernard Bergonzi (London: Penguin, 1985).

——. *The Nether World: A Novel,* ed. John Goode (Brighton: Harvester Press, 1974).

Haggard, H. Rider. *The Witch's Head* (London: Longmans, Green, 1900).

——. *King Solomon's Mines* (London: Cassell, n.d.).

——. *Allan Quatermain* (London: Longmans, Green, 1901).

——. *She* (London: Longmans, Green, 1918).

——. *Nada the Lily* (London: Collins, 1957).

Hardy, Thomas. *Tess of the d'Urbervilles: A Pure Woman,* Intro. C. Day Lewis (London: Collins, 1958).

——. *The Mayor of Casterbridge,* ed. Martin Seymour-Smith (London: Penguin, 1976).

Hawthorne, Nathaniel. *The Blithedale Romance,* Intro. Tony Tanner Explanatory Notes. John Dugdale (Oxford: Oxford University Press, 1991).

——. *The Scarlet Letter: A Romance* (Edinburgh: William Paterson, n.d.).

Henley, William Ernest. ed., *Lyra Heroica: A Book of Verse for Boys* (London: Macmillan, 1921).

Henty, George Alfred. *Out on the Pampas: or The Young Settlers* (London: Hodder & Stoughton, 1917).

——. *The Tiger of Mysore: A Story of the War with with Tippoo Saib* (London: Blackie, n.d.).

——. *With Clive in India* (London: Blackie, n.d.).

——. *By Sheer Pluck: A Tale of the Ashanti War* (New York: A. L. Burt, 1884).

Hudson, W. H. *Green Mansions: A Romance of the Tropical Forest* (London: Duckworth, 1925).

Hughes, Thomas. *Tom Brown's School Days* (Thomas Nelson, n.d.).

Jefferies, Richard. *Bevis: The Story of a Boy* (London: P. R. Gawthorn, n.d.).

Kingston, W. H. G. *Ben Hadden: or Do Right Whatever Comes of It* (London: Religious Tract Society, n.d.).

———. *In the Eastern Seas: A Tale for Boys* (London: Thomas Nelson, n.d.).

———. *Michael Penguyne: Fisher Life on the Cornish Coast* (London: Society for Promoting Christian Knowledge, n.d.).

———. *Peter Biddulph* (London: Sunday School Union, n.d.).

———. *The Rival Crusoes* (London: Griffith Farran Browne, n.d.).

Kipling, Rudyard. *Captains Courageous* (London: Macmillan, 1941).

———. *Kim*, ed. Edward W. Said (London: Penguin, 1989).

———. *Stalky & Co.* (London: Macmillan, 1924).

———. *Twenty-One Tales* (London: Macmillan, 1946).

Marryat, Frederick. *Masterman Ready* (London: Thomas Nelson, n.d.).

———. *Mr. Midshipman Easy* (London: P. R. Gawthorn, n.d.).

———. *Peter Simple*, ed. Ernest Rhys (London: J. M. Dent, 1944).

Maugham, W. Somerset. *Of Human Bondage: A Novel* (Melbourne: William Heinemann, 1950).

Melville, Herman. *Typee: A Peep at Polynesian Life*, ed. George Woodcock (London: Penguin, 1986).

Moore, Marianne. 'The Steeple-Jack', in *Salt and Bitter and Good: Three Centuries of English and American Women Poets*, Cora Kaplan, ed. (UK: Paddington Press, 1975).

Morrison, Arthur. *A Child of the Jago*, ed. P. J. Keating (London: Panther, 1971).

Mrs. Craik. *John Halifax, Gentleman* (T. Nelson, n.d.).

Ouida. *Under Two Flags* (London: Chatto & Windus, 1907).

Poe, Edgar Allan. *Selected Writings*, ed. David Galloway (London: Penguin, 1974).

Shakespeare, William. *The Tempest*, Arden edn, ed. Frank Kermode (London: Routledge, 1994).

Shelley, Mary. *Frankenstein: or The Modern Prometheus*, ed. Maurice Hindle (London: Penguin, 1992).

Shorthouse, John. *John Inglesant: A Romance* (London: Macmillan, 1896).

Stevenson, Robert Louis. 'The Beach of Falesá', in *Island Landfalls: Reflections from the South Seas*, ed. Jenni Calder (Edinburgh: Canongate, 1987).

———. *Dr. Jekyll and Mr. Hyde and the Story of a Lie* (London: Thomas Nelson, n.d.).

———. 'A Humble Remonstrance', in *Memories and Portraits*, Skerryvore edn (London: William Heinemann, 1925) 155–68.

———. *Kidnapped and Catriona*, ed. Emma Letley (Oxford: Oxford University Press, 1986).

———. *Treasure Island*, ed. Emma Letley (Oxford: Oxford University Press, 1985).

———. *Weir of Hermiston* (London: J. M. Dent, 1957).

Stevenson, Robert Louis and Lloyd Osbourne. *The Ebb-Tide: A Trio and Quartette* (London: William Heinemann, 1905).

Tennyson, Alfred. *Poetical Works of Alfred Lord Tennyson* (London: Macmillan, 1899).

Wells, H. G. *The Island of Doctor Moreau* (Daily Express Fiction Library, n.d.).

———. *The Time Machine* (London: Collins, n.d.).

———. *The War of the Worlds* (Daily Express Fiction Library, n.d.).

Zola, Emile. *Nana*, ed. Ernest Boyd (New York: Modern Library, 1927).

Secondary sources: critical texts

Allen, Jerry. *The Sea Years of Joseph Conrad* (New York: Doubleday, 1965).

Auerbach, Erich. *Mimesis: The Representation of Reality in Western Literature,* trans. W. R. Trask (Princeton: Princeton University Press).

Appleman, Philip. *Darwin* (New York: W. W. Norton, 1970).

Barber, Richard. *The Knight and Chivalry* (New York: Charles Scribner's Sons, 1970).

Barr, John. *Illustrated Children's Books* (London: British Library, 1986).

Becker, George. *Documents of Modern Literary Realism* (Princeton: Princeton University Press, 1963).

Beer, Gillian. *The Romance* (London: Methuen, 1986).

Berthoud, Jacques. *Joseph Conrad: The Major Phase* (Cambridge: Cambridge University Press, 1978).

Billy, Ted. *Critical Essays on Joseph Conrad* (Boston: G. K. Hall, 1987).

Bivona, Daniel. *Desire and Contradiction: Imperial Visions and Domestic Debates in Victorian Literature* (Manchester: Manchester University Press, 1990).

Blatchford, Robert. *Merrie England* (London: Walter Scott, 1894).

Boehmer, Elleke. *Colonial & Postcolonial Literature: Migrant Metaphors* (Oxford: Oxford University Press, 1995).

Boyle, Ted E. *Symbol and Meaning in the Fiction of Joseph Conrad* (London: Mouton, 1965).

Brantlinger, Patrick. *Bread and Circuses: Theories of Mass Culture as Social Decay* (London: Cornell University Press, 1983).

———. *Rule of Darkness: British Literature and Imperialism 1830–1914* (Ithaca: Cornell University Press, 1988).

Caracciolo, Peter. *The Arabian Nights in English Literature: Studies in the Reception of The Thousand and One Nights into British Culture* (London: Macmillan, 1988).

Cauldwell, Christopher. *Romance and Realism* (New Jersey: Princeton University Press, 1970).

Cott, Jonathan. *Victorian Color Picture Books* (London: Allen Lane, 1984).

Cox, C. B. *Joseph Conrad: The Modern Imagination* (London: J. M. Dent, 1974).

Darras, Jacques. *Conrad and the West: Signs of Empire,* trans. Anne Luyat and Jacques Darras (London: Macmillan, 1982).

de Groot, Joanna. '"Sex" and "Race": The Construction of Language and Image in the Nineteenth Century', in *Sexuality and Subordination: Interdisciplinary Studies of Gender in the Nineteenth Century,* eds Susan Mendis and Jane Rendall (London: Routledge & Kegan Paul, 1989).

Digby, Kenelm, *The Broadstone of Honour: or, Rules for the Gentlemen of England* (London: Printed for C. & J. Rivington, 1823).

Drabble, Margaret, ed. *The Oxford Companion to English Literature* (Oxford: Oxford University Press, 1985).

Erdinast-Vulcan, Daphna. *Joseph Conrad and the Modern Temper* (Oxford: Clarendon Press, 1991).

Fincham, Gail and Myrtle Hooper. *Under Postcolonial Eyes: Joseph Conrad After Empire* (Cape Town: University of Cape Town Press, 1996).

Ford, Ford Madox. *Joseph Conrad: A Personal Remembrance* (London: Duckworth, 1924).

Gailey, Harry A. *Clifford: Imperial Proconsul* (London: Collins, 1982).

Gilmour, Robin. *The Idea of the Gentleman in the Victorian Novel* (London: George Allen & Unwin, 1981).

Girouard, Mark. *The Return to Camelot: Chivalry and the English Gentleman* (London: Yale University Press, 1981).

Graham, Kenneth. *English Criticism of the Novel 1865–1900* (London: Oxford University Press, 1965).

Graver, Lawrence. *Conrad's Short Fiction* (Berkeley: University of California, 1969).

Gray, H. B. *The Public Schools and Empire* (London: Williams & Norgate, 1913).

Green, Martin. *Dreams of Adventure, Deeds of Empire* (London: Routledge & Kegan Paul, 1980).

Guerard, Albert J. *Conrad the Novelist* (London: Harvard University Press, 1979).

Hampson, Robert. *Joseph Conrad: Betrayal and Identity* (London: Macmillan, 1992).

Hewitt, Douglas. *English Fiction of the Early Modern Period 1840–1940* (London: Longman, 1988).

Higgins, D. S. *Rider Haggard: The Great Storyteller* (London: Cassell, 1981).

Honey, J. R. de S. *Tom Brown's Universe: The development of the public school in the nineteenth century* (London: Millington, 1977).

Hunter, Allan. *Joseph Conrad and the Ethics of Darwinism: The challenges of science* (London: Croom Helm, 1983).

Hunter, Jefferson. *Edwardian Fiction* (London: Harvard University Press, 1982).

Jackson, Holbrook. *The Eighteen Nineties: A Review of Art and Ideas at the Close of the Nineteenth Century* (Harmondsworth: Penguin, 1950).

James, Henry. *The House of Fiction*, ed. Leon Edel (London: Rupert Hart-Davis, 1957).

Jameson, Fredric. *The Political Unconscious: Narrative as a Socially Symbolic Act* (London: Methuen, 1981).

Johnson, Bruce. *Conrad's Models of Mind* (Minneapolis: University of Minnesota Press, 1971).

Jordan, John O. and Robert L. Patten, eds. *Literature in the Marketplace: Nineteenth-Century Publishing and Reading Practices* (Cambridge: Cambridge University Press, 1995).

Katz, Wendy. *Rider Haggard and the Fiction of Empire: A critical study of British imperial fiction* (Cambridge: Cambridge University Press, 1987).

Keating, Peter. *The Haunted Study: A Social History of the English Novel 1875–1914* (Glasgow: Fontana Press, 1991).

Knox-Shaw, Peter. *The Explorer in English Fiction* (London: Macmillan, 1981).

Krenn, Heliéna. *Conrad's Lingard Trilogy: Empire, Race, and Women in the Malay Novels* (London: Garland, 1990).

Kuehn, Robert E., ed. *Twentieth Century Interpretations of Lord Jim* (Englewood Cliffs, New Jersey: Prentice-Hall, 1969).

Larkin, Maurice. *Man and Society in Nineteenth Century Realism: Determinism and Literature* (London: Macmillan, 1977).

Lee, Robert F. *Conrad's Colonialism* (Paris: Mouton, 1969).

Lucas, John. *The Melancholy Man: A study of Dickens's novels* (Brighton: Harvester, 1980).

Mangan, J. A. *Athleticism in the Victorian and Edwardian Public School: The Emergence and Consolidation of an Educational Ideology* (London: Cambridge University Press, 1981).

———. *The Games Ethic and Imperialism: aspects of the diffusion of an ideal* (Harmondsworth: Penguin, 1986).

Mangan, J. A. and James Walvin, eds. *Manliness and Morality: Middle-class Masculinity in Britain and America 1800–1940* (Manchester: Manchester University Press, 1987).

McClure, John A. *Kipling and Conrad: The Colonial Fiction* (London: Harvard University Press, 1981).

Miller, Karl. *Doubles: Studies in Literary History* (London: Oxford University Press, 1985).

Moore, Gene M. *Conrad's Cities: Essays for Hans van Marle* (Amsterdam and Atlanta: Rodopi, 1992).

———. *Conrad on Film* (Cambridge: Cambridge University Press, 1997).

Muir, Percy. *Victorian Illustrated Books* (London: B. T. Batsford, 1971).

Najder Zdzislaw, ed. *Conrad's Polish Background: Letters to and from Polish Friends,* trans. Halina Caroll (London: Oxford University Press, 1964).

———. *Conrad Under Familial Eyes,* trans. Halina Caroll (Cambridge: Cambridge University Press, 1983).

———. *Joseph Conrad: A Chronicle* (Cambridge: Cambridge University Press, 1983).

Newbolt, Henry. *Poems: New and Old* (London: John Murray, 1919).

Newsome, David. *Godliness and Good Learning: Four Studies on a Victorian Ideal* (London: John Murray, 1961).

Nordau, Max. *Degeneration* (New York: Howard Fertig, 1968).

O'Hanlon, Redmond. *Joseph Conrad and Charles Darwin: The influence of scientific thought on Conrad's fiction* (Edinburgh: Salamander, 1984).

Parry, Benita. *Conrad and Imperialism: Ideological boundaries and visionary frontiers* (London: Macmillan, 1983).

Raskin, Jonah. *The Mythology of Empire: Rudyard Kipling, Joseph Conrad, E. M. Forster, D. H. Lawrence and Joyce Carey* (New York: Random House, 1971).

Richards, Jeffrey. *Happiest Days: The Public School in English Fiction* (New York: Manchester University Press, 1988).

Roussel, Royal. *The Metaphysics of Darkness: A Study in the Unity and Development of Conrad's Fiction* (Cambridge, Massachusetts: Johns Hopkins Press, 1971).

Rowbotham, Judith. *Good Girls Make Good Wives: Guidance for Girls in Victorian Fiction* (Oxford: Basil Blackwood, 1989).

Runciman, Steven. *The White Rajahs: A History of Sarawak from 1841 to 1946* (London: Cambridge University Press, 1960).

Ruskin, John. *Sesame and Lilies and The Political Economy of Art* (London: Collins, n.d.).

Said, Edward W. *Culture & Imperialism* (London: Chatto & Windus, 1993).

———. *Orientalism: Western Conceptions of the Orient* (London: Penguin, 1978).

———. *The World, The Text, and the Critic* (London: Faber and Faber, 1984).

Sandison, Alan. *The Wheel of Empire: A Study of the Imperial Idea in Some Late Nineteenth and Early Twentieth-Century Fiction* (London: Macmillan, 1967).

Saveson, John E. *Joseph Conrad: The Making of a Moralist* (Amsterdam: Rodopi, 1972).

Schwarz, Daniel R. *Conrad: Almayer's Folly to Under Western Eyes* (London: Macmillan, 1980).

Seymour-Smith, Martin. *Rudyard Kipling: The Controversial New Biography* (London: Papermac, 1980).

Sherry, Norman. *Conrad's Eastern World* (London: Cambridge University Press, 1966).

———. *Conrad: The Critical Heritage* (London: Routledge & Kegan Paul, 1973).

Smiles, Samuel. *Self-Help* (London: John Murray, 1875).

Springhall, John. *Youth, Empire and Society: British Youth Movements, 1883–1940* (London: Croom Helm, 1977).

Stern, J. P. *On Realism* (London: Routledge & Kegan Paul, 1973).

Stevenson, Lionel. *The History of the English Novel* (New York: Barnes & Noble, 1970).

Storry, Mike and Peter Childs. *British Cultural Identities* (London: Routledge, 1997).

Stott, Rebecca. *The Fabrication of the Late-Victorian Femme Fatale* (London: Macmillan, 1992).

Street, Brian V. *The Savage in Literature: Representations of 'Primitive' Society in English Fiction 1880–1920* (London: Routledge & Kegan Paul, 1975).

Stromberg, Roland. *Realism, Naturalism, and Symbolism: Modes of Thought and Expression in Europe, 1848–1914* (London: Harper & Row, 1968).

Tanner, Tony. *Conrad: Lord Jim* (London: Edward Arnold, 1969).

Thorburn, David. *Conrad's Romanticism* (New Haven: Yale University Press, 1974).

Vance, Norman. *The Sinews of the Spirit: The Ideal of Christian Manliness in Victorian Literature and Religious Thought* (Cambridge: Cambridge University Press, 1985).

Vicinus, Martha. *A Widening Sphere: Essays on the social history of women* (London: Indiana University Press, 1977).

Watt, Ian P. *Conrad in the Nineteenth Century* (Los Angeles: University of California, 1979).

———. *The Rise of the Novel* (London: Chatto & Windus, 1974).

Watts, Cedric. *A Preface to Conrad* (Harlow: Longman, 1982).

White, Andrea. *Joseph Conrad and the Adventure Tradition: constructing and deconstructing the imperial subject* (Cambridge: Cambridge University Press, 1993).

Wise, Thomas J. *A Bibliography of the Writings of Joseph Conrad (1885–1921)* (London: Dawsons of Pall Mall, 1964).

The World's Greatest Paintings: Selected Masterpieces of Famous Art Galleries, ed. T. Leman Hare (London: Odhams Press, n.d).

Journals and papers

Achebe, Chinua. 'An Image of Africa', *Massachusetts Review* 18 (1977), 782–94.

Allen, J. de V. 'Two Imperialists: A Study of Sir Frank Swettenham and Sir Hugh Clifford', *Journal of the Malayan Branch of the Royal Asiatic Society*, 37.1. (1964), 41–73.

The Athenaeum Review, no. 3526 (25 May 1895).

Bevan, Ernest Jr. 'Marlow and Jim: The Reconstructed Past', *Conradiana* 15:3 (1983), 191–202.

Braun, Andrzej. 'The Myth-Like Kingdom of Conrad', *Conradiana* 10:1 (1978), 3–16.

Browne, Andrew K. M. 'An Original for "Gentleman" Brown?', *Conradiana* 26:1 (1994), 76–9.

Conroy, Mark. 'Ghostwriting (in) "Karain"', *The Conradian* 18:2 (1994), 1–16.

Davidson, Arnold E. 'The Abdication of Lord Jim', *Conradiana* 13:1 (1981), 19–34.

Driver, Felix. 'Geography Triumphant? Joseph Conrad and the Imperial Adventure: A review essay', *The Conradian* 18:2 (1994), 103–11.

Drouart, Michele. 'Gunrunning, Theatre and Cultural Attitude in Conrad's "Karain"', *Span* 33 (Christchurch, New Zealand, 1992), 134–49.

Dryden, Linda. 'Conrad and Hugh Clifford: "An Irreproachable Player on the Flute" and "A Ruler of Men"', *The Conradian* 23.1 (1998), 51–72.

———. '*Heart of Darkness* and *Allan Quatermain*: Apocalypse and Utopia', *Conradiana* 31:1 (1999), 3–24.

Dunae, Patrick A. 'Boys' Literature and the Idea of Empire, 1870–1914', *Victorian Studies* 24 (1980), 105–21.

Gasiorek, Andrzej. '"To Season with a Pinch of Romance": Ethics and Politics in *Lord Jim*', *The Conradian* 22.1 and 2 (1997), 75–112.

Gekoski, R. A. '*An Outcast of the Islands*: A New Reading', *Conradiana* 2:3 (1974), 47–58.

Gordan, J. D. 'The Rajah Brooke and Joseph Conrad', *Studies in Philology* 35 (1938), 613–34.

Haggard, H. Rider. 'About Fiction', *Contemporary Review* li (1887), 173–80.

Hampson, Robert. 'Encountering the Other: Race, Gender and Sexuality in Joseph Conrad's Early Malay Fiction', *Tenggarra: Journal of Southeast Asian Literature* 32 (1994), 108–18.

Huttenback, Robert A. 'G. A. Henty & the Vision of Empire', *Encounter* 35 (1970), 46–53.

Inniss, Kenneth. 'Conrad's Native Girl', *Pacific Coast Philology* 5 (1970), 39–45.

Kerr, Douglas. 'Crowds, Colonialism and Conrad's *Lord Jim*', *The Conradian* 18:2 (1994), 49–64.

McClintock, Anne. 'Maidens, Maps, and Mines: The Reinvention of Patriarchy in Colonial South Africa', *South Atlantic Quarterly* 87 (1988), 147–92.

McCracken, Scott. 'Reading Masculinity in Lord Jim', *The Conradian* 17:2 (1993), 17–38.

McLauchlan, Juliet. 'Almayer and Willems—"How Not To Be"', *Conradiana* 11:2 (1979), 113–41.

Mongia, Padmini. 'Narrative Strategy and Imperialism in Conrad's *Lord Jim*', *Studies in the Novel* 24 (1992), 173–86.

———. '"Ghosts of the Gothic": Spectral Women and Colonized Spaces in *Lord Jim*', *The Conradian* 17:2 (1993), 1–16.

Naidis, Mark. 'G. A. Henty's Idea of India', *Victorian Studies* (1964), 49–58.

Nelson, Claudia. 'Sex and the Single Boy: Ideals of Manliness and Sexuality in Victorian Literature for Boys', *Victorian Studies* (1989), 525–50.

Newell, Kenneth, B. 'The Yellow Dog Incident in Conrad's *Lord Jim*', *Studies in the Novel* 3 (1977), 26–33.

O'Connor, Peter D. 'The Function of Nina in *Almayer's Folly*', *Conradiana* 7:3, 225–32.

Roberts, Andrew Michael, 'Introduction', *The Conradian* 17: 2 (1993), v–xi.

Saveson, John E. 'Conrad's View of Primitive Peoples in *Lord Jim* and *Heart of Darkness*', *Modern Fiction Studies* 16 (1970), 163–83.

Simmons, Allan. 'Ambiguity as Meaning: The Subversion of Suspense in *Almayer's Folly', The Conradian* 14. 1 & 2. (1989), 1–18.

———. '"Conflicting Impulses": Focalization and the Presentation of Culture in *Almayer's Folly', Conradiana* 29. 3. (1997), 163–72.

The Spectator (28 April 1888), 569–71.

Stockwell, Anthony. J. 'Sir Hugh Clifford's Early Career (1866–1903)', *Journal of the Malaysian Branch of the Royal Asiatic Society* 49.1. (1976), 89–112.

Turnbaugh, Roy. 'Images of Empire', *Journal of Popular Culture* 9 (1975), 734–40.

Young, Vernon. 'Lingard's Folly: The Lost Subject', *Kenyon Review* 15 (1953), 522–39.

Index